Advanced Masterclass

CAE

NEW EDITION

Student's Book

Tricia Aspinall

Annette Capel

with Structure
sections by
Kathy Gude

OXFORD

UNIVERSITY PRESS

Contents

Exam Factfile   pages 5–8

Exam Factfile

The Certificate in Advanced English (Cambridge Level 4) has five papers. Each paper is worth 20% of the total marks and you will receive an overall grade based on your performance across the five papers. There are three pass grades – A, B and C – and three fail grades – D, E and U (unclassified).

Paper 1 Reading (1 hour 15 minutes)

In Paper 1, you have to read four texts and answer between 40 and 50 questions. The length of CAE reading texts can be from 450 words to 1,200 words, depending on the task involved, but the total amount of reading is always around 3,000 words. The texts are taken from a variety of sources including magazines, newspapers and non-fiction material. They are 'authentic' texts in that they have not normally been edited and are usually presented in their original form. You write your answers on special answer sheets and must do this within the total time allowed for the paper.

Task type	Task format	Masterclass example
Parts 1 and 4 Multiple matching	There are always two separate texts, one on a single page (Part 1) with 8–12 questions, and one double page with 15–20 questions (Part 4).	
	The task involves one or more of the following:	
	• matching headings to parts of the text	Unit 2, pages 28–29
	• matching topics to parts of the text	Unit 6, pages 74–75
	• matching statements to parts of the text	Unit 8, pages 102–103
	Test focus: ability to skim a text for overall meaning, and to scan for specific information.	
Part 2 Gapped text	This is an incomplete text with 6 to 8 paragraphs missing. You have to select the missing paragraphs from a choice which includes one extra paragraph.	Unit 7, pages 92–93
	Test focus: understanding of the organization of a text.	
Part 3 Multiple-choice	A text followed by between 5 and 8 multiple-choice questions with four options.	Unit 3, pages 34–37
	Test focus: detailed comprehension of a text and your ability to interpret it.	

Paper 2 Writing (2 hours)

In Paper 2, you have to answer two questions, each requiring an answer of around 250 words in length. You have to write a particular text type for a specified reader. The text type is always indicated in the question in bold (for example **article**, **letter**, **report**) and the target reader of the piece of writing is clearly specified.

The paper has two parts: Part 1 and Part 2. Part 1 consists of one compulsory task. In Part 2 you must complete one task from a choice of four.

Scripts are assessed both in terms of language and task achievement; each answer is given a mark of between 0 and 5.

Task type	Task format	Masterclass example
Part 1	This is a compulsory question consisting of one or two written tasks. You have to process written material of up to 400 words and use information selected from this input in your answer. The input may include one or more text types, including formal or informal letters, informal notes, reports, questionnaires and articles. *Test focus*: ability to select and summarize information from the input, as well as ability to write a specified text type for a target reader.	Unit 2, pages 26–27 (formal letter) Unit 5, pages 70–71 (report) Unit 7, pages 94–95 (formal and informal letters)
Part 2	You have to answer one question from a choice of four. One question will always be work-oriented. The range of text types includes:	
	• article	Unit 9, pages 119–120
	• character reference	Unit 13, pages 166–167
	• competition entry	Unit 4, pages 56–58
	• guidebook entry	Unit 8, pages 106–107
	• leaflet	Unit 11, pages 144–145
	• letter	Unit 3, pages 39–40
	• report	Unit 14, page 179
	• review	Unit 6, pages 79–80
	Test focus: overall command of English and ability to write one of the text types above for a target reader.	

Paper 3 English in Use (1 hour 30 minutes)

Paper 3 consists of six parts, with a total of between 70 and 80 items. You write your answers on special answer sheets and must do this within the total time allowed for the paper.

Task type	Task format	Masterclass example
Part 1 Vocabulary cloze	This is a multiple-choice cloze. You are given a short text of approximately 200 words with 15 gaps and four options for each gap. *Test focus*: vocabulary	Unit 2, pages 22–23

Task type	Task format	Masterclass example
Part 2 Grammar cloze	This is a short text of approximately 200 words with 15 gaps. You have to complete each gap with one word. *Test focus*: grammar	Unit 12, pages 150–151
Part 3 Error correction	You are given a short text with numbered lines, most of which contain an error. Errors are of one of the following types: • spelling and punctuation • unnecessary word *Test focus*: ability to proofread written English, as well as spelling and punctuation	Unit 1, page 17 Unit 4, page 49
Part 4 Word formation	You are given two short texts which contain gaps in most of their lines. For each gap, a word is given in capital letters, and you must form another word from this to fill the gap. *Test focus*: vocabulary	Unit 3, page 45 Unit 10, page 131
Part 5 Register transfer	This consists of two texts. One is a short text in either a formal or informal register, and the second is a gapped text in a contrasting register. You have to complete the second text using the information from the first text. *Test focus*: style and register	Unit 13, pages 164–165
Part 6 Phrase gap	You are given a longer text of approximately 300 words, with a number of gaps and a set of phrases / short sentences. You have to fit the correct phrases / short sentences into the text. *Test focus:* text structure and cohesion	Unit 6, pages 83–84

Paper 4 Listening (about 45 minutes)

The actual listening test lasts approximately 35 minutes and you are then given 10 minutes to transfer your answers to a special answer sheet. The paper has four Parts and between 35 and 40 questions in all.

Task type	Task format	Masterclass example
Part 1	You will hear one person speaking and must complete sentences or notes. There will be around 10 gaps to complete. The recording is heard twice.	Unit 2, pages 21–22
Part 2	You will hear one person speaking and must complete sentences or notes. There will be around 10 gaps to complete. The recording is heard once only. *Test focus*: understanding and application of specific information from the recording.	Unit 6, page 82

Task type	Task format	Masterclass example
Part 3	You will hear more than one person speaking and must show an understanding of the content, especially the attitudes or opinions of the speakers, by answering multiple-choice questions, identifying statements made by a speaker, making short notes or completing sentences. The number of questions depends on the task type. The recording is heard twice. *Test focus*: overall understanding of content, including the attitudes and opinions of the speakers.	Unit 3, page 41 (identifying statements) Unit 8, page 100 (multiple-choice questions)
Part 4	You will hear five short extracts of different people speaking and must complete two multiple matching tasks or a single multiple choice task. There are always 10 questions to complete. The recording is heard twice. *Test focus*: ability to identify overall context, opinions and topics.	Unit 4, page 50

Paper 5 Speaking (about 15 minutes)

The Speaking test is taken in pairs or groups of three, with two examiners present. One examiner acts as an assessor and does not participate in the test at all.

You are assessed on your general language ability and not on your personality or world knowledge. The examiner who is assessing you awards you between 0 and 8 marks each for fluency; accuracy; range; pronunciation and task achievement. A global impression mark of between 0 and 8 is also awarded by each examiner and the total marks are then scaled down to a mark out of 40. There are four parts to the test.

Task type	Task format	Masterclass example
Part 1	You and another candidate have to ask each other questions about yourselves in an introductory way. *Test focus*: ability to introduce yourself and respond to questions.	Unit 1, pages 10–11
Part 2	You have to take turns with another candidate to do tasks related to photographs or other visual material. *Test focus*: ability to describe and comment on a visual prompt, and use turn-taking skills.	Unit 3, page 44
Part 3	In Part 3, you have to discuss a topic or problem with another candidate and arrive at a conclusion. *Test focus*: skills of negotiation and persuasion, and ability to reach an agreement or to 'agree to disagree'.	Unit 8, page 101
Part 4	You and another candidate have to discuss the topics introduced in Part 3 in greater depth with the interlocuter. *Test focus*: ability to explain, summarize and develop the discussion you had in Part 3.	Unit 11, page 142

Loud and Clear

Listening and Speaking *Face to Face* ▼

Introduction

1 Look at these statements.

Face-to-face communication minimizes the risk of misunderstanding. Consequently, the video phone will be a huge asset to society.

Mobile phones are a public nuisance and should be banned.

Do you agree with the views expressed?

2 Do you think we have become better communicators with all the high-tech aids we have today? Give reasons for your answer.

Listening

1 How good a listener are you? Which of these could apply to you during a typical conversation? Tick the boxes and then compare your results with another student.

Do you hear what I'm saying?

Day-dreaming about something completely unrelated ☐

Losing interest in what another person is saying ☐

Finishing off sentences for slow or boring speakers ☐

Misinterpreting, either deliberately or by accident ☐

Filtering the message – hearing what you want to ☐

Butting in before you have heard all the facts ☐

Trying to change the subject prematurely ☐

Fidgeting and causing other distractions to the speaker ☐

2 The following words are all to do with qualities a good listener may have. Can you provide the related adjectives or nouns?

Noun	alertness	_____	restraint	_____
Adjective	_____	attentive	_____	respectful

Complete these sentences about good listeners, choosing suitable nouns or adjectives from those above.

1 Janet was very _____ in the meeting today – she picked up a lot of mistakes in the accountant's report!

2 Even if you find what he says boring, show him the _____ he deserves.

3 I thought you were very _____ just now – I would have told them to shut up and mind their own business!

4 If you pay _____, this won't take long to explain.

5 John is a particularly _____ interviewer and gives the impression that he is very interested in what people are saying.

6 She showed a lot of _____ in staying calm during such a confrontation.

6.1 page 194   When you see this reference in a unit, it means that you can find a related list of words at the back of the book.

3 Listen to the recording called *Varied Speech* and number the topics in the order that you hear them.

Pausing _____   Quantity _____   Volume _____   Speed _____   Tone _____

Listen again to check your answers. Do you agree with the final observation about parents who are good listeners? Give reasons for your answer.

4 Now you are going to hear some short extracts of people talking. Match descriptions a–d to each main speaker. Can you guess what each speaker does for a living?

Speaker 1   a slow, dull, monotonous
Speaker 2   b hesitant, evasive, pauses a lot
Speaker 3   c fast, dominant, very little turn-taking
Speaker 4   d calm, concerned, respects the listener

Speaking

Part 1

Exam tip ▼

Part 1 of the Speaking test is an introductory phase, where you must talk about yourself and ask your partner questions about themselves. It is important to take turns with your partner, so that you each have an equal opportunity to speak.

1 Ask another student questions about the following topics:

- their current job or studies
- their favourite free-time activity
- something they really hate doing
- something unusual they would like to do.

Make notes of the answers to your questions and then introduce that person to another pair, referring to your notes if necessary. Aim to speak for about 30 seconds.

2 How could you improve the fluency of your introduction and avoid repeating yourself? Look at these conversation linkers and use some of them in a revised introduction.

Another very interesting side to X is his / her …   In addition to …, X is also …

Moving on to another of X's …   *Changing the subject a little, X is a …*
On the other hand, X believes …

Finally, X's ambition is to …   *One more thing needs to be said about X …*
Last but not least, X …

Practise the revised introduction with another pair.

3 Look at the cartoon strip. Think about the content and how far it mirrors real life.

Student A should talk for about one minute describing the sequence of events illustrated.

Student B should not interrupt Student A but use appropriate pause fillers, such as *I see*, to show you are listening.

Now change roles. Student B, talk for about one minute. Address the question 'how far does it mirror real life?'.

Part 3

4 Here are some turn-taking strategies for balanced conversations.

Speaker

- Invite your partner to contribute.
  Do you think that's true?
  Is this the case in your own experience?
  You have some ideas on this, don't you?
- Control the amount you say at each stage.
- Introduce deliberate pauses, to allow your partner to contribute.

Listener

- Use a pause as an opportunity to introduce a statement of your own.
- Make eye contact with the speaker to indicate that you have something to say.
- Use a subtle gesture, such as hand movement, as a cue for you to speak.

5 Form groups of three. You are going to discuss a cartoon strip. One student will act as an observer, taking no part in the conversation but monitoring it for turn-taking. The two participants should try to make sure that they speak equally, using the turn-taking strategies given above. At the end, the observer should report back to the other two, giving suggestions if necessary on how the dialogue could have been more balanced.

Now look at the cartoon on page 197. What does it tell you about the way people communicate in society? How does the main character respond to this?

The Nature of the Reading Process

To understand the nature of the basic differences between the techniques used by slower readers and the more effective techniques used by efficient readers, we must first understand the nature of the reading process.
5 If you stand at a window overlooking a busy road and watch a car pass you from left to right, your eyes will appear to move smoothly because they are focused on the car. If, however, you wait until there is no traffic and try to follow an imaginary car as it moves from left to
10 right anyone who watches your eyes while you do this will tell you that they move in a series of small jerks. This is what happens when you read. As your eyes move from left to right along a line of print, they make a series of small jerky movements, stopping momentarily on each
15 word or group of words. These pauses are called 'fixations' and each one lasts for about a third of a second.

The slow reader finds that he has to fixate on every word in order to understand what he reads. The efficient reader, on the other hand, has learned to widen his 'eye span'
20 and to see written material more in terms of groups of words than as single words. There are many films and mechanical devices available which claim to be able to help any reader to widen his eye span, but no one has yet been able to produce evidence that they are any more
25 effective than simply trying to read faster. In fact, as you usually cannot read faster without widening your eye span, then, if your reading speeds increase as a result of trying to read faster, you have widened your eye span without necessarily realising it. One follows naturally
30 from the other. ■

Gordon Wainwright, *Rapid Reading*

300 words

Introduction

 300 words

1 At an advanced level, you will come across quite long texts, so you need to be able to read efficiently. Have you any idea how many words on average you read per minute?

Wherever you see this symbol, make a point of timing your reading. Divide the number of words by the number of minutes you have taken, and record your wpm (words per minute).

According to the text, what technique would an efficient reader use?

2 Check your comprehension of the text by agreeing or disagreeing with the following statements.

1 When you read, your eyes move smoothly along a line of text.
2 Your eye span is the number of words you are able to process at a time.
3 Increasing your reading speed will widen your eye span.

3 Look at the word in *italics* below. How many words can you take in at the same time on either side of the word?

You can increase your reading *speed* significantly without comprehension loss.

Reading

1 Look at these phrases. Discuss your interpretation of their meaning with another student.

1 incomplete success
2 real counterfeit diamonds
3 genuine imitation leather
4 economically non-affluent people

How would you describe this type of language?

The world of
DOUBLESPEAK

Farmers no longer have cows, pigs, chickens, or other animals on their farms: according to the U.S. Department of Agriculture, farmers have *grain-consuming animal units*. Attentive observers of the English language also learned recently that the multibillion dollar stock market crash of 1987 was simply a *fourth quarter equity retreat*; that airplanes don't crash, they just have *uncontrolled contact with the ground*; and that President Reagan wasn't really unconscious while he underwent minor surgery, he was just in a *non-decision-making form*. In other words, doublespeak continues to spread as the official language of public communication.

Doublespeak is a blanket term for language which pretends to communicate but doesn't, language which makes the bad seem good, the negative appear positive, the unpleasant attractive, or at least tolerable. It is language which avoids, shifts, or denies responsibility, language which is at variance with its real meaning.

We know that a toothbrush is still a toothbrush even if the advertisements on television call it a *home plaque removal instrument*, and even that *nutritional avoidance therapy* means a diet. But who would guess that a *volume-related production schedule adjustment* means closing an entire factory in the doublespeak of General Motors, or that *energetic disassembly* means an explosion in a nuclear power plant in the doublespeak of the nuclear power industry?

THE HOME PLAQUE REMOVAL INSTRUMENT

The euphemism, an inoffensive or positive word or phrase designed to avoid a harsh, unpleasant, or distasteful reality, can at times be doublespeak. But the euphemism can also be a tactful word or phrase; for example, "passed away" functions not just to protect the feelings of another person but also to express our concern for another's grief. A euphemism used to mislead or deceive, however, becomes doublespeak.

Jargon, the specialized language of a trade or profession, allows colleagues to communicate with each other clearly, efficiently, and quickly. Indeed, it is a mark of membership to be able to use and understand the group's jargon. But it can also be doublespeak – pretentious, obscure, and esoteric terminology used to make the simple appear complex, and not to express but impress. Lawyers and tax accountants speak of an *involuntary conversion* of property when discussing the loss or destruction of property through theft, accident, or condemnation. So, if your house burns down, or your car is stolen or destroyed in an accident, you have, in legal jargon, suffered an *involuntary conversion* of your property.

> ‘When a company initiates
> a career alternative enhancement
> program, it is really laying off
> 5000 workers’

A final kind of doublespeak is simply inflated language. Car mechanics may be called *automotive internists*, elevator operators *members of the vertical transportation corps*; grocery checkout clerks *career associate scanning professionals*. When a company *initiates a career alternative enhancement program*, it is really laying off 5000 workers; a *negative patient care outcome* means that the patient died.

These last examples should make it clear that doublespeak is not the product of careless language or sloppy thinking. Indeed, serious doublespeak is carefully designed and constructed to appear to communicate but in fact to mislead. Such language is highly strategic, and it breeds suspicion, cynicism, distrust and, ultimately, hostility. If we really believe that we understand doublespeak and think that it communicates, we are in deep trouble.

William Lutz, *The World of Doublespeak*

3 The article mentions these different kinds of *doublespeak*:

the euphemism   jargon   inflated language.

Can you define each of them in your own words? Look back at the article to see if your definitions were correct.

4 Some of the *italic* phrases in the article contain compound adjectives ending in *-ing*. For example, *grain-consuming animal units, non-decision-making form*.

Compound adjectives such as these are formed with the present participle. For example,

grain-consuming   smooth-talking   off-putting.

Match each compound adjective in 1–8 to an adjective in a–h with a similar meaning.

1	hard-wearing	a	convenient
2	record-breaking	b	interminable
3	labour-saving	c	outstanding
4	hard-hitting	d	extensive
5	good-looking	e	durable
6	never-ending	f	attractive
7	mouth-watering	g	direct
8	far-reaching	h	appetizing

Writing   *Writing it Right*

Introduction

It is not always easy to get your message across in the right way. If you sound rude or tactless in a piece of writing, you will have a negative effect on your reader. If you fail to give a clear picture of something, you will confuse rather than inform.

Have you ever written a letter and immediately regretted sending it? What effect do you think it had on its reader?

Writing

Exam tip ▼

The ability to produce different types of writing is an important skill for CAE Paper 2. The style and register you choose will be determined by the text you are asked to produce and who you are writing for.

1 As you read through any CAE writing task, you should consider carefully:
- who the target reader or audience is.
- what style and register would be appropriate.
- what particular points you are asked to cover.
- what type of text is required.

When you have finished you should read through and edit your work. It may help if you remember this checklist. ▶

W Who for?
R Register?
I Include …
T Text type
E Edit!

2 Say where you think extracts A–F are taken from, who they might have been written for and why.

A

'Betsy Byars, an American, writes about children in realistic, often daunting situations. Her books are very funny and she writes in a direct, economical style. This way of writing suits her view of childhood, which is never sentimental.'

B

Tucked away in a quiet part of Somerset, the remains of **Cleeve Abbey** are remarkably well preserved.

There are many fascinating details to look for: medieval tiled flooring in the original dining hall, a magnificent fifteenth-century timber roof, and some unusual wall paintings.

C

Your advertisement offers 'tailor-made holidays in small groups'. In fact, there were over fifty people on our particular tour! Because the company has misled us in this and other respects, I would like to request financial compensation.

D

date: 7 June

Further to your memo concerning the Sales Meeting, I now have all the information on conference centres to hand. This document will evaluate the three possible sites in relation to geographical location, transport, accommodation, in-house facilities and cost.

E

Anyway, let me tell you about Jim. I was amazed when he phoned, after such a long time. We met in town the next day. It was really weird — he acted as though he'd only been away for five days, rather than five years!

F

AS STUDENTS WE ARE ALWAYS FACED WITH THE NEED TO ECONOMIZE

There are several ways to do this which are fairly painless and won't result in your having to lead a dull and miserable life as a result! Why not reconsider some of the things you take for granted?

Do you really need to take the bus every day?

WALKING OR CYCLING IS GOOD FOR YOU!

3 Answer these questions for each extract. Compare your views with another student.

1 Is the register formal, informal or neutral?
2 Is the tone personal or impersonal, serious or light-hearted?
3 Does the extract concentrate on facts or opinions?
4 Does it contain a lot of descriptive language?
5 Does the extract require the reader to take any immediate action?

4 Vocabulary choice can also influence the style of a piece of writing, because some words are only appropriate in a certain register.

Look at the following sets of words, each of which has a similar meaning. The underlined word in each set has been used in one of the extracts above. Find it and try to substitute the three other words. Do any seem inappropriate for the extract?

1	<u>amazed</u>	astonished	bowled over	staggered
2	conned	deceived	fooled	<u>misled</u>
3	assess	<u>evaluate</u>	judge	size up
4	abnormal	bizarre	odd	<u>weird</u>
5	boring	dreary	<u>dull</u>	monotonous
6	great	<u>magnificent</u>	splendid	superb
7	amenities	<u>facilities</u>	resources	services
8	corny	emotional	nostalgic	<u>sentimental</u>

5 Although phrasal verbs may sometimes be used in formal writing, they are much more common in informal texts. Look at these sentences. Decide which of the words or phrases in *italics* best complete each sentence.

1 Expenditure on recruitment has *gone up* / *increased* substantially since 1994.

2 I'm really exhausted – think I'll *turn in* / *retire* for the night.

3 Can you try to *find out* / *ascertain* what's the matter with Anna?

4 Our company would be pleased to *fix up* / *arrange* accommodation for you.

5 Please take a seat and *hang on* / *wait* until the doctor is ready to examine you.

6 Dave never stops eating – he had a huge breakfast and now he's *polished off* / *consumed* my last packet of biscuits.

7 The aim of this report is to *pin down* / *specify* five areas where improvements could be made.

8 Julie's visit will have to be *put off* / *deferred* until the house is ready.

9 The Managing Director will be *dropping in on* / *visiting* these offices on the 16th of March.

10 Adam was *told off* / *reprimanded* by his mum for coming home late.

11 I'm really sorry to *let you down* / *disappoint* you over our hols, but I can't make those dates now.

12 The Principal had no more appointments so couldn't *get out of* / *avoid* attending the meeting.

6 Write a postcard to a close friend to postpone an invitation you had previously made. Apologize, giving reasons for your change of plan and inviting your friend on another day.

Write around 50 words. Remember to use phrasal verbs where appropriate.

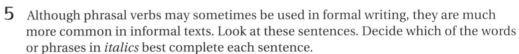 **1** page 193

Editing

Exam tip ▼

In Part 3 of Paper 3, you will have to proofread a short text for errors (either grammatical errors or spelling and punctuation errors). Work through the text line by line and make sure you read each line carefully. A few lines will be correct.

Editing skills are essential for good writing and also an important part of Paper 3. It is therefore useful to build in a checking stage for all your written work.

1 Skim read the text below. Who has it been written for?

2 Now look carefully at the text. Decide whether any of the following have been omitted or wrongly used:

- full stops
- commas
- speech marks
- apostrophes
- brackets
- capital letters.

Write the correct version alongside the line. Tick any lines that are error-free. Three examples have been done for you.

A PERSONAL VIEW

Telling a Story

In whatever way you approach the teenage novel, you will find it vital, to do some research into teenage behaviour This research will help to ensure that your characters speech is convincing. You may want to write, in the first person, because this seems to offer an easy method of getting inside, the main character. Although this is effective when it works well, there are pitfall's. First, there is the obvious snag that the narrator cant be everywhere at once and some incidents have to be told at second-hand (this can become clumsy. Second, if you try to reproduce exactly the way some characters' might really write or speak, the use of slang or jargon may make the text less convincing, because it sounds dated. Third some writers believe the narrative, is equally unconvincing unless there is some good reason for one of the characters to be telling the story. Nadia wheatley feels strongly about this. What annoys me about a lot of novels is that its not often explained *why* the character writes I can't do that. I have to justify it.'

0	✓
0	*vital to*
0	*behaviour.*
1	
2	
3	
4	
5	
6	
7	
8	
9	
10	
11	
12	
13	
14	
15	
16	
17	

3 Have you ever been put off reading a novel because of its style? What kind of books do you prefer and why?

Structure *What do you Mean?*

Sometimes inappropriate grammar or vocabulary leads to a breakdown in communication. In groups of three or four, discuss the questions in sections **A–K** below. These questions will be answered in more detail as you work through the grammar sections in this course.

A How do the words in *italics* affect the meaning of these four sentences?

1 The personnel department *might* give you a reference.
2 The personnel department *could* give you a reference.
3 The personnel department *would* give you a reference.
4 The personnel department *should* give you a reference.

B Match statements 1–3 to the possible meanings in a–c.

1 If I phoned home every day, I'd run up huge phone bills.
2 If I'd phoned home every day, I'd have run up huge phone bills.
3 If I phone home every day, I'll run up huge phone bills.

a I might phone home every other day, then the phone bills won't be so expensive.
b I don't phone home every day because phone calls are expensive.
c I didn't phone home every day because phone calls were expensive.

C What were the students' exact words in these sentences?

1 The students said they'd try to work harder.
2 The students said they were trying to work harder.
3 The students said they'd tried to work harder.

D Match statements 1 and 2 to the implied meanings in a and b.

1 The children who had attended nursery school settled down quickly in primary school.
2 The children, who had attended nursery school, settled down quickly in primary school.

a All the children had attended nursery school and they all settled down quickly in primary school.
b Only the children who had attended nursery school settled down quickly in primary school. Those who did not go to nursery school did not settle down.

E Match questions 1 and 2 to the possible meanings in a and b below.

1 How long did you live in France?
2 How long have you lived in France?

a The listener is still in France.
b The listener has lived in France and is now living somewhere else.

F Match statements 1–3 to the possible explanations in a–c below.

1 I can't meet you for lunch tomorrow. I'm visiting my aunt.
2 I'm going to try and look in on my aunt. I haven't seen her for ages.
3 I know! I'll visit my aunt tomorrow. I haven't seen her for ages!

a The speaker is making a decision to visit her aunt.
b The speaker is expressing an intention to visit her aunt.
c The speaker is talking about an arrangement which has already been made – to visit her aunt.

G What information is the speaker giving about Martin?

1 I wish Martin wouldn't tell lies.
2 I wish Martin weren't so rude.
3 I wish Martin hadn't moved in next door.

H Read the sentences in 1–3 and answer the questions.

1
a   We saw the young dancer rehearse for the opening night.
b   We saw the young dancer rehearsing for the opening night.

Which statement means that you saw:

• the whole performance?
• only part of what was actually happening?

2
a   Paul remembered setting the alarm clock for six o'clock.
b   Paul remembered to set the alarm clock for six o'clock.

Which statement refers to:

• something which happened **after** Paul remembered?
• something which happened **before** Paul remembered?

3
a   I tried to talk to my boss to explain how I felt about the job.
b   I tried talking to my boss to explain how I felt about the job.

Which statement means that:

• the speaker talked to his boss?
• the speaker didn't talk to his boss?

I Match statements 1–6 to the explanations in a–f. More than one answer may be correct.

1   I joined the class so that I could improve my English.
2   I joined the class because my English wasn't good enough to help me get a job.
3   My English was so good that I didn't need to join a class.
4   I joined the class although I spoke English much better than the other students.
5   I'll join the class as long as I don't have to work too hard!
6   Maria speaks English as if she's been speaking it all her life.

The speaker is telling you:

a   on what condition she will join the class.
b   for what reason she joined the class.
c   how somebody does something.
d   what her intention was when she joined the class.
e   what happened as a result of something else.
f   what might have prevented her from joining the class but did not.

J Match statements 1–3 to the explanations in a–c.

1   John used to work in a hospital.
2   John was used to working in a hospital.
3   John got used to working in a hospital.

a   He might have come across some problems at first but in the end he was able to cope with it.
b   He worked there in the past but does not now.
c   He was accustomed to working there – it presented no problems for him. Possibly he had been there for some time.

K Match statements 1–3 to the explanations in a–c.

1   A well-known artist painted my portrait.
2   My portrait was painted by a well-known artist.
3   I had my portrait painted by a well-known artist.

a   The speaker is emphasizing **who** arranged for the portrait to be painted.
b   The speaker is stating a fact.
c   The speaker is emphasizing **what** the artist painted and **who** painted the portrait.

Now compare your answers with those of the rest of the class.

Fighting Fit

Listening and Speaking *Alternative Therapies* ▼

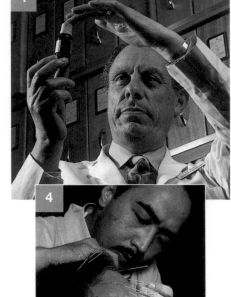

A

Iridologists examine the eye for irritation or deposits in nerve fibres, which they say correspond to inflammation or infection in the body. They also claim to detect inherent weaknesses, and can discover whether a person has a predisposition for certain illnesses.

B

Aromatherapy uses essential oils from plants, which are diluted with a carrier oil before being rubbed into the skin. Different plants are supposed to have different healing properties. Like other massages, it's soothing, pleasant and relaxing.

C

Homeopathy is based on the principle of using 'similars' or 'like to treat like'. A German doctor, Samuel Hahnemann, found that using substances at extreme dilutions and shaking them violently produced a correspondingly more powerful effect. This process of 'potentizing' has become the key feature of homeopathy.

D

In acupuncture, needles are inserted at an acupuncture point, then aligned with energy pathways called 'meridians', which connect internal organs with points along the body's surface. The needles are rotated clockwise or anti-clockwise, according to whether energy is to be stimulated or damped down.

Introduction

1 The pictures illustrate various kinds of alternative medicine. Read the descriptions above and match them to the pictures.

2 What makes these various treatments different from more conventional medicine? What treatment could be offered in their place?

3 Choose one alternative therapy which you find particularly interesting. Make a list of the reasons why you would or would not want to try it, then discuss your reasons with your partner.

Listening

Part 1

1 You are going to hear an acupuncturist talking about his work. Before you listen, read the sentences. Then, as you listen, focus on the answers in 1–10 and listen out for any differences in wording on the tape.

Exam tip ▼

Part 1 of Paper 4 is often a sentence completion task. You must fill in the gaps in sentences with information that you hear. A gap can be filled by a maximum of four words. You may have to change the wording in some way to fit the grammar of the sentence.

Acupuncture

In Chinese medicine, *chi* is the (1)_____*energy flow*_____ of the body.

Healthy people have an (2)_____*even flow*_____ of *chi*.

Acupuncture can make a person's energy flow (3)_____*more balanced*_____ again.

Before starting treatment, the acupuncturist reviews the patient's

(4)_*medical history*_.

He also takes the patient's (5)_____*pulse*_____.

By doing this, he can decide whether the patient's body is being affected by either

(6)_____*blockages or surges*_____ of energy.

The body's energy flow can be (7)_____*increased or reduced*_____ by inserting and twisting the needles.

The Chinese (8)_____*use*_____ acupuncture as an anaesthetic.

According to the acupuncturist, conventional medicine is becoming less

(9)_____*personal*_____.

Some people prefer acupuncture to conventional treatment because they believe

they are in (10)_____*better control*_____ of their bodies.

2 Now look at the extracts from the tapescript and compare them closely with answers 1–6.

Chi – the body's energy flow.
If you have an even flow of *chi* you are in good health.
It is then possible to readjust a person's flow of energy if it has become unbalanced.
Before I treat anybody I take some time to study a patient's medical history. I also read the body's pulses.
From this information I can decide if there are any blockages in the flow of energy or indeed any surges of energy.

Look at the rest of the tapescript and underline the relevant extracts for answers 7–10.

... It is at this point that I decide where I'm going to insert the needles. These needles increase or reduce the flow of energy when they are inserted and twisted
5 at the appropriate meridian points. Don't worry – it doesn't hurt and you won't bleed!

Now, I believe that acupuncture can benefit most people suffering from disease or who are in pain. In China it is used as
10 an anaesthetic. I myself used it on my wife when she was having our last child. It certainly seemed to reduce her need for pain-killers.

I run two practices. There is great
15 interest and I have a long waiting list. I think the reason for this is partly because conventional medicine has become increasingly impersonal. Ordinary doctors are over-worked and don't have enough
20 time to spend on each patient. It's often easier and quicker for them to hand out pills than to give proper personal attention.

What acupuncture does is to encourage the body to heal itself, which
25 is, after all, a natural tendency. There is nothing drastic about the treatment, and I think people feel more in control of their bodies than when they are subjected to all that high-tech equipment in a modern
30 hospital.

3 Now prepare to listen to another recording about treatments for migraine.
Before you listen, read the sentences, noting the words before and after the gaps.

Alternative therapy and migraine

Migraine is a growing problem, particularly among people who (1)_____.

A migraine can also be brought on by certain foods and wine, or if a person doesn't
(2)_____.

Painkillers are a (3)_____ way to treat migraine, but they don't always work.

In alternative therapy, the use of (4)_____ relieves mild attacks.

During acupuncture, (5)_____ four needles to the face has a quick effect.

To keep a patient free from attacks, it is usually sufficient to have (6)_____.

Many people don't (7)_____ hypnosis.

The intense relaxation causes the attack to (8)_____.

4 Listen to the recording and complete the sentences. Then listen to the tape for a
second time to check your answers.

English in Use

Part 1

1 Look at the extract below. It is taken from a magazine called *Me and My Health*,
where the actress Maureen Lipman talks about her lifestyle. What part of speech are
the underlined words?

I never seem to stop. I'm not so much a workaholic as the (1) <u>original</u> 'girl who can't say no'. Not only have I never learned to organize my time, I need the deadline to pass before I get going. Then I wonder why I feel (2) <u>exhausted</u>! I'm very good at whipping up false energy.

Without (3) <u>sufficient</u> rest, though, I start to look grey and then, apart from a good night's sleep, the only thing that brings me back to life is meditation. I find that 20 minutes' meditation is (4) <u>equivalent</u> to a night's sleep and that keeps me going.

2 In each set (1–4) there is the correct answer and three incorrect 'distractors'. In pairs,
choose two sets each and explain why the other words cannot be used.

1	A	innovative	B	first	C	foremost	D	<u>original</u>
2	A	apathetic	B	<u>exhausted</u>	C	gruelling	D	spent
3	A	<u>sufficient</u>	B	severe	C	acceptable	D	minimal
4	A	compatible	B	alike	C	<u>equivalent</u>	D	proportional

Exam tip ▼

Part 1 of Paper 3 is
a vocabulary cloze. You
are asked to complete a
text by filling in each gap
with a suitable answer,
from a given choice of
four words. Remember
that all four choices will
be the same part of
speech.

3 Now look at how the article continues and underline the words in 5–10 below which best fit each space. For each one, say what part of speech is tested and explain why you think the alternative words do not fit.

> ❛Somehow though, I never get around to meditating on a daily (5)_____. I'm no good in the morning. By the time I've managed to get up and repair the (6)_____ of the night, half the day's gone. When it comes to food, I'm a hostess's nightmare. As I (7)_____ from migraine, I avoid cheese and stimulants like coffee, red wine and spirits, which are generally (8)_____ to trigger an attack. I only eat rye bread, as the gluten in wheat makes me feel bloated and ropy. I've (9)_____ countless migraine 'cures', from the herbal remedy *feverfew* to acupuncture. Acupuncture (10)_____ balance the system, but nothing stops the attacks.❜

5	A	way	B	basis	C	routine	D	manner
6	A	damages	B	wrecks	C	ravages	D	ruins
7	A	complain	B	suffer	C	experience	D	ache
8	A	foreseen	B	maintained	C	regarded	D	thought
9	A	tried	B	experimented	C	searched	D	proved
10	A	assists	B	improves	C	restores	D	helps

Vocabulary

Confusable words

1 Stimulant, stimulus

Do you know the difference between these two words? Which one appeared in the vocabulary cloze in the previous exercise? Match 1–5 to a–e below.

1 Williamson tested positive for the banned
2 Unemployment has been a major drawback in rural life and a
3 Many people believe that alcohol is a
4 A certain cinema and its environs were both
5 We hope that the books will provide a

a stimulant because most drinkers seem to become more outgoing.
b stimulus to migration to urban areas.
c stimulus for dialogue and serve as catalysts for improvement.
d stimulant ephedrine following Neath's opening league game.
e stimulus and setting for my juvenile adventures.

2 Treat, cure, heal

These verbs have all occurred in this section. Choose one of the verbs to complete each of the following sentences, using a suitable form.

1 Different remedies may have to be used before the patient can be _____.

2 The whole family should be _____ even if symptoms are not present.

3 The wounds, in some instances, may take time to _____.

4 The patients can usually be _____ if they are _____ in time.

5 Andrew is carrying niggling injuries which are proving slow to _____.

6 Within three weeks, her skin had _____.

7 Any secondary bacterial infection may need to be _____ with antibiotics.

8 Her condition had been improved but not _____ by the treatment.

Speaking
Part 3

1 Look at the pictures in this specialist holiday brochure. What type of holiday do you think is being advertised? Read the brochure to see if you were right.

ATSITSA *holidays on the*
beautiful Greek island of Skyros

Situated right by the sea in the idyllic, pine-forested Atsitsa Bay, Atsitsa is a unique adventure. Its holistic programme, run by some of the world's most experienced facilitators,
5 aims at relaxing and revitalising the whole person.

Participants choose up to three courses each week from a wide range on offer: perhaps yoga, dance and windsurfing or dream work, self-awareness and juggling. The programme is full, to tempt people to explore new
10 directions along with familiar ones, but everyone is encouraged to do just as much or as little as they like.

Atsitsa is set up as a community, and everyone has a communal responsibility to contribute to the programme. Away from much that is taken for granted
15 in modern city living, people live simply, but comfortably, in tune with the rhythms of nature.

Atsitsa's holistic approach is rooted in the classical Greek notion that health and fitness do not depend simply on diet and exercise, but upon the harmony
20 of mind, body and spirit, oneness with the physical environment, and active participation in community life. Participants return home not only with new skills but often with a new approach to life, and the benefits – and the friendships – continue long after the
25 holiday has ended.

2 Now read what some reviewers have said about Atsitsa.

> People go to Club Med to forget themselves. At Atsitsa they hope to find themselves – or at least some interesting new and undiscovered bit.
>
> The Sunday Telegraph

> **O**ut there, under those deep blue skies, and surrounded by people I came to know better in seven days than many I had known for seven years, I was forced to swallow my cynicism. It worked.
>
> Vogue

> **I** saw the skill and care of the therapists, and the bonds which grew between people, enabling a special kind of trust and compassion. Sometimes it was a bit hard going – it's not a holiday for those who want a rest "away from it all". The experience, in fact, brings you closer to it all – to emotion, feeling, hurt and happiness and all the rag-bag of riches we carry around inside ourselves.
>
> Here's Health

> An unspoken philosophy prevails at Atsitsa that anyone can do anything and that age is irrelevant.
>
> The Observer

3 In pairs, discuss the advantages and disadvantages of going on an Atsitsa holiday. Try to use some of the adjectives given below.

+		**–**	
friendly	lively	prying, intrusive	boisterous
sympathetic	tranquil	callous, brutal	excruciating
intimate	exhilarating	claustrophobic	intense, threatening

6.3 page 194

4 Would you like to go on a holiday like this? Give reasons for your answer.

Writing *Sport for All* ▼

Introduction

1 Look at the pictures and discuss them with another student. What do they tell you about the nature of sport today?

2 Read this article once, timing yourself as you read. Do you think the people mentioned are experienced or inexperienced marathon runners? Why?

Over 8,000 runners from 90 nations come to New York City every November to run the marathon. They fill up about a third of the field in this, the largest international marathon in the world. And they fill New York's streets, shops and restaurants.

Marathon

You'll run into international runners everywhere in the days before and after the marathon. They don't just sit in their hotel rooms with their feet propped up, resting and carbo-loading on bread and
5 pasta. No, they've come to see the sights.

But why? Why do they come to New York, with its traffic, crime and congestion? Sure, the marathon offers an inspiring tour of the five boroughs of the city and enthusiastic support from throngs of
10 spectators, but other marathons offer a similar experience in environments less harsh than this one. What is the intrigue of New York? And what do the visitors who have come here to run do?

We decided to see for ourselves, so we followed
15 various contingents of runners around New York in the days before the marathon. We found that they were having lots of fun, some of them so much that we were amazed they were in any condition to make it to the starting line, much less run 26.2 miles.

20 LA DOLCE MARATONA

Take, for example, a 25-year-old architecture student from Italy. We caught up with him 72 hours before the start of the marathon at a posh party
25 at the Italian Trade Commission. As Andrew Arduini sipped on a glass of Soave, he recounted his day for us. He and seven of his friends had been discovering New York. Before he broke
30 out the slide projector, we had to interject:"Andrew, don't you have a marathon to run in two days? You've been walking all over creation, eating hot dogs, drinking wine... Don't you
35 read the training articles?""Well," he said, "I haven't really trained very hard. Next year, I'll come prepared."

THE FRENCH CONNECTION

About 60 blocks uptown, a group of
40 Parisian runners and their families were preparing for a pre-race meal that would have sent our nutrition columnist reaching for the stomach pump. They had arrived at what tour
45 operator Mark Klein calls their favourite destination in New York – Harlem. Specifically, Wilson's Bakery and Restaurant, a Harlem landmark since 1945, where pork, chicken and
50 cholesterol are served up in heaps. "I'm not sure they realize just what soul food is," chuckled Klein, as huge servings of fried chicken and ribs were dumped onto their plates.

55 ISLANDERS

They have a marathon in Bermuda, but still, a few of the members of that island paradise are enticed by New York and make the journey to run the race's
60 five boroughs. Unlike the French and Italian contingents – who could have practically started their own borough – the 36-person Bermudian presence was tiny. Still, they have an organized
65 support network here."We'll be cheering them at the corner of First Avenue and 68th Street," said Peter Lever of the Bermuda Track and Field Association."That's our official
70 spectator point."

INTERNATIONAL BREAKFAST RUN

Others run the marathon without support, embassy welcoming parties or group tours. For them, however,
75 there is always Saturday's International Breakfast Run – the one official event for all foreign entrants. Runners gather at the United Nations plaza and blend into one mass as they jog two miles up
80 to Tavern on the Green in Central Park, where they are served breakfast. A lot of carbohydrates are consumed. There is a marathon tomorrow, after all. And not just any marathon. "All
85 marathoners want to run New York," said one runner. "There is not another like it in the world."

New York City

John Hank, Runner's World

600 words

3 Have you ever taken part in a long-distance run? If you haven't, would you like to do so? Give reasons for your answer.

How do people train for a long run? What physical and mental skills are required?

Writing

Part 1, letter

Exam tip ▼

Part 1 of Paper 2 involves the reading of up to 400 words of text extracts, in order to complete a task based on the material. You must be able to include appropriate information from what you have read, without 'lifting' phrases. It is crucial for you to write in the correct register and you will often have to change what you have read into a different style, appropriate to the text type.

Understanding the task

1 Look at the writing task below. You need to think carefully about what the task involves. For example, in the club note on page 27, you are told that you do <u>not</u> need to include organizational details about the run itself (see the second sentence of the note).

You should read the information carefully in Section A – you will be penalized if you have misunderstood the task in any way.

Your town's small and friendly international club, of which you are a member, is organizing a 'Fun Run' for members. You have been asked to put together a letter for the other participants, giving practical suggestions for training and preparation in the time leading up to the event.

Look at the information about local fitness training facilities, together with a note you have received from the club committee. You must cover all the points referred to in the note. You may also include additional points of your own.

fitness centres

sport and recreation

gymnasiums &

■ **MB GYM**
Gym equipment, sauna, sunbeds, cardiovascular room and juice bar – run by top athlete.

■ **YMCA CITY GYM**
Extensively refurbished. Features fully-equipped, air-conditioned gymnasium, full-sized sports hall, sunbeds, relaxation area, restaurant facilities. Good range of classes, featuring step and slide training.

■ **BODIFIT**
New club with gym, steam room, sunbeds. Full range of classes, inc. aerobics, step, slide. Reduced rates for students.

■ **BODY MAINTENANCE**
Alternative facility – everything from aromatherapy to massage and osteopathy. Also sports injury treatment. With the 'Spice of Life' restaurant next door, an 'Alternative Night Out': steam bath with aromatherapy oils and vegetarian meal.

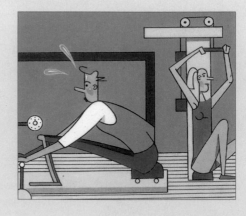

> Thanks for agreeing to write to members about the Fun Run _next month_. They already have all the info about when and where to meet on the day itself, but it would be really helpful for them to get some _training tips_ from you. We think they also need some encouragement, so make sure you emphasize the FUN!
>
> Here are some _suggestions for you to include_:
> – Group sessions at some of the local gyms (which ones?)
> – Swimming nights at the central pool (say when)
> – Jogging in the park (give precise times)
>
> We would also like to arrange a supper party the evening before the run. Could you decide where and include these details in your letter, please?
>
> Look forward to getting your letter!

Selecting ideas

2 Look at the underlined parts of the club note and its suggestions, then read the descriptions of gym facilities. Decide with another student which of the gyms would be suitable for group sessions and a supper party. More than one can be suggested.

Don't forget that you can add points of your own, as long as you have covered the required content. Discuss extra training possibilities with a partner. What other information might it be relevant to include, for example, diet, sleep, clothes?

Focusing on the reader

3 Decide on the register for your letter. There are some clues in the club note you have been sent and in the exam rubric. Can you find them?

Planning your answer

4 The plan below will help you organize your letter. In pairs, brainstorm useful language and add it to the plan.

- Introduction
  Why you are writing

- Paragraph on training
  Gym sessions, swimming, jogging
  Any additional suggestions

- Paragraph on supper party
  Details on where, what food, what time

- Ending
  Encouraging tone!

Writing

5 Now write your letter in about 250 words. Remember the **WRITE** ✎ checklist on page 14.

Checking

6 After you have finished writing, don't forget to go back and check your work. Carry out these procedures.

- Put yourself in the reader's place.

  Is your work clearly organized into meaningful paragraphs?
  Is the format suitable for the task type?
  Is the register appropriate?
  Is what you say informative and interesting? Could you include more details?

- Then check your work for grammatical accuracy, considering each of these areas:

  articles   prepositions   tenses   word order.

- Finally, check your writing for any spelling or punctuation errors.

  When you see this reference in a unit, it means you can find a related writing model in the back of the book.

✎ page 189

Reading *Bad Habits* ▼

Introduction

1 If you were in a public place, what would your reaction be if someone:

- played their personal stereo loudly next to you?
- threw litter down on the ground?
- parked their car on the pavement?

2 Do you consider all of these to be anti-social activities? Can you think of any other anti-social activities you would find offensive?

Reading

Multiple matching

1 The extract below is the first paragraph from a leaflet produced by the *Health and Safety Executive* in Britain. Skim through the paragraph quickly and decide:

- what the main theme is.
- who the leaflet is aimed at.

Exam tip

In Paper 1, there is a lot to read. There are always four texts giving a total of 3,000 words. You are not always expected to read these texts in detail. Reading at speed, using the skills of skimming and scanning, is essential if you are to finish the paper within the time allowed.

HEALTH AND SAFETY AT WORK

Employers should consider how to limit passive smoking at work. There are various methods of preventing or limiting exposure to smoke. Every workplace is different, and there is no universal solution. Full in-depth consultation with employees and/or their representatives is highly desirable for the smooth
5 implementation of policies designed to limit exposure to tobacco smoke. A policy is very much more likely to be accepted by all employees if they feel they have been properly consulted. It is important to take time and make sure that details of restrictions on smoking are worked out and agreed between management and employees, and if necessary arrange a transitional period or a step-by-step approach.

2   One type of multiple-matching task involves matching headings to paragraphs. Read headings A–H below carefully, so that you are sure what they are about. Then scan the text, summarizing each paragraph as you read. Match each heading with the correct paragraph.

You will not usually find exactly the same word in both the heading and the paragraph, but the content will be similar. In each paragraph, underline the word, phrase or sentence which helped you choose the correct heading. The first heading has been done for you as an example.

A   What is passive smoking?

B   How can passive smoking be a danger to health?

C   What about people who already have respiratory diseases?

D   What are the benefits to employers of taking steps to limit passive smoking?

E   Wouldn't it be best to totally prohibit smoking at work?

F   What is the evidence?

G   Why be concerned about smoking at work?

H   What about safety hazards from smoking at work and health risks for smokers?

1   **G**   **Why be concerned about smoking at work?**

10   Nowadays fewer people are smokers and attitudes to smoking are changing. Smokers are a minority in many workplaces. People have become more aware of the serious health risks faced by smokers themselves. There is increasing concern over the possible health effects of breathing other people's tobacco smoke. Work is one of a few situations where non-smokers may have to spend long periods in close contact with smokers.

2

15   When smokers and non-smokers share the same room, non-smokers cannot avoid inhaling some environmental tobacco smoke as they breathe. This is called 'passive smoking'. The smoke concerned is mainly 'sidestream' smoke from burning cigarettes, cigars or pipe tobacco, but there is also some smoke exhaled by smokers.

3

In some situations, a complete ban is justified for safety reasons. But elsewhere
20   the imposition by management without proper consultation of any measures to control passive smoking could lead to resentment among smokers and problems in enforcing the no-smoking rule.

4

This leaflet does not deal with the well-recognized safety hazards from smoking where there is a risk of fire or explosion. Nor does it discuss the health hazards to
25   individuals who smoke, particularly while working with substances such as lead or asbestos. Such hazards are covered by guidance on each subject.

5

It is now beyond doubt that smoking is a major cause of disease and premature death for smokers themselves. Tobacco smoke contains various substances that can cause cancer or other health problems. Raised levels of airborne harmful substances
30   are found when smokers' homes are compared with those of non-smokers. Still higher levels may occur in poorly ventilated indoor places of work where several people are smokers.

6

There have been many scientific studies on passive smoking. The results of this research were reviewed by the Independent Scientific Committee on Smoking and Health
35   in their Fourth Report. The Committee concluded that 'while none of the studies can on its own be accepted as unequivocal, the findings overall are consistent with there being a small increase in the risk of lung cancer from exposure to environmental tobacco smoke, in the range of 10%–30%'.

7

It has been recognized for some time that exposure to tobacco smoke can cause
40   discomfort and irritation to some people, particularly those who already have a respiratory disorder such as asthma. Passive smoking may cause more distress to this group than it does to most non-smokers.

8

Limiting or preventing smoking by an agreed and carefully implemented policy may improve employee morale, reduce arguments between smokers and non-smokers,
45   reduce time lost through sickness, and diminish cleaning bills. It will reduce fire risk.

Health and Safety Executive

3 Do you think smoking should be banned from public places, such as cinemas, restaurants, public transport? List your reasons why / why not and discuss them with another student.

Style

1 Look at this example from the leaflet:

It is now beyond doubt that smoking is a major cause of disease …

This use of the impersonal *it* to introduce statements is very common in formal pieces of writing, particularly where the emphasis is on presenting facts or evidence.

Choose appropriate phrases from the ones below to preface statements 1–3.

It is a fact that   It seems to be the case that   It is fully understood that

1 _____ people tend to live longer nowadays.

2 _____ a balanced diet is important, especially during pregnancy.

3 _____ the demand for fitness centres is growing.

2 Look at the structure of this sentence:

It seems inevitable that we will have more free time.
It + verb + complement + *that* clause

 **2.2** page 193

The complement in this case is an adjective. Can you think of other adjectives that are commonly used in this way?

3 Here is another example of this structure, again from the reading text:

It has been recognized for some time that exposure to tobacco smoke can cause discomfort …

A passive form is used with the impersonal *it* to emphasize that the fact about to be expressed is a commonly held view.

Finish these examples with similar factual statements about smoking.

1   It has recently been suggested that …
2   It cannot be denied that …
3   It is now agreed that …

11 page 195

4 The passive forms used above are all reporting verbs. Can you suggest more reporting verbs that could be used in this way?

Introduction

What are these advertisements trying to sell? Do you think they are successful in getting their message across? ▼

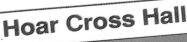

Slim Chance

Dieting is futile and downright dangerous reports Isabel Walker. In fact, many doctors now believe you would be better off staying
5 **overweight.**

Cross your heart and swear in all honesty that you have never ever been on a diet. If so, lucky you! You must be supremely confident about
10 your appearance, enviably restrained in your eating habits or blessed with an ability to eat what you like without gaining weight.

In a society whose most potent
15 icons are abnormally thin models, fat has become, quite literally, a dirty word – one of the earliest epithets to be hurled around the school playground. These days, children begin to restrict
20 their food intake as early as age nine. By fifteen, as many as one girl in three thinks she should be on a diet.

This obsession with losing weight fuels a multi-million pound slimming
25 industry which grows ever more inventive in its attempts to persuade veteran dieters that 'this one really works'. Meanwhile, it is obvious to many people that diets don't work – at
30 least, not in the long-term! If they did, we would be getting thinner, but in fact we are getting fatter.

 400 words

As many as nine (0)___*out*___ of ten dieters needn't have bothered
35 dieting at all as they put back the weight they lose; and up (1)_____ half end up weighing even (2)_____ than they did before. Most of these people see their problem
40 as a personal failure – they think they should (3)_____ been more strong-minded. This is a fallacy, however, for there is growing evidence (4)_____ many dieters get
45 locked into a losing battle with (5)_____ own bodies, which fight like mad to resist the starvation process. There is also a good reason (6)_____ believe that dieting
50 may be bad for you – particularly if it leads to regular fluctuations in weight. The phenomenon known (7)_____ 'yo-yo dieting' is now thought to represent as great a risk to
55 health, (8)_____ some respects, as the obesity which (9)_____ is designed to conquer.

These days, disillusioned dieters (10_____ advised by more and
60 more experts to throw away their scales and calorie counters and come (11)_____ terms with their physical appearance. There are of course some people (12)_____
65 problems are more serious and who really must lose weight. For those people, a healthy eating programme combined (13)_____ regular exercise is seen as (14)_____
70 safer and much more reliable route to success (15)_____ simply going on a diet.

Isabel Walker, Living

English in Use
Part 2

A Read the following extract from a magazine article, ignoring the spaces in the last two paragraphs. What points does the writer make about dieting?

B Look at the last two paragraphs of the article and supply the missing words by writing *one* word in spaces 1–15. The first one has been done for you as an example.

Modals and meaning

A   Modals, for example, *must*, *might* and *can*, are not usually tested in a cloze passage, but auxiliaries such as *be, have* and *do* may be. Why is this? The article on page 31 contained auxiliaries and several modals. Find eight modals in the article and list them in order of appearance.

Taken in context, which of the modals you have found:

1   expresses an obligation which might be fulfilled?

2   offers a logical explanation?

3   says something was done unnecessarily?

4   expresses a regret that something did not happen?

5   gives advice?

6   expresses an outcome based on an imaginary situation?

7   expresses a possibility?

8   expresses a necessity?

B   Use one of the following modals to complete sentences 1–8.

would   must   should   needn't   may

1   Even if I were angry, I _____ never speak to anyone like that!

2   The homework I'm setting you today _____ be handed in until Monday.

3   She hates the theatre here but she _____ go once in a while. It would help her learn the language.

4   This report is urgent – you _____ finish it by four o'clock.

5   _____ I help you with those bags?

6   You _____ phone back – just write a letter confirming our telephone conversation this afternoon.

7   It's difficult to say whether they'll accept the offer. They _____, they _____ not.

8   Tom _____ be caught in a traffic jam. He's never been as late as this before.

Look back at your answer to number 5. How is the modal used in this sentence?

Modals and the perfect infinitive

A   Some modals can be used with the perfect infinitive without *to* (except for *ought to*). Decide which of these modals can be combined in their positive and negative forms with the perfect infinitive.

	will	
	should	
	would	
They	might	have done it.
	need	
	could	
	must	
	can	

Which ones are not used in the positive?
How can we express the opposite of *must have done*?
Which could refer to something which might happen in the future?

B   Match sentences 1–6 with the explanations in a–e. More than one answer may be correct.

1   They couldn't / can't have done it.
2   They should have done it.
3   They would have done it.
4   They needn't have done it.
5   They ought to have done it.
6   They might / may not have done it.

a   They didn't do it.
b   They did it but it wasn't necessary.
c   I don't believe they did it.
d   I'm not sure if they did it or not.
e   They were willing to do it but they didn't.

C   Complete sentences 1–12 using one of the modals in B 1–6 in its correct form. They may be either positive or negative. More than one answer may be possible.

1   You _____ have eaten those strawberries. You know you're allergic to them!

2   Had I realized how damaging it was going to be, I certainly _____ have gone on that diet!

3   You _____ have gone back for my glasses. I've got a spare pair in my bag, but thanks anyway!

4   Try phoning the surgery. The doctor _____ not have left yet.

5   She didn't look well. That medicine she was taking certainly _____ have done her any good.

6   We _____ have written the essays. The teacher didn't even ask to see them!

7 I told you we _____ have gone to that party. I knew it would be absolutely dreadful.

8 They _____ have understood my directions. They've turned right instead of left!

9 He _____ have spoken to them about it already, there again he _____ not have.

10 I _____ definitely have informed you earlier if I'd known all the details.

11 A I've brought you some flowers.
   B Oh, you _____ have!

12 A I haven't brought that reference book with me.
   B Well, you _____ have!

Need

A What's the difference between the two statements below?

1 She needn't have gone on a diet – her body weight was exactly right for her height.
2 She didn't need to go on a diet – her body weight was exactly right for her height.

B Which statement sounds correct, which incorrect?

1 She need have gone on a diet.
2 She needed to go on a diet.

C Which question would you rarely hear?

1 Need she have gone on a diet?
2 Did she need to go on a diet?

Must, can't, mustn't, needn't

A What is the meaning of *must* in these two sentences?

1 He must be the new manager.
2 You must keep your feelings to yourself.

What is the opposite of 1?
What is the opposite of 2 when you are:

a giving somebody some advice?
b saying this is the wrong thing to do as it may be harmful?
c saying that there are alternatives one might like to consider?

What is the past of *must* in 2 above?

B Read the following dialogue then complete the gaps with *must, can't, mustn't* or *needn't* in their correct form.

John and Elaine have been sent to meet two important clients arriving at the airport. Unfortunately, they seem to have missed them.

John They're not at the reception desk so they (1)_____(wait) outside the main entrance.

Elaine They (2)_____(wait) outside the main entrance because it's locked!

John We'll ask the information desk to put out an announcement for them. We (3)_____ (find) them. We'll be in trouble if we arrive back without them!

Elaine They (4)_____(go) far because they were asked to wait, even if there was nobody to meet them right away.

John Well … we'll sit tight for a while. The flight's only just landed so we (5)_____(panic) just yet!

Elaine Hang on a minute. Actually, we (6)_____(bother) with that announcement after all. I think I can see them over there!

Practice

Complete 1–10 using a sentence containing a suitable modal. Several alternatives may be possible.

1 It was kind of you to take the trouble to come and see me in hospital but really you _____.

2 We made a mistake about the time of the appointment. I knew we _____.

3 I still haven't found that patient's file. I really _____.

4 Are you trying to tell me Julia's left her husband? She _____.

5 What? Me? Go on a crash diet? You _____.

6 If you looked at the instructions more carefully, you _____.

7 He hasn't phoned yet but it's still early. He _____.

8 I hate taking pills, but when I was ill I _____.

9 If you see a sign on a hospital bed saying 'Nil by mouth', the patient _____.

10 If you see a sign saying 'No admittance', you _____.

3 Getting to Know You

Reading *Silent Speech*

Introduction

1 Match these adjectives describing posture to each person.

round-shouldered   slouched   straight-backed   cowering

2 Does posture tell you anything about a person? Use some of these adjectives to speculate about each person's personality.

aggressive	lively	calm	dominant
expansive	flirtatious	insecure	nervous
self-confident	submissive	tense	outgoing

Reading

Multiple–choice
questions

1 What does the expression 'silent speech' convey to you? In pairs, compare your ideas. Read the introductory text to the magazine article to see if you are right.

2 Now skim read the whole article. As you read, think about these questions:

- Why is body language so important?
- How can it be used to your advantage?

Practical *psychology*

● Have you ever taken a dislike to someone for 'no reason at all'? Or ever wondered why one particular plain, dull person is swamped by a vast circle of friends and a busy social calendar? According to some psychologists the answer is simple – it's all down to body language.

Sheena Meredith explains some of the secrets of our 'silent' speech.

Body language, it seems, could be the key to all sorts of unsolved mysteries. Experts believe that our 'silent speech' – the way we move, small changes in appearance, posture and gestures – conveys far more meaning
10 than the words in any conversation. Body language can make or break any encounter, especially if you're feeling uncomfortable.

Sheena Meredith, Practical Health

Learning the Language

If body language doesn't match words, it makes us feel uncomfortable even if we can't identify why. Dr Desmond Morris, the world-famous animal and people watcher, calls these incongruities 'non-verbal leakage', the failure of our social 'mask', and being able to spot them can help us to make much more sense of our interactions.

Watching other people's body language can also help your own self-image. 'The main problem when people are insecure or lack self-esteem is that they imagine everyone else is secure,' he says. 'If you spot the tricks someone is using to intimidate you, they seem less threatening.'

So body language tactics are not to hide these signs of tension, but to gain mastery and confidence over the environment, to spot when others are being threatening or belittling, and take counter-measures. 'If you don't feel good about yourself, it's going to show. You can only fake it to an extent,' says psychologist Dr David Lewis, who teaches people how to use body language tactics to think themselves into a more confident manner.

Walk Tall

Anyone who's ever tried to change the way they move, say from being round-shouldered, knows that it takes a great deal of concentration – for a while. It can soon become as much of a habit as a slouched posture. And walking tall increases and creates confidence.

Another useful ploy to boost confidence before a tricky encounter is to look up at the sky or ceiling (if you're alone, stretch your arms up as well), then put your chin horizontal and lower your gaze, but keep your eyes and eyebrows in the same position. This simple change of facial posture can make you look, and feel, many times more confident.

'Echoes' of Friendship

Consider how you feel with true friends. There is a sense of relaxation, of freedom from the tension, power plays and uncertainty experienced during encounters with strangers. The key here is that you are of equal status. Among friends, there is a similarity of posture and a mimicry of movement, known as postural echo. It carries the message 'I am like you', making friends 'feel right' together.

Popular people seem to have a natural ability with postural echo, and it is often used by successful salespeople. The synchrony is missing in people with serious mental disturbances, and many normal people have poor postural echo. Perhaps because their parents were undemonstrative or unloving, they seem never to have absorbed the unconscious signals of co-operative movement. As the echo goes, so does the sense of rapport, and they themselves may find it difficult to make friends.

Minding your Language

People signal feeling and intent in body language. Jabbing a raised finger in conversation means power or anger. Turning the head, or crossing legs away from someone you're talking to – however animatedly – shows you don't want to be so involved.

Other 'barrier signals', like folded arms, may reveal a person's hostility or insecurity. Submission gestures like nodding and bowing are ritualised socially. We all start to edge away slightly, or sit forward in our chair, when we're too polite to say 'I'd like to leave', and most people will take the hint. Those who don't are likely to be labelled as monopolising bores.

Lies and Body Language

A whole new world opens up if you're aware of contradictory signals. If a friend who seems to be listening raptly is tapping her toes as well, change the subject – she's bored. No matter how charming the boss is being, those aggressive little foot kicks probably mean you'll not be given a pay rise. After a lovely evening, the man of your dreams says he'll call soon, but he isn't looking at you and his arms are folded – don't bother to wait by the phone.

Safe Space

The way we dominate space is an extension of body language. The more expansive we are, the more powerful, from the hands-behind-head, feet-on-desk pose, to the positioning of towels on a beach or books on a table. Furniture is often used to dominate, like the common ploy of forcing a visitor into a lowly position in the guise of having the most comfortable, squishy armchair.

Encroachments into strangers' territory, like placing your bag firmly on their desk or putting your coffee cup down near to theirs, make them nervous and increase your dominance in an encounter.

Close Encounters

The first four minutes of any encounter are critical, Dr Lewis says. When two people meeting make eye contact, both raise and lower their eyebrows in a flash greeting, which is known by experts as the 'eyebrow flash'. This may signal 'hello', a query, approval, thanks, agreement, flirtation, emphasis or occasionally disapproval.

During a conversation, direct gaze is needed for contact and to convey good intent, but it can also be threatening. Intense staring occurs at the heights of both intimacy and aggression. On the other hand, too short a gaze implies disinterest.

3 Can you say what the following words and phrases from the article mean, in your own words?

1   non-verbal leakage (line 16)   5   mimicry (line 57)
2   belittling (line 26)   6   edge away (line 81)
3   tactics (line 30)   7   take the hint (line 83)
4   ploy (line 41)   8   encroachments (line 100)

4   Multiple-choice options

Exam tip ▼

Multiple-choice questions test your ability to understand the detail and subtleties of a text. Unlike the multiple matching task that you met in Unit 2, here you should take more time, as you need to read the text in greater depth.

In the multiple-choice task, you need to apply skills of interpretation, both to what is in the text and to what exactly is stated in the multiple-choice options.

When you are answering multiple-choice questions and you are unsure which is the right answer, one strategy is to try to rule out answers which you know are incorrect. This 'process of elimination' helps you to evaluate all four options carefully. Look at this question:

1   Low self-esteem can be improved by

A   using body language to hide what you really feel.
B   using threatening behaviour to make others feel small.
C   recognizing that everyone else feels secure.
D   recognizing that body language need not be a threat.

To decide whether an option is incorrect, you first need to locate the parts of the text which are potentially relevant. Look at the underlined text from the section called *Learning the Language*.

Watching other people's body language can also help your own self-image. 'The main problem when people are insecure or lack self-esteem is that they imagine everyone else is secure,' he says. 'If you spot the tricks someone is using to intimidate you, they seem less threatening.'

So body language tactics are not to hide these signs of tension, but to gain mastery and confidence over the environment, to spot when others are being threatening or belittling, and take counter-measures. 'If you don't feel good about yourself, it's going to show. You can only fake it to an extent,' says psychologist Dr David Lewis, who teaches people how to use body language tactics to think themselves into a more confident manner.

Notice that options which use the same or similar words as those in the text do not necessarily produce the right answer! For example,

Option A picks up the word *hide* but in fact states the opposite of what is in the text.

Option B mentions the word *small* but is incorrect as the text refers to others doing the *belittling*.

Option C says that *recognizing that everyone else feels secure* is a solution but the text states that imagining everyone else feels secure is *the main problem*.

Option D is the correct answer as it reflects what is said in the text. Look at how the original wording has been changed in the option.

If you spot the tricks someone is using to intimidate you recognizing that body language

they seem less threatening. need not be a threat.

5 Now look at the following multiple-choice questions. Use the above technique to help you to decide on the correct options.

2   One of the ways to become more confident is to

A   relax more with friends.
B   imitate the facial expressions of others.
C   alter the way you walk.
D   avoid direct eye contact with people.

3   Some people have poor postural echo because they

   A   do not co-operate with their parents.
   B   do not mix with people of equal status.
   C   have not received the proper training.
   D   have not understood the signals in a relationship.

4   How can you show that you want to end a conversation?

   A   cross your legs
   B   move back a little
   C   fold your arms
   D   nod your head slightly

5   People dominate space in a meeting in order to

   A   give themselves an advantage.
   B   put other people at their ease.
   C   make themselves more comfortable.
   D   hide their own nervousness.

6   What should you try not to do in a *social encounter*?

   A   fail to return an eyebrow flash
   B   glance away while talking to someone
   C   look directly into someone's eyes
   D   appear too friendly and interested

6   Do you agree with the views in this text? How important is body language in the way we relate to other people? Discuss your answers with a partner.

Style

The organization of this text is typical of many 'general interest' articles. Consider the following features. Why is each one important to the success of the article?

- Each section has a short heading (sometimes well-known phrases).
  Walk Tall
  Close Encounters

- The first sentence of each section often encapsulates the content of that whole section.
  People signal feeling and intent in body language.
  The way we dominate space is an extension of body language.

- Key statements are often immediately exemplified.
  Anyone who's ever tried to change the way they move, say from being round-shouldered …
  A whole new world opens up if you're aware of contradictory signals. If a friend who seems to be listening raptly is tapping her toes as well …

- Quotes from specialists support the arguments made.
  Dr Desmond Morris … calls these incongruities 'non-verbal leakage' …
  'If you don't feel good about yourself, it's going to show. You can only fake it to an extent,' says psychologist Dr David Lewis …

Look out for these features in articles that you read. In Paper 2, you may be asked to write an article in either Part 1 or Part 2 and some of these features will be of use to you.

Writing *The Generation Gap* ▼

Introduction

THE TOMORROW PEOPLE

Japan is a country in turmoil: traditional values, attitudes and culture are being challenged by the nation's youth. *David Sandhu* reports.

Japan's old guard is under siege. As well as external international pressure to become a more open society, Tokyo's elders face a new, and more serious, threat to traditional Japanese values – the *shinjinrui*. Translated literally, *shinjinrui*
5 means 'new people': the first generation of Japanese teenagers to challenge authority, to do their own thing, to be young, rebellious and free. These new people grew up in a time of incredible national affluence during the 1980s. When the bubble officially burst in 1991, many young people actually benefited
10 by increased leisure time and the possibility of exploring alternative lifestyles.

 305 words

1 Look at this picture of a group of young people. With a partner, discuss what values and attitudes you think they may have.

2 The extract below is taken from an article about young people in Japan. Read the extract quickly to find the answers to these questions:

Who are the *shinjinrui*? What are their attitudes?

Micki Ebara, a young journalist working as a European correspondent, has noticed a fundamental difference in attitudes between her peers and their parents. 'My generation has a very
15 different view of the importance of work and money. The immediate post-war generation saw the creation of wealth as the most important thing in life, while people of my age have other concerns and priorities,' she says. 'I suppose we've learned to take economic prosperity for granted and don't feel the need
20 to be workaholics. Family life, leisure time, and holidays are much more important to Japanese people than before.'

'Young people don't get listened to by either parents or teachers'

As one Japanese teenager said: 'They (the older generation) think differently; they have staid ideas and won't listen to new ones. Young people don't get listened to by either parents or teachers.
25 Some older people think the young are getting very lazy.'

For Japanese young people these are exciting times, in many ways comparable to the USA during the 1950s and 1960s – the period of liberation for American teenagers – and, as the complex web of formal social structures begins to blur, the *shinjinrui's* time is here.

David Sandhu, *Young People Now*

3 Think about the relationships between young and old people in your country. In what way has there been a move away from the values and interests of the older generation?

4 Go back through the text and underline any words and expressions to do with the young and the old. Some of them may be of use in the writing task for this section.

Look at how the words *staid* and *rebellious* are used in the text. Can you supply the right word to complete the following sentences?

1 Jo was a _____ teenager who always used to stay out late.

2 Nowadays the major pop consumers are the _____ over-25s.

3 Simon had an edgy, _____ streak in his nature.

4 Jackie's a very restrained and conservative character. In fact, I'd say she was positively _____.

Writing

Sample account

Part 2, account

1 a Read the following letter. Why has it been written? If you were Julia Harrison, what would you do?

> Dear Mr Branston
>
> I am writing on behalf of the residents' association to inform you of our feelings regarding your behaviour. <u>We've really had just about enough of you.</u> Although we have tried to speak to you civilly on several occasions, you have always responded with a stream of verbal abuse.
>
> Ever since you moved in three months ago, you have shown very little consideration for the other residents of this building, despite numerous complaints. For the past six weekends in a row, you have held extremely noisy parties, which have not finished until the early hours of the morning. It's just not on! As you are aware, most of the people here are elderly or have very young children, and the noise keeps them awake all night. You don't have to be so noisy, do you? Last weekend the situation deteriorated further when two of your acquaintances were involved in a fight on the first floor landing. The disturbance was so bad that the police had to be called. What's more, your mates left the stairs in a terrible state — they even smashed two windows on their way out! We feel that this type of behaviour is intolerable.
>
> We strongly recommend that you arrange payment for the damage to the windows soon. If you don't and you carry on being a nuisance, we'll kick you out! Legal steps will be taken if necessary.
>
> Yours sincerely
>
> *Julia Harrison*

b Now read the letter again. It contains some inconsistencies in style. Can you find them? The first has been underlined for you as an example.

Now rewrite these sentences in a formal style. As you rewrite them, consider the following features:

- contractions
- use of phrasal verbs
- link words
- use of intensifiers
- use of the active and passive
- punctuation.

c Notice how the letter is organized.

- Introductory paragraph — *Reason for writing*
- Main paragraph — *Account of what has happened, beginning with the main complaint*
- Additional paragraph — *Request for action*
- Ending

Understanding the task

2 Now read this writing task. What exactly does it ask you to do? If you were really in this situation, what would you hope to achieve by writing such a letter to the company? Discuss your answers in pairs.

> You recently had a visitor from Britain staying with you for a month, as part of an exchange programme. You had asked for someone similar to you in age and interests, but the company that organized the trip actually arranged for a person of a very different age and background from yourself to stay with you. It was very difficult looking after this person, who had nothing in common with you and yet expected to be constantly entertained.
>
> Now that the visitor has left, you have decided to write to the company, describing the various problems you had, and suggesting that they should be more careful when matching people in future.

Bearing in mind the target reader, which of the styles in **1** would be appropriate for this letter?

Brainstorming ideas

3 Discuss with another student what this visitor could have been like, and what sort of problems might have arisen. Here are some aspects to consider. Add your own ideas.

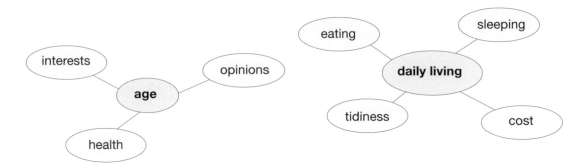

How many problems did you think of?

Planning your answer

4 Use the framework below to plan what you are going to write. You may like to use some of the suggestions given to begin each part of the letter. Decide approximately how many words each part requires, out of a total of 250.

*   Beginning the letter
    Dear Sir / Madam   Dear Mr / Mrs / Ms

    I am writing to you   regarding / concerning …
    *   with regard to …*

*   The visitor – what happened
    Although / Even though I had specifically asked you to …
    Despite / In spite of requesting …

*   Your recommendation to the company
    I suggest that …   I would urge you to …   I strongly recommend that you …

📖📖 **5** page 193

*   Ending the letter
    Yours faithfully / Yours sincerely

Writing

5 Now write the letter in about 250 words. Remember **WRITE** ✎

Check your piece of writing carefully. You should consider the accuracy of the grammar, spelling and punctuation, as well as the overall organization and effectiveness of your answer.

Listening and Speaking *Big Boys don't Cry*

Introduction

Can you think of situations that provoke extreme emotion, like the ones shown? Do men and women react in the same way in these situations?

Listening

Part 3

> **Exam tip** ▼
>
> Part 3 of Paper 4 tests your understanding of the views and attitudes being expressed in a listening text. The recording features two or more people. To help you answer questions about attitude, listen out for the intonation of the speakers.

 1 You are going to hear a discussion between a man and a woman about male and female attitudes to being ill. Before you listen to the tape, read the following statements quickly. As you listen, write *Y* (yes) or *N* (no) next to 1–7 according to whether the statements accurately reflect what the woman says or not.

1 The woman thinks that men believe they never have mild illnesses.

2 She expresses sympathy for injured football players.

3 She believes that most men try to hide their reactions to pain.

4 She thinks that men do not like to take time off work through illness.

5 She thinks that men prefer to be looked after by their mothers when they are ill.

6 She believes that women, unlike men, accept that they will experience some pain in life.

7 She thinks that women expect their partners to look after them when they are ill.

 2 Now listen again and check your answers. What is your reaction to the woman's views?

1 Read the article once only. What does the writer think about men crying in public?

Big boys do cry …
and they're heroes

Wimbledon 1992 will be remembered as the year the champion, his coach and his girlfriend all broke down in tears, and the winner and runner-up hugged each other on court in full view of 500 million spectators all round the world.

Is Andre Agassi heralding a new type of hero, the one who openly weeps and so tugs at the world's heartstrings? How many of us
5 watching also felt a tear come to our eyes as we witnessed his reaction?

Open displays of emotion, of course, are becoming common in world-class sport, at least among the
10 younger players. We've seen it among football players for the past few years. But so far, it's only the men who are shedding public tears.

Women seem to be getting tougher
15 while men are increasingly allowing their vulnerable sides to show, and not being ashamed of it, either.

According to Dr Brian Roet, author of *A Safer Place To Cry*, men who can
20 openly weep are the lucky ones, the emotionally healthy people. A common newspaper expression for people who are trying to cope with strong emotions is that they are
25 "fighting back tears". This is taken to mean that they are being brave. But how much braver if they can let the tears flow and allow everybody else to know what they are going
30 through.

Tears, Roet says, represent so many emotions: "They are a natural form of expression, like laughter. They can convey a multitude of feelings, such
35 as happiness, sadness, loneliness, fear, relief, anger, or frustration, and as such provide healthy pathways to the outside world.

"However, for some strange reason
40 society has designated this expression of emotion to be unsuitable and the feelings are forced to remain underground."

Many people, he says, have an
45 overbrimming lake of tears ever ready to flow just under the surface, yet they do their best never to let them come out, at least in public.

After 15 years in general practice, Dr
50 Roet came to realize that the inability to shed tears and show emotion was behind many of the illnesses he had been trying to treat. He now feels that providing a "safe
55 place" to cry is far more helpful to his patients than dispensing drugs. Many have not cried for years and at first are ashamed when the tears start to flow but, he says, it's only
60 when tears can come that emotional healing can take place.

"The only safe place for me to cry is in the cinema …"

"I hope that people will learn to respect tears. As we learn to laugh and cry naturally, without fear of
65 guilt, we develop peace of mind and the tranquillity that provides a healthy basis for the rest of our life."

But he admits he remains unable to shed them himself. "The only safe
70 place for me to cry is in the cinema, where the tears well up and flood over the most trivial situations."

"I believe now that I was told so much as a child that boys don't cry
75 that this imprint has sealed my tear ducts, except out of sight in the darkness of the make-believe cinema world."

Sporting stars who break down in
80 public remind us that there is nothing wimpy, nothing weak or loser-like about the ability to shed tears. Men who can cry easily are the real winners in life, those who are at
85 the same time confident and sensitive.

Agassi's tennis is wondrous, but it's his ability to cry and remind us that he is fully human rather than just a
90 tennis robot that will turn him into a world-class heart-throb.

Women always warm to a man who can cry. And perhaps the new breed of weeping sports stars will give
95 other men "permission" to cry, so that tears can become as natural a form of expression as smiling and laughter.

Liz Hodgkinson, *The Guardian*

 650 words

2   Do you agree with the writer's views? Why? Why not?

3   In the article, the writer uses the following words and phrases:

a   … when the tears start to *flow* … (line 59)
b   …. tears *well up* and *flood* … (line 71).

What do they mean?

The verbs in *italics* are usually associated with water. These verbs normally have a literal sense; however, it is also possible for them to have a metaphorical or figurative sense.

Look at the following examples of *flowing* below and decide whether the meaning is literal or metaphorical.

1   "… source of discontent," he says. "Once the oil starts **flowing**, the companies demand that the sub-contractors …"

2   … month which is extremely fast. Once the ideas start **flowing**, you don't want to block it by taking too much time …

3   … his contemplations of the turquoise **flowing** Nile were abruptly sullied by the tinny sounds of …

4   … while the European champion, confidence **flowing**, sprinted to 13 min 17.82 sec, a time he has never …

5   While the Honda's bodywork is smooth and **flowing**, the Kawasaki's is angular and punchy.

6   Above him, a full moon rode **flowing** black clouds in a charcoal sky, illuminating the …

7   The camera shows tourists **flowing** back and forth in front of the White House.

8   He divided her hair into three parts, three golden rivers **flowing** down from the hills to the plain.

4   In line 45 of the text, the writer refers to *an overbrimming lake of tears*. This is a good example of a metaphor, where the image of a lake is used to emphasize the extent to which a person may cry.

Here are some more metaphors using similar images. What type of situations could they be used to describe?

1   a sea of happy faces
2   a sea of campaign banners
3   rivers of fire
4   waves of rebellious children
5   pools of empty silence

Notice the common pattern of noun + *of* + noun. Look up the following words in your dictionaries and note down similar phrases using this pattern.

For example, *a stream of verbal abuse*.

a stream
torrents   of
floods

You may be able to use metaphors like these when you are talking about a scene in a picture (like the Speaking task on page 44) or when you are writing descriptions.

Speaking

Part 2

1 Look at the picture and read the statements made about it. Decide which statement would be the most suitable one to use first, giving your reasons. Which one might you use as a final statement?

a The scene reminds me of media coverage of the riots last year.
b This is a picture of a large and unruly crowd, who appear to be very angry about something.
c There are a number of banners, but I can't quite read the slogans on them.
d Just in front of the crowd there are …

2 You and another student are each going to look at a different picture. Student A, describe your picture in detail. You have about a minute to do this. When you have finished, ask Student B to talk about their picture.

Student B, listen to your partner's description first and then talk about two things that are similar in your picture and two things which are different. If you need to, you can ask Student A more questions.

After doing this, you should be able to say what your pictures have in common and in what way they are different. You may like to use some of the following language:

Similarities

They seem to have quite a lot in common, for example …
There isn't much difference between them …
Both of them …

Differences

Whereas yours is about X, mine is about …
They differ in several ways …
The main difference is …

 3 page 193

 **6.4** page 194

Don't forget to use prepositional phrases such as *in the foreground, in the top left-hand corner*, etc.

Student A look at picture **3A** on page 198.
Student B look at picture **3B** on page 200.

English in Use

Part 4

Exam tip ▼

Part 4 of Paper 3 tests your knowledge of word formation. You need to work out what part of speech is required in each gap. Sometimes, you will need to add a negative prefix to the word given in capital letters, to fit the sense of the text.

1 Sort these words into four groups, according to their part of speech. Which word is both a noun and a verb?

abandon	amount	basic	capacity	definition
eventually	frustrate	fundamental	insensitive	preference
reluctant	significantly	tolerance	unwillingness	vulnerable

2 Look at these prefixes. Which of them have a negative meaning?

co- de- dis- en- in- re- un- under-

Make new verbs from the ones below, using some of these prefixes. Explain how the verbs you have made differ in meaning from the original ones.

allow discover estimate exist please stabilize trap unite

What other words, with different parts of speech, are related to the verbs you have made?

3 Read the text below, ignoring the gaps for the moment. What action does it see as harmful in a relationship?

Compromise is no cure for conflict

The capacity to communicate openly and honestly in a relationship does not guarantee (0) _invulnerability_ to distress. At times, one person may (1)_____ the other, causing frustration and conflict. A compromise is normally reached, but this amounts to an (2)_____ strategy. Perhaps people should abandon the (3)_____ to smooth things over, in favour of an (4)_____ process, where more fundamental questions are asked. Though this may be very (5)_____ at the time, the airing of basic (6)_____ often leads each person to view the other more (7)_____ in the long run.

0	VULNERABLE
1	VALUE
2	AVOID
3	TEND
4	EXPLORE
5	PLEASE
6	GRIEF
7	SYMPATHY

4 Look at the example (0). What changes have been made to the word in capital letters to create the new word? What part of speech is this word?

5 Now look at gaps 1-8 and decide what part of speech is required in each. Then make suitable words from the ones given in capital letters, remembering to add negative prefixes where necessary. Check that each word makes sense in the gap.

6 In the exam, you will have to complete two texts in this way, giving a total of 15 gaps. Do the second text below, following the same procedure.

Jealousy

Jealousy can be one of the most (8)_____ feelings in any relationship. In jealousy, there is a perceived loss of (9)_____ ; if a partner is paying attention to someone else, that attention is being (10)_____ from you. Often, these feelings of jealousy remain (11)_____ , either for fear of (12)_____ the relationship or because of a basic (13)_____ to confront the issue. Jealousy endured in silence breeds (14)_____ , which in turn brings even greater (15)_____ to the sufferer.

8	AGREE
9	AFFECT
10	HOLD
11	SPEAK
12	STABILIZE
13	RELUCTANT
14	SECURE
15	HAPPY

Structure *It's Only Love* ▼

Introduction

Look at the picture. What do you think it could be illustrating?

English in Use

Part 2

A Read the following article quickly, ignoring the spaces in the first four paragraphs, then explain briefly what a love map is.

Do you think the love map is a useful idea?

B Now read the first four paragraphs of the article again and supply the missing words by writing *one* word in spaces 1–15. The first one has been done for you as an example.

A ccording to scientists' recent findings, there's simply (0)___*no*___ such thing (1)_____ random love. 'Nature has wired us for one special person,' insists Anthony Walsh, a psychologist in Idaho, USA.

Apparently we all carry (2)_____ unalterable, subliminal guide to our perfect partner (3)_____ our subconscious. When all the elements click into place, we fall in love. And, even (4)_____ we don't find a

10 perfect match, our brain circuitry will hunt for the next best thing – we (5)_____ not hooked, unless enough of the right bells ring.

From early childhood we gather information about the world and the people around us, slowly developing a map

15 (6)_____ our preferences. John Money of Johns Hopkins University in the USA has coined the phrase 'love map' (7)_____ describe the process. The love map gets (8)_____ tentacles round you at an early age. John Money reckons the age from five (9)_____

20 eight years is the crucial period for determining your destiny. As (10)_____ reach adolescence your love map begins to solidify, becoming quite specific. Our subconscious love template works overtime in the search (11)_____ the perfect match.

25 According to psychotherapist Dr Harville Hendrix, biologists and anthropologists (12)_____ mapped out the basics accurately enough – but he has gone one step further.

Hendrix insists that our love map provides far

30 (13)_____ than a route to our one true love: it offers a unique opportunity (14)_____ growth. His central premise (15)_____ that, during childhood and adolescence, most of us are hurt in some way. Almost everyone carries some form of unfinished business from

35 childhood. And so, 'We fall madly in love with someone who has both the positive and negative traits of our imperfect parents,' he says. Even tiny criticisms can lodge in the childish mind and return to haunt our adult relationships.

If you were constantly being told off for doing the wrong

40 thing, you would perhaps form the thought 'I can't do anything right', and you may constantly overreact if your adult partner is always criticising your behaviour. However, you will also find yourself following your parents' example and, if your partner doesn't perform as well as you expect, you may

45 criticise him in the way your parents criticised you.

It seems like a no-win situation. But psychotherapist Kati Blanc says not. 'The good part is that it does give you a challenge – a challenge to work things out, if you really want to grow as a person. If I've invited someone into my life,

50 albeit subconsciously, I am giving myself the challenge either to repeat the saga or to get out of it.'

Dr Hendrix believes that if one partner begins to change, the other will automatically respond. So even if our love map has clear directions, our destination is not fixed. We can opt

55 for the scenic route. ■

Jane Alexander, New Woman

⏱ **460** words

Conditionals in context

Look at these three types of conditional sentences.

1 If I see him, I'll tell him the good news.
2 If I found the perfect partner, I'd get married.
3 If you are enthusiastic about your work, you get better results.

Which of these sentences refers to something which:

a you know does not exist at this moment in time?
b is generally thought to be true?
c may very well happen in the future?

Which is usually referred to as the:

• 'zero' conditional?
• first conditional?
• second conditional?

Zero conditional

A According to Anthony Walsh:

When all the elements click into place, we fall in love.

Notice the tenses are both in the simple present. Underline five conditional sentences in the article with similar structures.

Why is the present continuous rather than the simple present used in one of the sentences?

B The conditional parts of the sentences you have found begin with either *unless, if* or *even if*. What is the difference between these words and expressions?

First conditional

A The first conditional suggests that, given certain circumstances, there is a possibility of something happening in the future. Find two examples of first conditional sentences in the article.

Which example suggests that it makes no difference whether something happens or not because the outcome will be the same?

B A variation on the first conditional

We can use the present perfect in the conditional part of the sentence to suggest that something may already exist or has already happened. Can you find an example of this type of conditional in the article?

Why is the tense in the main part of this sentence in the continuous form?

Second conditional

Look at these examples of the second conditional:

1 If I were the King or Queen of England, I'd give all my money to charity.
2 If you were to win $20,000,000 in a lottery, what would you do?

Which is used to refer to:

a a possible, but highly unlikely, future situation?
b a set of circumstances which you know very well does not exist now and never will?

Can you find an example of a second conditional in the article which is similar in meaning to the example in 1?

Practice

A   Cause and effect in conditional sentences

Form plausible conditional sentences using the conditionals and modals below, or an imperative.

If you're planning to stay here for a while	might
If we had time to study more	could
If we really loved each other	will
Unless you can agree	would
If you've had a row	should
Even if he were to apologize	Imperative,
Even if they begged me	eg tell/don't tell

Which conditionals suggest that it wouldn't make any difference if these things happened?

B   Tenses in conditional sentences

Complete the sentences with an appropriate form of the verb in brackets. You may also need to use a modal or an imperative. If the verb is in the imperative form, decide whether it should be positive or negative.

1 If I (be) ten years younger, I (take) a year off work and (travel) around the world.
2 (ask) them to the wedding unless you (want) to.
3 If I (see) her tomorrow, I (tell) her what you said.
4 If you (think) about becoming a vet, you (find) out what subjects you need to study.
5 If I (be) to ask you how old you are, you (answer) me?
6 If they (have) a little more common sense, they (not ask) such ridiculous questions all the time.
7 (accept) his proposal of marriage unless you (be) really sure you (make) up your mind.
8 Even if I (have) more time, I (not afford) to go out more than twice a week.

Can You Believe It ?

Listening and Speaking *Strange but True* ▼

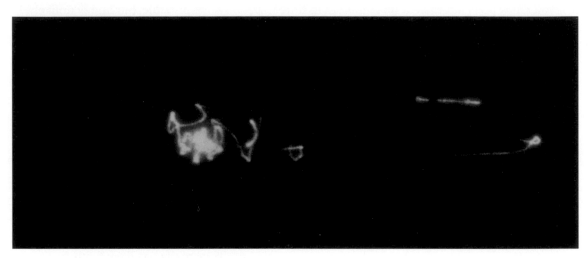

Introduction

1 What could this picture be?

Have you ever witnessed a strange phenomenon?

2 Read this account. Can you explain what the phenomenon is?

eye**witness**

GLADYS HUGHES of Colwyn, North Wales, was driving home in her car one June evening when she ran into a bank of mist rolling off the river. She
5 suddenly saw a glowing ball of translucent greenish light, about the size of a football, spinning forwards like a wheel, with four spikes of light radiating out from it. It slid up to about
10 a foot away from her side window.

Wondering if she had gone mad or if aliens were visiting from outer space, she slowed the car down, and, in perfect synchrony, the ball slowed down too.
15 She then accelerated and again the ball kept perfect pace. No matter what she did she could not shake the thing off, and only when the mist faded away did the ball suddenly shoot up and away out
20 of sight.

Fearing that her sanity would be questioned, Gladys didn't even mention this at home, but her husband had witnessed something similar – a glowing
25 green ball shooting up high into the sky, at about eight o'clock. And in the next few days, news seeped out that several others had witnessed the strange green light rocketing into the evening sky.

Paul Simons, *The Guardian*

3 If this experience happened to you, how would you feel afterwards and why? Here are words to help you:

elated   exhausted   nervous   perplexed   unaffected   terrified.

English in Use

Part 3

1 These are some of the grammatical areas that are tested in Part 3 of Paper 3.

- use of articles   *the, a / an*
- prepositions   *to, of*
- conjunctions   *while, as*

This proofreading task involves finding a word that does not fit in with the rest of the text, either because it is unnecessary or because the sense is wrong in relation to the text.

Look at the first part of this task, which has been completed. Say why some of the words in 0–4 are unnecessary. To do this, you will have to talk about the words before and after the errors.

Great Balls of FIRE

Some years ago, a professor of the electrical engineering	0 _____*the*_____
witnessed a glowing ball aboard a plane. It came floating	0 _____✓_____
down the aisle, gliding from out the cockpit and exiting	1 _____*out*_____
gracefully through the rear toilets. Several of electrical	2 _____*of*_____
workers have also witnessed strange glowing balls while	3 _____*while*_____
during their work, which often involves high voltage equipment.	4 _____✓_____

2 Now read the rest of the text. Make sure you read all of the words carefully. Write the words that are unnecessary in the space provided. Four of the lines are correct. Mark these with a tick, as shown above.

So what is the ball lightning? At a recent conference,	5 _____
scientific experts grew increasingly hot under their	6 _____
academic collars, their only explanations ranging from	7 _____
glowing micro-meteorites to fields out of energy that	8 _____
condense then into balls of light at their centre.	9 _____
Yet the sheer volume of evidence does point to one very	10 _____
neat theory. Many sightings must happen towards the end of	11 _____
a ferocious thunderstorm. The balls often precede a huge	12 _____
bolt of lightning. The current which leaks before that the	13 _____
flash is in the form of a glowing ball that is attracted to	14 _____
electrical equipment in too confined spaces – hence its	15 _____
floating into aircraft and houses.	

Listening

Part 4

Exam tip ▼

In Part 4 of Paper 4, you will hear five short extracts of different people speaking. You must answer 10 questions in all. Make sure you read through the questions before you listen.

1 Look at pictures a–h below. Decide with another student what they are illustrating, choosing from this list.

ball lightning   a UFO   the Northern Lights
an earthquake   a shooting star   a solar eclipse
corn circles   an avalanche

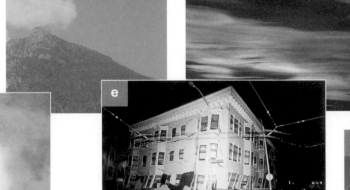

2 You will hear five people talking about phenomena they have witnessed. Decide what each person is talking about, choosing from a–h above.

Speaker 1_____   Speaker 3_____   Speaker 5_____

Speaker 2_____   Speaker 4_____

3 Now listen to the tape again and answer these questions.

1   What was it like in the cabin, according to Speaker 1?

    A   chilly   B   airless   C   damp

2   Why was Speaker 2 troubled by the event?

    A   Her room was damaged.
    B   It woke her up.
    C   She hadn't predicted it.

3   How does Speaker 3 sound?

    A   rather perplexed   B   totally calm   C   extremely elated

4   Why didn't Speaker 4's group expect to witness anything?

   A   It was the wrong time of day.
   B   The weather was getting cloudy.
   C   They had waited for so long.

5   Which word best describes Speaker 5's feelings?

   A   disappointed
   B   unenthusiastic
   C   insecure

Vocabulary

Phrasal verbs

In this section, you have come across phrasal verbs with *up* and *out* (for example, *shoot up* and *get out*). Here are some other verbs which combine with *up* and *out*. Fit the most suitable phrasal verb into the gapped sentences, choosing an appropriate tense.

run   break

up

take   **out**   make

1   Nobody believed Edward when he told them about the UFO. They thought he
    _____ the whole story.
2   She's been house-bound for so long, she really needs to be _____ for
    the evening.
3   After months of careful planning, the three convicts finally managed to
    _____ of the top security prison.
4   Would you mind going to the shops for me? I _____ of milk.
5   Her daughter _____ a huge phone bill without her knowledge.
6   The sea was so rough and stormy that they could barely _____ the
    island in the distance.

Speaking

Part 3

1   You have witnessed a possible UFO sighting. You and another witness are being
    interviewed about the event on local radio. Unfortunately, your accounts don't quite
    match! Listen to the other witness's version and interrupt tactfully if you think
    something is incorrect.

    Read the details and be ready to tell your side of the story. Student A, read extract **4A** on
    page 198. Student B, read extract **4B** on page 200.

    Student C (the interviewer) should prepare some questions to ask the other two.
    Cover these aspects:

    • when the event took place
    • where each person was
    • how many UFOs were seen
    • their size, shape, colour
    • how each person reacted.

2   Here are some suggestions for ways to interrupt. Which ones seem the most tactful?

   Excuse me, but that isn't quite right.   *Hang on, get your facts straight …*

   Just a minute! It wasn't like that at all …   *That's absolute rubbish!*

   No, no, you've got that wrong. Listen …   *What really happened was …*

   Could I just say something about that?   *I don't think I agree with you there …*

3   page 193
9.2 page 195

Reading *Lost and Alone*

Introduction

1 How much do you enjoy the company of other people? Could you survive alone on a desert island for a long period of time? How might such an experience affect you?

2 Which of these words relate to loneliness and isolation? What do the other words mean? Look them up in a dictionary if you are not sure.

solitary	remote	abandoned	exile
conceited	celebrity	deserted	weary
gregarious	eccentric	intimate	reclusive

Reading

Part 2

1 Read the opening paragraph of the text about Kaspar Hauser. Do you know anything about his life story?

> On Monday 26 May 1828, the Unschlitt Square in Nuremberg was almost deserted. At about five in the afternoon, a weary-looking youth dragged himself into the square. He was well-built but poorly dressed, and walked in a curious stiff-limbed manner. He held an envelope in his hand.

Exam tip ▼

Part 2 of Paper 1 is a gapped text. Your task is to complete the gaps in the text with the missing paragraphs. To do this successfully, you must understand the sequence and content of the text, looking out for linking words and reference markers.

2 Look at the next two paragraphs of the text. Read the notes about the highlighted parts.

> It contained two letters. The first began: 'I send you a lad who wishes to serve his king in the army. He was brought to me on October 7, 1812. I am but a poor labourer with children of my own to rear. His mother asked me to bring up the boy. Since then, I have never let him go out of the house.' The other stated that he was born on April 30 1812 and that his name was Kaspar. His father had been a cavalry soldier and was now dead.

> Taken to the police station, the boy accepted a pencil and wrote 'Kaspar Hauser'. But to other questions he answered 'Weiss nicht' – I don't know. The boy was locked in a cell, and his gaoler observed that he seemed perfectly contented to sit there for hours without moving. He had no sense of time, and seemed to know nothing about hours and minutes. It soon became clear that he had a very small vocabulary.

This sentence refers back to the envelope that was mentioned in the first paragraph.

In the sequence of events, taking Kaspar Hauser to the police station is logical. The reference to 'the boy' means that this event could not happen later in the story.

The next paragraph will probably refer in some way to Kaspar Hauser's vocabulary.

Now find the correct paragraph to follow on, choosing from A–F. You should only need to scan the paragraphs, looking for references to Kaspar's vocabulary.

A

It seems that all this attention and good living was not good for Kaspar's character; predictably, he became vain, difficult and conceited. Back in Nuremberg, his new guardian arranged for him to stay in the town of Ansbach, with a friend, Dr Meyer. Kaspar was to be guarded by a certain Captain Hickel, a security officer. Feeling he had done his duty, Stanhope disappeared back to England.

B

For as long as Kaspar could remember he had lived in a small room and its windows were boarded up. There was no bed, only a bundle of straw on the bare earth. The ceiling was so low that he could not stand upright. He saw no one. When he woke up he would find bread and water in his cell. Sometimes his water had a bitter taste, and he would go into a deep sleep; when he woke his straw would have been changed and his hair and nails cut. The only toys were three wooden horses. One day a man had entered his room and taught him to write his name and to repeat phrases like 'I want to be a soldier' and 'I don't know'. Shortly after this, he woke up to find himself in the baggy garments in which he had been found, and the man came and led him into the open air. He was abandoned somewhere near the gates of Nuremberg.

C

Then, only a few days before Christmas, Kaspar staggered into the house gasping: 'Man stabbed me ... knife ... Hofgarten ... gave purse ...' A hastily summoned doctor discovered that Kaspar had been stabbed in the side, just below the ribs. Hickel rushed to the park where Kaspar had been walking and found a silk purse containing a note, written in mirror-writing. It said: 'Kaspar will be able to tell you how I look, from where I came and who I am.' But Kaspar could tell them nothing about the man's identity. Hickel also revealed a fact that threw doubt on the story: there had only been one set of footprints – Kaspar's – in the snow. But when, on 17 December, Kaspar slipped into a coma his last words were: 'I didn't do it myself'.

D

Most people took the view that his life was in danger. He was moved to a new address, and two policemen were appointed to look after him. For the next two years Kaspar vanished from the public eye. But not from the public mind. Now the novelty had worn off, there were many in Nuremberg who objected to supporting Kaspar on the rates. Then a solution was proposed that satisfied everyone. A wealthy and eccentric Englishman, Lord Stanhope, took him off on a tour of Europe. Kaspar was again the object of endless interest.

E

He could say that he wanted to become a cavalryman like father – a phrase he had obviously been taught like a parrot. To every animal he applied the word 'horse' and he seemed to be fascinated by horses. He did not even seem to know the difference between men and women, referring to both as 'boys'. His knowledge of words increased from day to day, and as he learned to speak he was gradually able to tell something of his own story.

F

Suddenly Kaspar was famous; his case was discussed all over Germany. The town council decided to take Kaspar under their protection; he would be fed and clothed at their expense. The town council also appointed a guardian for its celebrity, a scientist named Daumer. Under his care, Kaspar finally developed into a young man of normal intelligence. Like any teenager, he enjoyed being the centre of attention. Then, a mere seventeen months after he had been 'found', someone tried to kill him. He was found lying on the floor of the cellar of Daumer's house, bleeding from a head-wound, with his shirt torn to the waist. Later he described being attacked by a man wearing a silken mask, who had struck him either with a club or a knife.

The Encyclopedia of Unsolved Mysteries

3 Scan the remaining five paragraphs to find links between them. Look in particular for:

- a sequence of events.
- references to people.
- repeated references to things or events.

Sort the paragraphs into the correct order.

4 Explain the meaning of these phrases from the text.

1 good living (paragraph A)
2 Feeling he had done his duty (paragraph A)
3 A hastily summoned doctor (paragraph C)
4 a fact that threw doubt on (paragraph C)
5 the public eye (paragraph D)
6 the novelty had worn off (paragraph D)
7 a mere seventeen months (paragraph F)

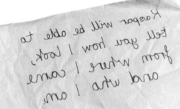

5 What do you think really happened to Kaspar Hauser:

- in his childhood?
- at the end of his life?

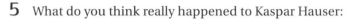

Style

1 The text reflects a narration of a sequence of events.

- Time references are used.
  One day a man …
  Shortly after this …

Find more examples of time references in the text.

- Specific events are described at the beginning of the paragraph, for clarity and effect.
  Taken to the police station, …
  Suddenly Kaspar was famous …

2 The text is not just a dry, factual account. The writer tries to bring some life to the story and engage the reader's interest.

- There are references to contemporary life.
  Like any teenager, he enjoyed being the centre of attention.

- The writer gives a point of view.
  It seems that all this attention and good living was not good for Kaspar's character …

- Simple quotations dramatize the story.
  '*Man stabbed me … knife … Hofgarten … gave purse*'.

Writing *Predicting the Future* ▼

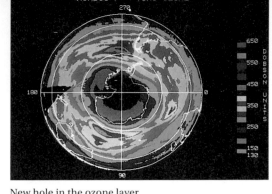

New hole in the ozone layer

Florida Hurricane

Nelson Mandela is freed

The Fall of the Berlin Wall

Introduction

Michel Nostradamus, who lived in France in the sixteenth century, wrote about his visions of the future. Many people have tried to interpret his verses. One author, Peter Lorie, claims that the events above are mentioned in the writings of Nostradamus. Match them to these dates and say whether you believe it is possible to predict such events.

1989   1990   1992   1995

In one of his books, Lorie interprets the verses to predict two more events. These are:

In 1998, someone, perhaps an amateur camera-person, happens across a group of creatures which evidently appear to be aliens 'from the sky' while on a road on Earth. Nostradamus goes so far as to describe the beings as having a 'broken, limping' movement. The aliens flee and return to their home world but the capturing of the images on film alters public opinion in regard to extra-terrestrial life.

Mars, our closest planetary neighbour, is visited for the first time by humans in 2000. A new technology is mentioned in the verse, heralded by the statement that it 'grows instead of lessens'. The new method of travel will not make use of the massively heavy and quickly expended fuels that lifted the moon rockets so laboriously out of the earth's atmosphere. The new form of propulsion will create the possibility of much longer and more economical space travel.

How valid is this kind of prediction, in your opinion?

Writing

Part 2, competition entry

Exam tip ▼

In Part 2 of Paper 2, you may be asked to write a competition entry. Remember that this is not a letter. The task may mention publication in a magazine or newsletter, or offer a 'prize' for the best entries. As in a real competition, it is important for your writing to be unusual and engaging if it is to be successful.

Sample entries

1 a Read the following pieces of writing and the competition to which they refer. Which one do you think would be the winning entry?

TRAVEL BACK IN TIME

Which famous person from the past would you most like to meet and why?

Imagine you could travel back in time – what questions would you ask the person and how would you like to spend your time with him or her?

The winning entry will receive a year's subscription to *Living History* magazine.

Entry A

Alexander the Great was the son of King Philip II of Macedonia. When Philip was murdered he became king. He was only 20. I would like to meet him because he was a great general. I am very interested in his story and I am studying it. Sometimes it is incredible to read about what happened in the past. History can teach us a lot about life, I think. Alexander the Great conquered all the land between Egypt and India. He was 33 when he died. That is not very old but it was different in those times. I would like to spend some time with him. I would like to meet him after he had won a battle.

I would ask Alexander the Great a lot of questions.

He founded the city of Alexandria, which became a great port and a centre of Greek culture and learning. I would like to ask him about that city. When he fought a battle he usually had fewer soldiers than his enemy. I would like to ask him how he won those battles. I really would like to meet Alexander the Great. I hope I can win this competition because I am a student of history. I think your magazine is a very good magazine for history students.

Alexander the Great – unequalled through time

A successful general, the creator of a huge empire and the cultural ambassador of his generation – imagine what could be learned from Alexander the Great! If time travel existed, it would be a privilege to meet this powerful man, and spend some time in his company.

There is so much he could explain to me. What, for example, was the secret of his military success? So well-trained were his soldiers that even when they were outnumbered by the enemy, they were victorious. We know about his strategy from history books, but what motivated him in his campaigns?

Culturally, he left a huge legacy in the city of Alexandria, which he founded. Did he enjoy this other success, away from the battlefield?

How did he cope with the untimely death of his father, who was callously murdered when Alexander was only 20? As a result of this, responsibilities were thrust upon him at a very early age.

If I could spend some time with him privately, I would tactfully ask him about his feelings and try to get to know him as a person. He was only 33 when he died. I am also 33 and I have done very little in comparison to him! Would we have anything in common, I wonder? It would be fascinating to find out.

Entry B

b What are the successful ingredients in the winning entry? Compare the following aspects in the two pieces.

- Does the piece fulfil the requirements of the competition?
- Is there a title?
- How well organized is each piece?
- How strong is the opening sentence?
- What is the average sentence length?
- How are questions used in each piece?
- Is there any repetition?
- Is all the material relevant to the task?
- Is there a personal angle?
- How is each piece concluded?

c Look at some of the language used in the better entry.

• Giving extra information	*A successful general, …*
• Sentences starting with *So* for emphasis	*So well-trained were his soldiers that …*
• Conditional sentences	*If I could spend some time with him privately, I would …*
• Using adverbs to introduce a topic	*Culturally, he left a …*

 **8.1** page 195

Remember that adverbs like the last example above are always formed from adjectives. They often come at the beginning of a sentence, or are used in combination with an adjective. For example,

<u>Physically</u>, I felt very fit but, <u>psychologically</u>, I was a wreck.

It is quite possible that there are other beings that are <u>technologically superior</u> to ourselves.

They also combine frequently with the word 'speaking'. For example,

The film is very successful, <u>visually speaking</u>.

Understanding the task   **2**   Now look at this writing task. What period of time does it cover?

> You see the following announcement in an international magazine and decide to enter the competition.

WHAT will life be like a hundred years from now?

And **HOW** will today's lifestyle be viewed by those living in the 22nd century?

back from THE FUTURE

Think about your answers to both of these questions and then write us an original entry of around 250 words. We would like you to write to us 'from the future', contrasting your life in the year 2100 with life as it used to be in the 'past' that is today!

The three best entries will be published in our Spring issue.

Brainstorming ideas   **3**   Brainstorm your ideas about life in the future. Here is a picture to help you get started.

3 page 193

Now discuss the variety of ways in which you could contrast this lifestyle with that of today. Remember that you are going to be writing in the year 2100!

Focusing on the reader   **4**   Discuss how you could make your piece of writing more appealing to the reader. Consider these aspects:

- Title and opening sentence. Try to think of a relevant but intriguing title that will engage the reader. Your opening sentence should then develop from the title, perhaps revealing more about the content of the piece of writing as a whole. Look back at how this was done in the sample entry.

- Use of questions. Remember how questions were used in the sample entry to introduce a topic. Using questions sparingly to contrast the two different lifestyles will make your writing more original.

- Description. Use adjectives to make your writing more vivid and informative. Avoid repeating the same words and phrases.

- Choice of tenses. Look at the grammar section to review the different past tenses which can be used.

Planning your answer   **5**   Decide how you are going to organize your writing, separating your ideas into suitable paragraphs. Remember to include a forceful ending. (Don't be tempted to finish like sample entry A!) Finally, look again at the language that was highlighted in **1**c.

Writing   **6**   Now write your entry for the competition, in about 250 words. Remember **WRITE** ✎.

Introduction

The picture opposite is a 'still' from a film. What is happening in the picture and what might be causing it? If someone told you that supernatural causes were responsible for what is happening, how would you react?

English in Use

Part 2

A Read the text ignoring the spaces, then, with a partner, discuss the arguments for and against the existence of poltergeists.

B Look at the last two paragraphs of the article. Supply the missing words by writing *one* word in spaces 1–15. The first one has been done for you as an example.

Poltergeists

Poltergeists are associated with a range of seemingly inexplicable physical occurrences, such as strange noises and movement of objects, over a period of time.

In 1967, William Roll, then Director of the Psychical Research Foundation of North Carolina, was able to observe poltergeist effects associated with a 19-year-old boy, Julio. Julio was working as a shipping clerk in Miami. This was a job
5 which involved, among other things, working in a warehouse that was used for storing small, fragile objects. Although Julio was used to handling these delicate objects, when he was in the warehouse, they used to fly off shelves, and Roll noted that certain objects would do this much more frequently than
10 others. He experimented by putting those objects in different places from where levitations appeared to occur frequently, and keeping them under constant observation.

Roll's observation of one incident goes as follows:

At 11.27 am a glass from Tier 2 broke. This glass had been
15 12 inches from the edge of a shelf with several things in front of it. At that time Julio was working nearby but had no visible contact with Tier 2. The glass was four feet from his back. It moved away from him. Nothing in front of the glass was disturbed, so it must have risen at least two inches to clear
20 everything.

This is the type of evidence (0)___*which*___ must be considered carefully (1)_____ trying to evaluate poltergeist phenomena. Probably 95% of cases reported to researchers are, however, not (2)_____ a second visit.
25 Reports of strange goings-on may come (3)_____ lonely, isolated people who really only want (4)_____ to talk to. Sometimes, a precise cause of apparently inexplicable events can be found.

For (5)_____, one investigator studied the claim of an
30 old lady (6)_____ the spirit of her recently deceased husband could switch her bedside lamp on or off (7)_____ her request. Indeed, the investigator saw the light go on and off (8)_____ direct human touch, just (9)_____ the woman described, and mostly when she
35 asked for this (10)_____ happen. Checking the flex, plug and socket showed (11)_____ that would explain this bewildering event. Dismantling the lamp, however, revealed the cause: a thermal switch had accidentally been incorporated into the circuit near the bulb, (12)_____
40 the lamp to wink on and off. The woman, missing her husband and not used to living (13)_____ her own, had presumably learned to time (14)_____ requests to coincide (15)_____ the natural time cycle of the lamp switching on and off.

Eysenck and Sargent, Explaining the Unexplained

Tenses in accounts and narratives

A

1 The five sentences below all contain tenses which can be used in accounts and narratives. Can you name the tenses?

a Julio was working as a shipping clerk in Miami.
b Julio was about to start work as a shipping clerk in Miami.
c Julio worked as a shipping clerk in Miami.
d Julio had been working as a shipping clerk in Miami.
e Julio had worked as a shipping clerk in Miami.

2 Which tenses can be used to give background information about a story in the past?

3 Which tense can be used to relate events in a story or give an account of something?

4 Which tense implies that the action had not yet taken place?

5 Which tense can be used to show that one action happened before another in the past?

6 Which tenses can be used to emphasize the fact that the action continued for some time?

B Complete the following sentences with a suitable form of the verb in brackets, using one of the tenses in **A**.

1 Night (fall) when the Morrisons suddenly (spot) a strange glow in the sky.

2 The young girl (work) in the shop for several months before she (notice) that things often (move) from one place to another.

3 After these strange occurrences, Mary (decide) to look for another job. She (go) to every employment agency in the area but she (have) no luck.

4 At that time, Julio (work) in the warehouse and I (do) research into poltergeists.

5 John (place) the glass on the shelf, (make) a note of its exact position and (be) just about to go home when the burglar alarm (go) off.

6 While the coach (travel) along the motorway last night, something very strange (occur).

7 The occupants of the house (say) that they (never notice) any strange noises in the attic until the night the terrible storm (break).

8 The children (play) upstairs and I (have) a bath when suddenly we (hear) the sound of breaking glass.

9 Everything (run) smoothly for many years when the strange sequence of events (start) to happen.

10 Julio's boss (be) just about to suggest that the explanations (sound) implausible when he (change) his mind.

Past perfect, simple past

A What is the difference between these two pairs of sentences?

1 Barry knew it was wrong to steal.
2 Barry knew it had been wrong to steal.

3 Sally never saw the film.
4 Sally had never seen the film before.

B Look at the paragraph which gives Roll's account of one incident, and at the last paragraph of the article. What happened:

1 before the glass broke?
2 before the investigator began to look into the strange case of the lamp?

C Which tense, the simple past or the past perfect, would you use for the verbs in brackets?

1 By midnight, I (finish) the work and (be) ready to hand it in the next day.

2 Until last week, the research he (be) involved in (prove) inconclusive.

3 The scientist (point) out that the book he (write) the previous year (be) already out-of-date.

Practice

Now complete this extract about *déjà vu* with a suitable form of the verb in brackets.

Déjà vu is a feeling of having experienced a present situation before. I have been teaching students in the same college for many years now, but I remember one occasion in particular when I (experience) this disturbing phenomenon.

A few years ago I (teach) a student Physics in an upstairs lecture room where I (never teach) before. I (reach) the part of the lesson where we (discuss) radioactivity when I (be) swamped by a feeling of *déjà vu*. I (know) I (be) about to refer to a book in my office. I also (know) that on a previous occasion I (go) to collect it from the office. I (turn) to my student and (ask) him if we (do) the work already. He (look) puzzled and (reply) that we (not do) anything like it before. However, my awareness of the experience (not make) the *déjà-vu* feeling go away, even when I (try) not to repeat the pre-set pattern.

Used for, used to, be / get used to, would

A The following information appears in the article:

1 The warehouse was used for storing small objects.
2 Julio was used to handling these delicate objects.
3 The objects used to fly off the shelves.
4 Certain objects would do this much more frequently than others.

Which of the verb forms above mean:

a often did this?
b that was its purpose?
c was accustomed to?

Which verb form does not exist in the present with the same meaning?

B In which of the following sentences could you use *would* instead of *used to*?

1 William Roll used to be the Director of the Psychical Research Foundation of North Carolina.
2 William Roll used to spend hours reading books about supernatural phenomena.

What is the difference between the two forms?

C What is the difference between these two sentences?

1 Julio was used to handling delicate objects.
2 Julio got used to handling delicate objects.

How would you express these sentences:

a in the interrogative?
b in the negative?
c in the present?

Practice

A Complete these sentences with *used for, used to, be / get used to* or *would*. In some sentences more than one answer may be possible.

1 My parents hated living in a big city but they eventually _____ it.
2 Michael doesn't smoke now but he _____.
3 When my Italian friends first arrived in this country they found it difficult to _____ the climate.
4 This cabinet was _____ filing documents.
5 Leaving home was difficult for Frank. His mother had always done everything for him and he just _____ looking after himself.
6 _____ your brother _____ live in the USA?

7 _____ your brother eventually _____ living in the USA?
8 When James was a student in Paris he _____ save up for days to go and buy a cake and a cup of coffee in a real café!
9 The teacher never _____ be so bad-tempered!
10 It was a question of _____ a different way of life.
11 When we were children, we _____ swim in the river near where we lived.
12 Originally, the building _____ housing rare books.

In which sentences could you not substitute *would* for *used to*? Why not?

B Write a short paragraph outlining how life has changed over the last century. Use some of these prompts to help you describe what life used to be like:

transport   eating habits   communication
family life   entertainment   health care   fashion

All Walks of Life

Listening and Speaking *Lifestyles* ▼

Introduction

1 Read the title of the article below. What do you think it could be about?

2 Skim read the article and see if your prediction was correct. What view of the travelling way of life is expressed? Do you agree with it?

These children are taught to survive

The criticism generally levelled at "New Age travellers" who do not send their children to school every day is that somehow we are unfit to teach our own children. That we are depriving them of a "proper" education
5 and a "normal" life.

In fact, while some of us have been made homeless or unemployed and taken to the road as a survival tactic, many have made a conscious and positive decision to live in this way, not because "the system" has failed us
10 personally (many of us are well-qualified) but because it is clearly misguided and is failing so many. It would be foolish to disregard everything taught in schools. Our children need to know how to read and write, handle numbers, and experience music, sports, art and craft work. But I
15 cannot agree that all children should know certain prescribed facts and acquire certain prescribed skills at certain ages.

Our way of education is a kind of insurance. If we accept that adult life may involve having at least some periods
20 with very little money, with a lot of time on our hands, perhaps without a secure place to live, that skills have to be adapted and developed to compete in the job market, then our children are equipped better than most. They may not all know what happened in 1066 by the age of eight
25 and three-quarters, but most understand how to light a fire, build a tarpaulin shelter, find cheap food and clothing, saw and chop wood, handle and care for animals and deal with other children and adults in a variety of real situations.

Our way of education is a kind of insurance

Visitors unused to life on site are often struck by the
30 "adultness" of our young children. Three- and four-year-olds mix freely with adults, pay social calls without their parents, might get involved in feeding chickens, milking goats, mending engines, making pastry, jewellery and wood burners. As well as learning "skills" and "information", they
35 learn to accept a lot of people and their different behaviour. The feeling of common shared humanity, that we are all part of one "family", is important in the travelling community, and instead of striving to conform to a norm or compete for position, children are encouraged to accept
40 that we are all different but all due respect in our own way.

Esmeralda Greenslade, *The Guardian*

380 words

3 The phrases below have been taken from the article. In pairs, discuss what you think they mean.

1 unfit to teach (line 3)
2 taken to the road (line 7)
3 "the system" has failed us (line 9)
4 compete in the job market (line 22)
5 equipped better than most (line 23)

6 mix freely (line 31)
7 common shared humanity (line 36)
8 striving to conform (line 38)
9 compete for position (line 39)

4 Which of these phrases describe the lifestyle of the travellers?

Listening
Part 2

1 You are going to listen to a radio news broadcast in which the newsreader is talking about a recent clash between travellers, the police and local residents. Before you listen, read through the incomplete notes below and think about the type of information you will need to complete each gap.

2 Now listen to the broadcast. Fill in the missing information with no more than three words in each gap. Listen to the tape once only!

BROADCAST NOTES

Update on summer solstice celebrations:

travellers heading for (1)_____

police report build up of traffic

Situation in Shepton Mallet:

travellers are (2)_____

north of the town

Complaints by local residents:

(3)_____

gardens trampled

(4)_____

Traveller's claim:

(5)_____

vehicles not (6)_____

Exam tip ▼

Remember that you may have to write in note form. After you have completed each gap, make sure that the words you have added make sense in the sentences or notes.

---

3 How would you feel if a group of travellers came and set up camp near you? What would be the attitude of other people you know? In groups, discuss how the situation could best be handled.

Speaking

Parts 2 and 4

1 Compare and contrast

You should do this activity in pairs. You are each going to look at a different picture. Student A, describe your picture in detail. In particular, say as much as you can about:

- what the people are doing.
- what the people are wearing.
- what kind of people they might be.
- the surroundings.

Student B, listen carefully. Pick out five things which are different in your picture. You can ask your partner questions about their picture to help you.

Some of the following phrases may be useful if you want to check details about your partner's picture:

I'm not sure what you mean by …
Could you tell me a bit more about …?
What did you say about …?
How would you describe …?

3 page 193
6.4 page 194

Student A, look at picture **5A** on page 198.
Student B, look at picture **5B** on page 200.

2

What do the pictures tell you about the lifestyles of the young people in them? In what ways are they different?

3 Explain and discuss

With your partner explain what the concept 'lifestyle' means. Think of ways of completing the following phrases:

To me 'lifestyle' means …
'Lifestyle' is not something …
When people talk about 'lifestyle' …

4

Now describe your own lifestyle. Look at the adjectives and adverbs below. Combine the adverbs on the left with the adjectives on the right to form questions to ask each other. For example,

Would you describe your life as fairly organized?

fairly	energetic
extremely	organized
reasonably	relaxed
very	demanding
quite	quiet

If you could change your lifestyle, what changes would you make?

English in Use

Part 5

1 Look at the extract from a radio interview below. It is with a policewoman who has been involved in an incident with some New Age travellers. Following this is a newspaper report about the incident. The interview is in informal, spoken English, while the newspaper report is in a more formal and written style.

Read both texts and then look at the two examples which have been done for you in the newspaper report.

As you can see, you only need to use a few words (never more than two) to fill the gap. The meaning should remain as close as possible to what the policewoman said, although the words you use should not be the same as the ones that appear in the first text. Think of other ways of filling these first two gaps without using the actual words from the interview.

Interview with a Policewoman

'It was absolute chaos, they really messed things up! It was about 8.30 last night when it was decided we had to try and move the convoy off the motorway.

5 It was taking up all four lanes of the motorway, including the hard shoulder, right up to the service station near junction 11.

About 50 officers set off towards the
10 vehicles but they just started throwing stones and rocks.

Fortunately, we didn't get hurt but we had to go back and get our riot shields. We then managed to discuss things with the
15 travellers who eventually agreed to break up and go off in three different directions.

In the meantime, of course, there were delays to traffic in both directions so we had to shut off the north-bound lanes, just
20 in case.

What we are trying to do is to keep an eye on these convoys and prevent them from camping illegally on common land this holiday weekend.'

---

2 Now fill in the gaps in the news report.

Police pelted with stones by travellers blocking M5

Police were pelted with stones last night after they (1)_*attempted to*_ move a convoy of travellers blocking the M5 motorway.

The convoy (2) _*was blocking*_ all four lanes of the motorway, including the hard shoulder, as far as the service station at junction 11.

As 50 officers (3)_____ the vehicles, stones and rocks (4)_____. (5)_____ was injured, and after retreating to obtain riot shields, officers

(6)_____ with the travellers, who agreed, after nearly four hours, to break up the convoy into groups and (7)_____ in three different directions.

During the delay, heavy traffic built up on the south-bound side, and the north-bound lanes (8)_____ near the service station as a precaution.

The flare-up was the latest in a cat-and-mouse game, with the police (9)_____ the convoys in an operation which aims to prevent illegal camps on common land (10)_____ the holiday weekend.

'Children begin by loving their parents. After a time they judge them. Rarely, if ever, do they forgive them.'

Introduction

Look at the quotations about family life.
What do they mean and do you agree with them?

'Happiness in marriage is entirely a matter of chance.'

'Parents are the last people on earth who ought to have children.'

'Marriage is the waste-paper basket of the emotions.'

Reading

Part 3

1 One way to approach multiple-choice questions is to skim through the questions before reading the text. Don't look at the options (A, B, C or D) until you have read the article.

Look through the questions below, scan the article, then write brief answers to the questions.

1 What does the writer compare earthquakes to?
2 What was the writer scared to do?
3 What do British therapists believe about family breakdown?
4 Can you sum up the findings of recent research in Britain?
5 What conclusion has John Gottman reached about happy marriages?
6 Why might staying in a bad marriage be bad for your health?

All that's left is **A BAND OF GOLD**

California, as we all know, is a land prone to earthquakes, in which the ground splits asunder beneath one's feet and one is likely to lose one's bearings. Luckily for us, such physical events do not extend far beyond that state and we learn about disasters only through our news bulletins.

But the US, and California in particular, is a major source of dramatic psychological movements which first shake that country and then sweep eastward
10 towards Europe. The energy of these waves may be diminished by the Atlantic crossing, but Britain absorbs the main impact. Even after the resulting waves
15 arrive here, social changes have continuing effects in the US, extreme changes often generating a backlash or antidote which arrives here later.
20 Marriage and the family may have begun to come apart in the US earlier than in Britain, but the first reports of an antidote to family breakdown – family
25 therapy – were coming ashore in the fifties when I was training,

though I did not feel bold enough to get my feet wet and try it myself until 1962.
30 A recent swing of the pendulum in the US, still taking place, is moving not only public but professional opinion away from divorce towards the view
35 that marriages should, if at all possible, be sustained for the sake of the children, even at the cost of the continued unhappiness of the spouses.
40 No doubt these changes of view will soon affect us too as the waves arrive, but in Britain

nobody has reached any conclusions yet. Recent
45 research in Britain compared those children whose parents had divorced with those whose parents had sustained an unhappy relationship. It found
50 that in those families where the parents had split up, half of the behavioural problems of the boys, and some of the girls, were present before the
55 divorce.
Even in the US, some experts are not following the new tide. John Gottman and

other researchers suggest that
60 children from intact homes where there is high conflict do worse in the long run than children of divorced parents, though the latter may appear
65 more disturbed in the early years after the break-up before they 'bounce back'.
I have outlined in a previous article Gottman's
70 claims to be able to predict the future success or failure   of marriages with extraordinary accuracy, by observation of simple reactions such as the ▶

2 Now look at the options in 1–6 below. Which are nearest to your answers in **1**?

Read the article again to check your choices.

1 What does the writer compare earthquakes to?

    A   psychological theories
    B   news bulletins
    C   crossing the Atlantic
    D   the institution of marriage

2 What was the writer scared to do?

    A   get married
    B   get divorced
    C   learn about family therapy
    D   encourage people to stay married

3 What do British therapists believe about family breakdown?

    A   It should be avoided at all costs.
    B   It should be avoided if children are involved.
    C   They are undecided about its effects.
    D   They are critical of the American findings.

4 Which of the following sums up the findings of recent research in Britain?

    A   Boys from divorced families have more behavioural problems than girls.
    B   Problems amongst children from broken homes can be present before divorce.
    C   Children of unhappy parents who do not divorce have more problems.
    D   Children whose parents divorce have more academic difficulties.

5 What conclusion has John Gottman reached about happy marriages?

    A   Women express their angry feelings more readily.
    B   There are more good times than bad times.
    C   Both partners are likely to engage in fierce disagreements.
    D   Issues which could lead to arguments are avoided.

6 Why might staying in a bad marriage be bad for your health?

    A   It raises the blood pressure.
    B   It increases the heart rate.
    C   It reduces bone density.
    D   It affects the immune system.

75 rise in heart rate and blood pressure during arguments.

His research has now led to some further interesting conclusions, and he challenges
80 the commonly held view that couples who fight all the time and those who avoid conflict at

'As to divorce, it is an unpalatable truth that some marriages cannot and should not be saved'

any cost are the ones more at risk of marital failure. He found
85 that in happy marriages the commonly expressed view that men are less emotionally expressive than women did not apply. His research also
90 suggests that anger between spouses is not harmful except when it is accompanied by more lethal emotions like contempt or disgust; indeed,
95 'blunt, straightforward anger seemed to immunize marriages against deterioration ... disagreements and fights seem necessary in some degree in all
100 good marriages, and avoidance of confrontation often results in avoidance of intimacy'.

Marriages, he says, 'seem to thrive on, proportionately, a
105 little negativity and a lot of positivity'. As to divorce, it is an unpalatable truth that some

marriages cannot and should not be saved.
110   'Not only do patterns of toxic marital interaction keep the body in a state of unhealthy physical arousal, they create a psychological climate of
115 helpless misery ... these bone-deep states of arousal can no longer be willingly controlled ... Not only is it fatuous to suggest they just 'try harder' at this
120 juncture, it may even be bad for their health – witness our data suggesting that staying in a hostile, distant marriage actually compromises the
125 immune system, increasing susceptibility to illness.'

Dr Skynner, *The Guardian*

635 words

Vocabulary

Expressions

1   What metaphor does the writer use in the second paragraph of the article? In what way do you think it could be described as an 'extended metaphor'?

2   Look at the figurative expressions below which have been taken from the article. Can you explain what they mean?

1   coming ashore (line 25)
2   to get my feet wet (line 28)
3   following the new tide (line 57)
4   'bounce back' (line 67)
5   create a psychological climate (line 113)

Which of them have a connection with the metaphor in the second paragraph? Say what this connection is.

3   There are many expressions in English which use words to do with the weather. See if you can understand the meaning of the expressions in these sentences.

1   I'm feeling a bit *under the weather* as I think I've got a cold coming on.
2   Sarah accused me of *making heavy weather of it* but, actually, it really was hard work.
3   This year his business has managed *to weather the storm,* but I'm afraid that next year things are going to get tougher.
4   Unfortunately, as soon as David *got wind of* my plan to sell the car, he put a stop to it.
5   The old lady said she always *saved* some of her pension *for a rainy day*.
6   There was *a storm of protest* in Parliament when the Chancellor announced new tax increases.

Suffixes

4   In the article, you came across some of the following words. Each word contains a suffix. Group them into nouns, adjectives and verbs.

harmful	popularize	observation	reliable
disagreement	happiness	behavioural	ability
attractive	helpless	relationship	

5   Read through sentences 1–11 and insert the correct form of the word in brackets. Look back at the noun, adjective and verb groups in **4** to help you decide on the word ending.

1   Mike's extremely _____; he never hides his feelings. (demonstrate)

2   The two French chefs went into _____ and opened a restaurant in Mayfair. (partner)

3   'This office equipment badly needs to be _____. Look at this typewriter – it's completely out of date!' (modern)

4   After working together for several days, their initial _____ disappeared. (shy)

5   When talks between the two governments broke down, military _____ seemed inevitable. (confront)

6   After moving house, changing job, and getting married, Susan reflected on what an _____ year it had been. (event)

7   'There's no point in trying to negotiate improved working conditions, the situation is _____ – we must all go out on strike!' (hope)

8   I must admit that I find Simon's sarcasm absolutely _____! (detest)

9   There was a strong sense of _____ in the village; most families had lived there for generation after generation. (continue)

10   Joe was extremely nervous about his driving test, so passing it the first time was quite an _____. (achieve)

11   It was only when the company went bankrupt that the extent of its _____ problems were revealed. (finance)

Writing *Socializing* ▼

Introduction

1 In pairs, look at the examples of social activities above. Which of these activities would you enjoy and which would you not enjoy? Explain why.

2 Is there more to socializing than meets the eye? Read the extracts below and discuss whether you can sympathize with the points of view put forward.

A

Football provides everything: a common language, a way of making contact, a common pool of experience and a massive gallery of male role models, presented as being conveniently one-dimensional. What might seem to an onlooker to be a boring obsession is, to an anxious child, a place of refuge in a sea of uncertainty.

B

She is a strange girl. I like her but she doesn't fit in. You know that if everyone is wearing shorts this year and thinking about going to Thailand, she will be in designer jeans and off to the States with Virgin Atlantic. Actually, she doesn't want to be one of the crowd. She likes to be different. Only sometimes it can be annoying. There was an excruciating occasion when we invited her to a party. We'd specially asked people she gets on with to be there. I think she realized. She ignored them all and spent the whole evening talking earnestly to my mother about house plants!

C

'A terrible social paralysis grips me when I'm faced with the gaps in my knowledge. I have sat in agonies at numerous dinner parties, fiddling nervously with my bread roll, not being able to contribute a word to the animated conversation that is going on around me. Why does everyone know about opera except me? Should I venture an opinion? What should I ask? If I speak now, will my voice sound strange? Has everyone given me up as a complete bore?'

Writing

Part 1, report

Sample report

1 **a** Many people join clubs or societies as they like to feel part of a group of like-minded people. Read this extract from a report and briefly summarize the aims of each paragraph.

> After a significant fall in membership last month, I was asked to investigate and evaluate the current state of the <u>Latino Club</u>, a Latin American dancing club. This report looks at some of the problems based on information provided by the club, and on a questionnaire completed by its members.
>
> Since last year, membership has dropped by 30%. There are several factors to blame for this: firstly, many people mentioned bad organization and the lack of publicity for social events. Predictably, this lack of information has led to low attendance, which means that members have little opportunity to meet and mix with new people.
>
> Secondly, club facilities, including dancing tuition, were universally criticized as substandard. Unprofessional, lazy instructors were mentioned, and people complained about over-priced refreshments. However, although facilities have deteriorated, the cost of membership has risen, resulting in a lot of bad feeling. Consequently, many members are not renewing their subscription.
>
> Another important factor is the club's profile in the community. Over the past six months, this has fallen dramatically, largely due to the lack of local advertising as well as to the club's old-fashioned and unappealing image. The situation has been made worse by the opening of the new Jazz dance club <u>Groove</u>, which offers more competitive membership fees and a series of free trial dance lessons.
>
> To sum up, I would strongly recommend that <u>Latino Club</u> …

b Underline the words and phrases which:

- introduce the subject of the report.
- introduce a personal opinion.
- link together and order ideas.
- introduce the conclusion.

c Read the report through again and finish the concluding paragraph, making appropriate recommendations.

Understanding the task

2 Look at the task, then read the information given in the three documents below and on the next page. Decide on the theme and purpose of the report, and the target reader.

In response to a local newspaper article about the rise in vandalism and lack of social activities for young people in the area, the Council has decided it needs to investigate the situation before proposing plans to develop a new leisure centre. A questionnaire has been sent to young people asking for their opinions on the local facilities available. You have been asked to write a report based on the response to the questionnaire and the criticisms expressed in the articles.

Vandalism in city centre

AT a meeting last night to discuss the spate of break-ins and vandalism affecting the city centre, the point was made by several shopkeepers that the lack of leisure facilities and the rising number of unemployed youngsters in the town were partially to blame for the problems affecting the region.

The regional manager of *Silhouette*, a national chain of clothing and fashion accessories, claimed that wherever there was a significant lack of social amenities such as sports facilities, and evening entertainment such as theatres, cinemas and clubs, there was always a significantly higher level of what could only be described as 'mindless damage to property'.

▶▶

Sports hall price rise fear

COUNCILLOR Johnson has raised the matter of the sale of the sports hall to *Equip Leisure Ltd* suggesting that the move would result in higher prices and less availability to the less well-off. It was confirmed today that *Equip* would be the new owners of the sports hall and were planning to improve the facilities by extending the site to make room for a night club and restaurants.

We would be grateful if you could complete this questionnaire and return it to the manager of MARS MARKETING at the address given on the reverse.

Name *Jane Conron*

Age *19*   Occupation *Clerical Officer*

Which sports do you do regularly?
swimming

Which sports would you do if facilities were available?
tennis, basketball

Would cost be a significant factor in your choice of sport?
yes

What other leisure activities do you enjoy?
dancing, restaurants, cinema, theatre

What other leisure activities would you like to see made available in your area?
more discos for young people, restaurants open late, night-clubs

Would cost be a significant factor in your choice of leisure activity?
yes

If you have any other comments relating to these areas, please put them in the box below.

> *I do not earn very much, so most things are too expensive except on an occasional basis. There is not much to do in the evening except go to pubs. For the younger people, there is nothing. The swimming pool closes at 7 and the one club in town is for those over 18, and anyway it's terribly old-fashioned. On the whole, I find restaurants round here are too expensive for people like me.*

Selecting ideas

3 Before you begin the task, underline the significant facts you would want to include in the report. Ask yourself these questions:

Do any of the facts in the documents support or contradict each other?
Make a list.

What will your conclusions be and what recommendations will you make?

Planning your answer

4 Here is a structure for you to follow.

- Introduction — *The reason for the report*
  The aim of the report

- Findings — *Report any repeated views*
  Suggest ideas or underlying reasons for requests

- Recommendations — *Type of leisure facilities*
  Importance of pricing
  Availability to young people

7.1 page 194
11 page 195

- Conclusion — *Give a balanced view*

Writing

5 Now write your report in about 250 words. When you have finished, check your work carefully. Remember **WRITE**.

page 191

Structure *Preconceptions* ▼

Introduction

What, in your view, gives people social status? Look at the pictures and discuss what you think a status symbol is.

Reading

A Read the text quickly, ignoring any errors you may notice, and think of a suitable title.

A friend of mine worked in a council housing department in the north east. On one occasion she had to deal with an ageing rag-and-bone man who had been relocated from his suburban caravan home of
5 fifty years to the top of a high rise block of flats. The old fellow reluctant to surrender his mobile abode, settled in grudgingly, and pretty soon complaints found their way to the housing office. Well you see we hear all these funny grating and grinding noises coming from the flat at all
10 hours. Whenever he uses the lift it seems like hours before its free – and there's a strange sort of country-type smell in there – always

Aware that prejudice can colour a person's perceptions the housing officer set out to the block of flats one evening
15 ready to pacify the neighbours and show them the error of their ways. But when she arrived in the lobby, she found the lift occupied. Its that dirty old fellow love, whispered a tenant through the crack of a door. He goes up and down in the lift all night long. Don't bother waiting. Why don't
20 you use the stairs? It'll be quicker, you'll see

The housing officer tackled the staircase to meet the elderly resident on the seventeenth floor. The lift doors opened slowly to reveal the old man and a secret cohabitant – his trusty old bag-of-bones horse fresh from a
25 run-around outside.

Good heavens! stammered the housing officer. Are you mad What d'you think youre doing with that horse in here?

The old man was furious.

Eh What do you mean The horse cant, well … poor animal
30 – he has to use the lift. In his condition, all those stairs would kill him.

B Read the text again more carefully. Some necessary punctuation marks (for example, apostrophes in contractions and possessives, commas, question marks, full stops and direct speech marks) have been omitted. Can you punctuate the text correctly?

Comprehension

In pairs, discuss answers to the following questions.

1 How did the old man feel about leaving his former home?

2 Why did his neighbours complain to the housing authorities?

3 What did the housing officer feel might have been behind the complaints made by the old man's neighbours?

4 Why was the old man's reaction to the housing officer's question unusual?

Direct and reported speech

A The passage contains several examples of direct speech: statements, advice or instructions, and questions. List the examples under the appropriate heading below. One example is given for each category.

Statements
'Well, you see, we hear all these funny grating and grinding noises coming from the flat at all hours.'

Advice or instructions
'Don't bother waiting.'

Questions
'Are you mad?'

B Now look at these sentences. What kind of changes need to be made to these sentences in order to report what the speakers said?

1 'I'm worried about the test tomorrow,' said Peter.
2 'Don't touch this switch, children,' said the teacher.
3 'Have you finished this book or not?' Tom asked his
   father.

Constructions after reporting verbs

A Match the nine reporting verbs on the left to one or more of the constructions on the right. For example, 1 can be matched with e, f and g.

1	asked	a	that somebody should do something
2	insisted		
3	added	b	that somebody did something
4	suggested	c	somebody that
5	told	d	to somebody that
6	complained	e	somebody if / whether they did something
7	explained		
8	whispered	f	somebody (not) to do something
9	wondered		
10	replied	g	if / whether somebody did something
11	accused		
12	advised	h	somebody of doing something

B Now report the direct speech from the reading text, bearing in mind the changes that need to be made, and supplying a suitable reporting verb from the list in **A**. You do not have to report every word the speaker says. Try and use your own words to convey or summarize what the speakers said.

C You could have reported the last thing the rag and bone man said in this way:

The old fellow then said the horse had to use the lift, because in his condition all those stairs would kill him.

Why is it not necessary to change *would* when reporting direct speech?

Why is it not necessary to change the words in *italics* in these reporting sentences?

1 'You need to plan for the future.'
   They say you *need* to plan for the future.

2 'Unemployment is currently falling.'
   Government officials say that unemployment *is* currently falling.

3 'They're in love!'
   If you look at me like that, people will say we *are* in love!

4 'They could / would / might / take the exam.'
   The headmaster says / said they *could* / *would* / *might* take the exam.

5 'They can / may / will take the exam.'
   The headmaster says / said they *can* / *may* / *will* take the exam.

6 'If I'm going to be delayed, I'll phone.'
   He says if he*'s* going to be delayed, he*'ll* phone.

Adverbs

A Which of the adverbs below convey:

1 a lack of enthusiasm?
2 a loss of self-control?
3 a more positive attitude?

grudgingly	eagerly	tactfully
furiously	angrily	aggressively
patiently	reluctantly	politely
generously	emotionally	hesitantly

B Report these comments using the suggested prompts, a suitable reporting verb, and a suitable adverb.

1 'I'm not a punk – never have been and never will be.'
   Polly _____ .

2 'Mrs Thompson, would you care to look through the plans before the meeting?'
   The secretary _____ .

3 'Don't mention this matter to anyone, Frank. It's extremely delicate!'
   The managing director _____ .

4 'Prime Minister, may I put it to you that your policies have failed! Why doesn't the Government admit it has made mistakes?'
   The leader of the opposition _____ .

5 'Well, if pressed, I would probably have to say that I am not in favour of the new anti-terrorist measures.'
   The Ambassador _____ .

6 'I've never, well, er…, really given marriage any serious thought.'
   Sally _____ .

7 'That's it! I'm sorry but I've had enough. I just can't take any more.'
   The secretary _____ .

8 'If I were you, I'd take the lift,' said the porter to the hotel guest.
   The porter _____ .

Practice

Do you remember the brief conversation between the housing officer and the rag and bone man? Think of a short, unusual or interesting conversation you had with someone recently and tell a partner what was said. It could be:

- an argument or misunderstanding.
- something which happened at home, at work, in the street.
- an exchange of ideas or information.
- a humorous exchange.

6 Culture Vultures

Reading *Time Out*

Introduction

Do you like going out to events like these? Why? Why not? How much do you think being part of an audience influences your experience of such events?

Reading

Multiple matching

1 Look quickly at the text opposite. Where might you find it? Who is it written for?

2 The events A–J are among the events featured in the text. Read questions 1–12 only, then look at the comments in **3** below.

Which events can you see in Oxford this week? 1_____ 2_____

Which event is currently taking place in Scotland? 3_____

Which musical event is touring Britain? 4_____

Which event can you only see on Wednesday? 5_____

Which film is showing with another by the same director? 6_____

Which event do you not have to pay for? 7_____

Which events are about people from the past? 8_____ 9_____

Which events are tragic in content? 10_____ 11_____

Which event has been specially written for someone? 12_____

A	The Small Back Room
B	Dominic Muldowney
C	National Ballet of St Petersburg
D	Square Rounds
E	California Man
F	Jazz in Golden Square
G	Unforgiven
H	Sugar
I	Leonardo
J	Il Trovatore

Exam tip ▼

In Paper 1, you may be asked to match headings or brief descriptions of content to specific paragraphs, or to match appropriate items from a list to a set of questions or statements. This will involve scanning the text rather than reading every word.

3 Questions 1–4 are about *where* an event is taking place. What about question 5?

Now look at the layout and format of the text. You only need to read the words in brackets to find the answers to 1–5. Where will you find the answer to question 6?

What key word answers question 7? Look for it as you scan the whole text.

Questions 8–12 deal with content, so you will need to scan whole paragraphs to find the answers. Read each question carefully to determine the type of entertainment involved. You may be able to eliminate several paragraphs in this way.

4 Match the events A–J to questions 1–12. You will need to use some more than once. Try to do this matching exercise within ten minutes.

The List

OPERA & CONCERTS..

● BBC SYMPHONY
New season starts with the unlikely combination of composers Vaughan Williams and Steve Martland, introducing a British music series and a radical ticket policy: all seats £9. *(RFH, tonight.)*

● IL TROVATORE
New Scottish Opera production with soloist Lisa Gasteen as Leonora. *(Glasgow, Theatre Royal, from Tues.)*

● DOMINIC MULDOWNEY PREMIERE
An Oboe Concerto, commissioned by the LSO for its own principal oboist. Conductor Michael Tilson Thomas. *(Barbican, Wed.)*

CINEMA

● CALIFORNIA MAN
Finding a Neanderthal man in a block of ice, school-friends Harold and Stoney thaw him out and enrol him in Encino High, where his spaced-out expression and inarticulate grunts pass for normal. Humorously, artistically and intellectually challenged teen fun. *(PG; Odeons Marble Arch and Kensington.)*

● UNFORGIVEN
Ageing killer Clint Eastwood takes on sheriff Gene Hackman and wreaks a violent revenge in his most sombre western yet. *(15; Empire Leics Sq and all over London.)*

● THE SMALL BACK ROOM AND THE TALES OF HOFFMANN
A fine Michael Powell double-bill – bomb-disposal and operatic fantasia – followed by a discussion with the director's widow, film editor Thelma Schoonmaker. *(Everyman, today only.)*

THEATRE

● SQUARE ROUNDS
Playwright Tony Harrison returns to the National with a piece of doomsday drama highlighting the dangers of science, in which an experiment to boost fertility in Europe ends in mass fatality. *(Olivier, opens Thurs.)*

● LEONARDO
Yes, it's the song-and-dance version of Leonardo da Vinci's life, written by Greg and Tommy Mueller and Russell Dunlop. Having its West End premiere next year. *(Old Fire Station, Oxford, opens Thurs.)*

● SOMEONE WHO'LL WATCH OVER ME
A heart-breaking hostage drama, with fine performances by actors Stephen Rea and Alec McCowen. *(Vaudeville.)*

JAZZ

● MAL WALDRON
Veteran pianist whose work has graced the bands of Charles Mingus, Billie Holiday and Eric Dolphy, and now a distinguished solo performer. *(Jazz Cafe, Tues.)*

● JAZZ IN GOLDEN SQUARE
Free all-day event, in the Soho Jazz Festival, featuring pianist Bheki Mseleku, the all-women Latin band Candela, avant-funkateers Microgroove, tapdancer Will Gaines, and the Ed Jones Quartet. *(West Soho, Sat.)*

ROCK

● THE NEVILLE BROTHERS
A one-stop visit from big brother Aaron and his maverick Louisiana rock-soul quaverers. Amusing trousers guaranteed. *(Hammersmith Odeon, Sat.)*

● SUGAR
Jaunty but accessible power-trio, centred on the prolific, revitalized talent of ex-Husker Du lead guitarist Bob Mould – the master of introspective guitar overload. *(London Town & Country, tonight; Birmingham University, tomorrow; Brighton Pavilion, Fri.)*

DANCE

● NORTHERN BALLET
Tour continues of *A Christmas Carol*, a new work by Christopher Gable based on the Dickens tale, with music by Carl Davis. *(Theatre Royal, Bath, to Sat.)*

● NATIONAL BALLET OF ST PETERSBURG
Stars from the Kirov and Bolshoi alternate as principals. *(Apollo, Oxford, Thurs; International Centre, Bournemouth, Fri & Sat.)*

5 Find words which mean the same as these in the entries specified.

1	extreme (*BBC Symphony*)	6	increase (*Square Rounds*)
2	defrost (*California Man*)	7	upsetting (*Someone Who'll Watch Over Me*)
3	vacant (*California Man*)	8	acclaimed (*Mal Waldron*)
4	inflicts (*Unforgiven*)	9	lively (*Sugar*)
5	gloomy (*Unforgiven*)	10	productive (*Sugar*)

6 Go back over the whole text for useful vocabulary relating to these sets. Some words will appear in more than one set.

Films	Plays	People
western	*comedy*	*principal*

Now add these words to the same sets.

soundtrack	romance	cast	stage set
special effects	screenplay	plot	tragedy
hero	villain	protagonist	block-buster

Vocabulary

Order of adjectives

1 Look at these phrases. Can you say why the adjectives in *italics* are in the order they are in? What do the first adjectives of each pair have in common?

a *thoughtful British* playwright   a *stunning young* musician

2 Now look at 1–6. Are the adjectives in the correct order?

1	a powerful new film	4	a blue ancient vase
2	a large bulbous nose	5	a rotund mature artist
3	an overpriced cylindrical sculpture	6	a long cream exquisite dress

3 When several adjectives are used to describe people or things, which order do they normally follow? Use the categories below.

Colour   Quality   Shape   Size   Age

 6 page 194

4 Now write descriptive phrases for 1–4 below, using at least two adjectives to describe each picture.

Speaking

1 Today's big-budget movies often use all the devices available to them to ensure success at the box office, especially if the initial idea is a bad one. Now it's your chance to turn a bad idea into a block-buster.

Read the summary of the screenplay. Do you think *Save the Earth* is the best title?

Plot

Act One sets up the conflict – three good guys, plenty of bad guys.

Good guys Jake, the hunky scientist whose computers are telling him that an eco-disaster is imminent; Kumchika, a rain forest medicine man whose mystical powers are telling him the same thing; Daphne, the gorgeous anthropologist who will bring them together.

Bad guys All those big business polluter types who want to put a toxic waste dump in the middle of the rain forest. Meanwhile, the weather on Earth is going crazy: heat waves in Iceland, a cold spell in Mexico.

Act Two sees Jake in the rain forest. He's hit on the head during a storm, rescued by the native Indians and nursed back to life by Daphne. Jake and Daphne fall in love. Jake starts listening to Kumchika's wise words. The three heroes decide to take their eco-message to America but, before they can leave, the polluters kidnap Kumchika to silence the heroes.

Act Three starts with the shoot-out rescue of Kumchika and a series of ever-worsening ecological disasters: floods, tornadoes, landslides. Our heroes go on TV and announce Kumchika's prescription: all people must band together and chant a traditional hymn, which asks nature to save us from ourselves.

Conclusion is an international montage of togetherness, as people join hands and chant. It works: earthquakes swallow toxic waste dumps and volcanic dust blocks out the sun, reversing global warming. Daphne and Jake are together ever after.

Analysis Weak idea, some action, great special effects opportunities. With star power, could be big.

STEVEN SEAGAL JULIA ROBERTS

Can a motion picture change the course of human history?

SAVE THE EARTH

2 Now decide as a group how you can transform it into a box office hit. Here are the angles you should cover:

The stars Decide which actresses and actors should play the lead roles and why.

The message This film needs a powerful image for the ultimate hard sell. Can you improve on this one?

The merchandising Here are a few of the items that carried the *Jurassic Park* name. Which objects would be suitable for this film? Can you suggest other merchandising?

3 Now present your ideas to the class and decide which team has the winning formula.

Writing *In My Opinion ...* ▼

Introduction

1 Look at the following adjectives and decide which are positive and which are negative.

under-rated	pretentious	moving	intricate
perceptive	trivial	exquisite	phoney
unconvincing	subtle	compelling	wooden

Now listen to a radio discussion about the film *Things Change*. Tick the words in the list that are used.

Are the reviewers' comments mostly positive or negative?

2 Look at the tapescript on page 206 and listen to the piece again. The underlined parts of the script show the expressions used by the speakers to introduce their opinions. Could you use all these in a formal written review? If not, how would you rewrite them to make them more appropriate?

3 What was the last film you went to see? Tell another student what you particularly liked or disliked about it.

English in Use
Part 1

1 Skim read the review, ignoring the spaces. How would you describe the attitude of the reviewer?

Schlock of the New

DOUBLETAKE: Collective Memory and Current Art – the title alone is enough to cause serious (0)_____, but together
5 with the essays and statements in the accompanying catalogue, it induces total (1)_____.

At least the pamphlet issued as a guide to the exhibition is marginally
10 more (2)_____. It will leave you in no doubt about the inflated pretensions and muddled thinking which have produced this show of installations, photography, painting and sculpture
15 by 23 mostly young artists. These artists, we read, "challenge us by pushing our (3)_____ of the world around us beyond familiar limits". They also "dig deep into the common

20 memories of our culture, our biology and our technology, to see how these (4)_____ the way we understand the present and shape the future". It makes you think they're all (5)_____ for the
25 Nobel prize.

Until you see the work, that is. Displayed here are the products not of the inquiring, creative intellect, but of minds in the pursuit of whatever is
30 trivial, affected, (6)_____, egotistical or preposterous. Admittedly, the packaging is often appealing, but even

before the unwrapping begins, you know the box is empty.

35 New art, as the exhibition guide quite reasonably (7)_____, has a history of getting on people's nerves. But it doesn't necessarily follow that everything (8)_____ is new, art, or,
40 indeed, important. Novelty is not the same as originality, and incomprehensibility isn't always an indication of quality. There is little danger that DOUBLETAKE will ever find its place in
45 the collective memory. **G**

250 words

2 Read the review again carefully, and underline the words in 1–8 which best fit each space. The first has been done for you as an example.

0	A	<u>misgivings</u>	B	fear	C	horror	D	worries
1	A	doubt	B	mistrust	C	query	D	disbelief
2	A	conceivable	B	intelligent	C	clever	D	comprehensible
3	A	feeling	B	conviction	C	understanding	D	belief
4	A	fix	B	establish	C	choose	D	determine
5	A	candidates	B	applicants	C	winners	D	contestants
6	A	self-possessed	B	self-assured	C	self-respecting	D	self-indulgent
7	A	asserts	B	tells	C	insists	D	announces
8	A	upsetting	B	annoying	C	distracting	D	inflaming

3 Would you go and see this exhibition?

Writing

Section B, review

Sample review

1 a Skim read this review of a novel called *The Secret History.* What positive and negative points does the reviewer mention?

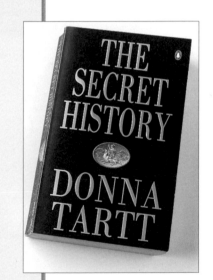

The Secret History is a powerful first novel by an American writer, Donna Tartt. Set in New England, it is the portrayal of an élite group of privileged and self-assured college students. The story is told by fellow student Richard Papen who has recently transferred to the college from California. Richard is eventually accepted into the group, and slowly becomes aware of their terrible secret, which is to change his own life forever.

The Secret History is rich and detailed in plot, providing many layers for the reader to explore. Predominantly, it is a murder mystery, which is so intricately constructed that it will hold your attention right up to the final page. The book is most moving at times, while at others it is immensely amusing. Additionally, for anyone with a background in classics, the book contains yet another layer of vivid references to Ancient Greece to be savoured and enjoyed.

As for characterization, Donna Tartt is extremely successful in forging the different identities of the clique of students, as well as introducing some delightful cameo characters such as tranquillized parents and spaced-out hippies. She is unusually perceptive about New England college life, and contrasts its rich sophistication with the less privileged West Coast viewpoint of the narrator most skilfully.

My only reservation about this book is its length. At over 500 pages, it is just a little too long. In spite of this, I literally could not put it down! I highly recommend The Secret History, which is a truly magnificent achievement from this new young novelist.

Which tense is used to describe the story-line? Why?

b Read the review again. Find examples of:

- adverbs that are used to intensify adjectives, in order to strengthen the writer's opinion, for example, *extremely successful.*
- adverbs that introduce or specify information, for example, *additionally.*

 **6.2** page 194
9 page 195

Understanding the task   **2**   Now look at this writing task. Think about the target reader before choosing an appropriate register.

> You have seen this announcement in a magazine. Write the review you enter for the competition.

STUDENT CRITICS
WANTED

We are looking for student critics to help judge this year's International Drama Award. To enter the competition, you should submit a 250-word review of a recent film or play that you have seen.

The winning entrants will attend **Festival of Arts** at our expense and join a team of professional judges in assessing the Festival productions on stage and screen. Their reviews will also be published in the next issue of *International Student* magazine.

Brainstorming ideas   **3**   Choose a film or play to review and decide whether your views about it are mainly positive or negative. Prepare some notes, including a short description of the plot and a list of your opinions. Cover all these points:

- Title of film / play
- Actors / actresses / director / producer
- Summary of plot
- My opinions + / –
- Recommendation.

Using your notes, tell another student about the film or play you have chosen to review. State your views clearly, grouping the main positive or negative points together. When outlining your opinions, try to use some of the adjectives and verbs from the cloze and the model. Remember the ways of introducing an opinion you noted in the introduction.

> Exam tip ▼
>
> Don't forget that a review demands **opinion** as well as description. It is not appropriate in CAE only to give details of the plot and describe what happened.

Planning your answer   **4**   Look back at the sample review on page 79. Can you identify the main function of each paragraph? Use the framework to help you plan your own review.

Writing   **5**   Write the review using about 250 words. When you have finished check your answer carefully. Remember **WRITE** ✎.

✎ page 192

Introduction

1 *The media can be a dangerous weapon.*

What do you think this statement means? Do you agree or disagree?

2 Skim read the article and summarize the views expressed.

MEDIA REVOLUTIONS

It's only rock 'n' roll – or is it ?

She calls it "empty" TV. "When I see teenagers come into the house and flop down in front of MTV, I want to be sick," says Bombay housewife Anupama Pant. To Pant and other critics, MTV isn't simple entertainment. It's a non-stop barrage of Western pop culture making small-screen addicts of kids from Manila to Bombay.

Music Television Asia is a 24-hour satellite station devoted almost exclusively to airing popular music videos. It has already had a huge impact, particularly in India, where it has lifted the music industry to new heights overnight.

To its fans, MTV is the latest in hip. To its foes, it's the latest in hype, a way for big record companies to boost sales – a cultural air strike from the West. Many Asians worry that they will lose their identity to the Western way of life.

"We're not here to change the world," says MTV veejay (video jockey) Danny McGill. "We're just here to put on videos. It's just pop music." But is it? Thirty years ago rock 'n' roll supplied young Westerners with anthems for a social revolution. So while MTV appears to be turning the generation gap into a chasm in India, other nations have taken steps to beat back its march. Singapore and Malaysia restrict ownership of satellite dishes and censor broadcasts. "We have not allowed an open sky," says the Malaysian Information Minister. "The media can be a dangerous weapon."

> "We're not here to change the world"

All across the region, MTV is pumping up local music scenes. Before MTV aired its video, mainland Chinese heavy-metal band Tang Dynasty was languishing in obscurity. Since being "advertised" on MTV, it has sold more than half a million copies of its album in China alone.

Fans and foes alike might agree that MTV is shaping young minds, not vice versa. Veejays with charisma are a key part of the appeal. Their formula: a blend of Western hip and Asian good looks. In some cities, the veejays are more popular than the artists. McGill says he has received 5000 fan letters. T-shirts he wears on-screen one week are on the streets the next. His first visit to Bombay is now an MTV legend. "Word got out that I was there," he recalls. "One group of girls camped out for two days. They started crying when they saw me. I said, 'What are you so excited about? It's no big deal.'" Clearly, for many young Asians it is. ■

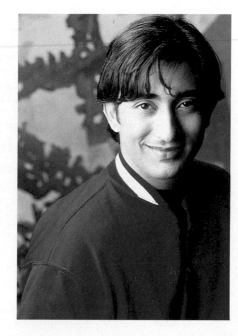

Asia week

 410 words

3 Can you explain what is meant by *To its fans, MTV is the latest in hip. To its foes, it's the latest in hype* (line 19)?

Do you watch MTV or similar channels? What are your own views on satellite broadcasting?

Listening

Part 2

Exam tip ▼

In Part 1 or 2 of Paper 4, you may have to complete a table with appropriate information. Look carefully at the table before you listen, to see exactly what is required.

1 You will hear a presenter talking about the evening's programmes on satellite TV. Your task is to complete the information in the listings below.

First look at the table. The numbering 1–12 shows you the sequence of the information you are going to hear. What type of information is missing?

2 The presenter refers to two of the programmes like this:

Sky One is screening *September* …

… at 10.15 there's *Tartan Extra* …

Listen out for the names of channels or times, which may cue the names of the missing programmes.

3 Now you are ready to listen. Complete the table, using no more than four words in each gap. You will hear the recording once only.

When you have finished, compare your answers with those of another student.

FRIDAY 14 MARCH

Satellite Highlights

SKY one

8.00 September
Drama set in Scottish Highlands.
(1)_____
mini-series.

10.00 Star Trek
The Enterprise welcomes a
(2)_____
on board.

SKY sports

(3)_____
International cricket coverage from Perth.

10.00 (4)_____

10.15 Tartan Extra
(5)_____
Scottish football.

SKY movies

8.00 Toys
(6)_____
starring Robin Williams.

10.05 (7)_____
Jeff Goldblum and Forest Whitaker as
(8)_____.

SKY movies gold

8.00 (9)_____
Romantic drama with Sean Penn.

SKY travel

6.30 and **9.00**
(10)_____
Dream holidays.

7.30 and (11)_____
Caribbean Vacation
Featuring
(12)_____
trips and extended cruises.

English in Use

Part 6

Exam tip ▼

Paper 3, Part 6 is designed to test your awareness of how a text is structured. You have to select suitable phrases or clauses to fill six gaps, from a set of ten options. Check that each phrase or clause fits the gap grammatically and follows on in meaning.

1 Read the text below. Who is Derek Walcott?

The underlined parts show some phrasal and clausal structures that may be tested. Decide in each case which function – a or b – the word *and* has.

a linking two phrases   b linking two clauses

Which words helped you to decide this?

Voice of a
Carnival Culture

Derek Walcott is by now established as the grand old man of Caribbean letters. Born on the tiny island of St Lucia in 1930, he had his first play, *Henri Christophe*, staged
5 there when he was 20. As both playwright and poet, he bridges the classical European / American and the indigenous Caribbean traditions. Brought up in both the British imperial heritage and the folklore
10 of the islands, he is equally at ease writing in a formally structured English and fluent Trinidadian dialect.

He was, in his early days, also a painter and his vivid visual sense informs much of
15 his work. In *The Last Carnival,* one character is an artist and the visual images give the production a dreamy sense of its Caribbean location.

With two white grandfathers, and having
20 been brought up a Methodist in a Roman Catholic community, Walcott is ideally placed to express the Caribbean's confusions of cultural identity – a recurring theme of both his poetry and plays.

Robert Thornber, *The Guardian*

2 Look at the first paragraph. The use of the verb *bridges* in line 6 tells you that two phrases are going to be linked together in the sentence. Which words signal the two underlined phrases in the next sentence?

3 In the second paragraph, could the two underlined parts be changed round within the sentence?

4 Why is the underlined part in the third paragraph within commas?

5 Now try this similar question 5 task, where you should select suitable phrases or clauses from A–J to fill in the gaps. Remember that not all the options will be required. One answer has been given as an example.

Japanese Noh Theatre

Michaael Macintyre, *The Shogun Inheritance*

In returning to the roots of Japanese theatre, a deep love of nature is to be found. The first dances were offerings to the gods of nature, acts of worship performed
5 in Shinto shrines, (0) _J_ . The solemn art of noh also began as a form of Shinto ritual, (1)_____. At the Itsukushima shrine on the Inland Sea near Hiroshima, the noh stage was built at the edge of the shore, (2)_____.
10 The outstanding personality in the history of noh was Zeami, the most famous actor (3)_____. In 1374, Shogun Yoshimitsu attended a performance in which Zeami and his father Kan'ami were taking part. He was
15 captivated by Kan'ami's acting (4)_____, then eleven years old, that he became their patron.

At the close of the medieval period, the noh play found a new patron in Hideyoshi, the general who had risen from the rank of foot
20 soldier to become the unifier (5)_____. Hideyoshi developed a passion for noh. He commissioned plays set in his own time, with himself as chief protagonist and hero. In a final manifestation of egomania, he even took
25 to the stage (6)_____.

A and so taken by the physical charms of Zeami
B and, at high tide, appeared to float on the water
C and undisputed ruler of all Japan
D and its plays were performed in natural settings of great beauty
E and performed the central role himself
F and at the Grand Shrine of Ise it is played in the open air
G and made use of the art to enhance his own prestige
H and it epitomized the artistic ideals of the late Middle Ages
I and playwright of his time
J and so too were the magic antics of simple puppets

Speaking

Part 2

1 You are going to look at a set of pictures. Your partner has the same set, but they are in a different order. Take it in turns to choose a picture and describe it in as much detail as you can. You should listen carefully to your partner and decide which picture is being described, giving reasons for your choice.

Here are some ways of describing parts of a picture that may be unclear, or that you may be unsure about:

I can just make out a …   *I'm not sure, but there seems to be a …*
There's something that looks like a …   *This is a small detail, but I think I can see a …*
It looks as if there might be …   *Perhaps I'm wrong, but I think there could be a …*

Use some of these expressions, and also look back at the Speaking section in Unit 3 (page 44) for other useful language.

 **6.4** page 194

Student A, look at the pictures on page 199. Student B, look at the pictures on page 202.

2 Think of a carnival or festival that you know about. Why is it held? Describe the event to another student.

Structure *Virtually Real?*

Introduction

Describe what is happening in the picture below.

BEFORE THE ADVENT OF TELEVISION WALLPAPER PLAYED AN IMPORTANT ROLE IN EVERYDAY LIFE

© Glen Baxter

Today, it is easier than ever before to bring entertainment into your own home. Whether through radio, television, video, satellite broadcasting or cable transmission, there is no need to leave the house. Say why you think this is desirable or undesirable.

Reading

Read the article about Virtual Reality and make a note of:
- what VR can do now.
- what VR may or will be capable of doing in the future.

Will and going to

A The following sentences about the future of Virtual Reality appear in the article.

1 *… in VR we won't be bound by boring restrictions …*

2 *… the virtual body will be able to follow every nuance of movement.*

3 *… it is going to become impossible to tell the difference.*

4 *… sound is going to be one of the first things to improve …*

What is the difference in meaning between the use of *will* and *going to*?

B What does *going to* express in this sentence and how is it different from the meaning in **A** above?

After all the hard work I've been doing, I*'m going to* have a proper holiday this year!

Imagine saying to a friend, "Sorry! I can't come over this afternoon. I'm taking part in the Formula One Grand Prix and the big race starts in five minutes' time!". What you would be referring to, of course, is not a real race, but a Virtual Reality session!

Virtual Reality does not aim to be the next best thing to being there; it aims to be indistinguishable from it. Indeed, the boundaries between real and virtual are about to be eroded completely. As technology improves, with lasers projecting directly onto the retina of the eye, touch-sensitive body suits and 3-D surround sound, it is going to become impossible to tell the difference.

VR technology uses computers to work directly on the senses to create an illusion of 'being there', even if 'there' exists only in the computer. The hope is that one day we will be doing 'virtually' the things we cannot do in real life – because in VR we won't be bound by boring restrictions like the laws of physics.

VR systems at present assume that reality is, literally, in the eye of the beholder: they rely almost entirely on goggles to create the illusion of a virtual world. Seeing may be believing, but a better virtual body would be able to touch and hear the virtual world. Judging by the current work in progress, sound is going to be one of the first things to improve in new-generation systems. And that isn't all! In tomorrow's virtual realities, the virtual body will be able to follow every nuance of movement.

Ultimately though, the distraction and mechanical clumsiness of suits, goggles and screens may outweigh the illusion they create. Researchers are now looking for more intimate links between real and virtual bodies. Really taking advantage of the senses would mean plugging a computer straight into the nervous system. American VR entrepreneurs are on the verge of launching arcade 'pods', which will provide the VR experience without headgear.

Perhaps the ultimate form of virtual entertainment would be to create a virtual city. Those who have tried it say that Do-It-Yourself world-building is the most entertaining kind of VR. In the future, it is highly likely that we will not only be building castles in the air – we'll be living in them too – virtually!

HYPE or hyper-reality?

Browning and Barrett, *Focus*

C *Will* and *shall* can also be used to express one or more of the following:

a   an offer
b   a promise
c   announcing a decision
d   willingness and determination.

What do *will* and *shall* express in these sentences?

1   I **will** pass my driving test this time.
2   Lend you the money? Of course I will.
3   Shall I carry those bags?
4   Well, it's quite expensive to buy a new TV. I know! We'll rent one instead.
5   We shall send you a copy of our new brochure as soon as it is available.
6   I'm sorry we weren't able to take you to the ballet for your birthday, but we'll make up for it another time!

D Complete the following sentences using either *will*, *shall* or *going to* and the word in brackets.

1   We (send) your travel documents two weeks prior to departure.
2   Your sister (help) you to write the essay if you feel you really can't do it by yourself.
3   It seems inevitable that the government (increase) taxes again this year.
4   We (be) delighted to accept your very generous donation to our charity.
5   (you / really / accept) Mark's proposal of marriage?
6   It's a difficult choice to make. We (ask) mum what she thinks about it!
7   Look at the red sky! I think (be) a fine day tomorrow!
8   I promise I (buy) you a new dress for the party!
9   We both know the company's in a financial crisis but the question is – what, if anything, (we / do) about it?
10 Give my consent to the project? That is something I (never do).

Present continuous, simple present, future continuous, simple future

A What's the difference in meaning between these two sentences?

1   What are you going to do this weekend?
2   What are you doing this weekend?

Which question might be followed by an invitation? Why?

Which question is a way of asking what someone intends to do, but has maybe not yet planned?

B The following sentences appear in the article:

1   *I'm taking part in the Formula One Grand Prix and the big race starts in five minutes' time!*
2   *... one day we will be doing 'virtually' the things we cannot do in real life ...*

Why does the writer use these tenses to talk about the future?

When would you have to use the simple future instead of the future continuous?

C Complete the following sentences using either the simple future or the future continous and the words in brackets.

1   I can't really say whether I (work) this weekend or not.
2   This time next week we (be) in sunny Spain!
3   This time tomorrow my brother (fly) to Portugal.
4   In future the human race (have) to take more care of the earth's resources.
5   I wonder what we (do) twenty years from now!
6   Who knows what science (be) able to achieve in the next decade or so?
7   Perhaps one day we (all / live) on other planets.
8   It (seem) strange not going into the office next week!
9   Next thing you know the government (tell) us what we should spend our money on!
10 By the way, I forgot to tell you. We (travel) down to London next weekend.

About to and on the verge of

Can you find one example of *about to* and *on the verge of* in the article on page 85?

What effect does the writer create by using these expressions instead of *going to*?
Is there any difference in meaning between these two expressions?

Practice

In small groups, ask and answer questions about your future plans, arrangements or predictions for some of the following:

• your arrangements for the coming holiday
• pollution in the next few years
• the use of computers in the next millennium
• your career plans
• the world's population
• the number of cars on the road in years to come
• your arrangements for a forthcoming celebration
• what to do when the lesson is over
• whether to buy something expensive or save your money.

7

Welcome to the Real World

Listening and Speaking *Starting Out* ▼

Introduction 1 Here are six adults talking about the careers advice they had at school. Look at the pictures and their captions. How many quotes can you match to the pictures? Which words in the captions or quotes help you to do this?

choices

CAREERS

A

At school they were only interested in people who were going to university. I always knew I wanted to do something like acting or being in front of a camera. They quashed the idea of me going to drama school. I suppose they had no resources to tell me how to go about it.

B

I don't see how a complete stranger can help you choose your career. Surely you need someone who knows you quite well. I didn't know what I wanted to do. I was interested in films and music, and I thought things would just fall into place. When I left school, I took a year off and started clubbing solidly.

C

Even at the age of 14, I knew I could do things for myself, could make them happen in the real world. That's the real test – after you leave the classroom. Other people can't tell you your strengths and weaknesses; you have to work them out for yourself.

D

I went to a school that was very sports-oriented, but the teachers always advised us to concentrate on getting good exam results first. It was good advice, and I started a degree, but I didn't finish my course because Leicester offered me a contract in the middle of it.

E

There was no careers advice whatsoever in my school. Maybe some students did have a teacher talk to them, but there were no lessons or anything formal. I certainly didn't get any useful information about becoming an actress, although it was my headmistress who actually spotted what she called my 'potential'. She told me I should go on the stage.

F

I was too busy at school to listen to careers advice. In 1967, just before I left, the headmaster came up to me and said, 'I predict you will either go to prison or become a millionaire.' He was absolutely right. But I've never stopped worrying about the first half of his sentence.

1 Owner of the legendary Joe Bloggs Jeans Company

2 Owner of the successful Virgin airline

3 Football player

4 TV presenter

5 Disc jockey and pop star

6 Actress

2 Read the quotes again to find words or phrases that are similar in meaning to 1–5.

1 repressed (quote A)
2 necessary means (quote A)
3 happen by themselves (quote B)
4 aptitude or talent (quote E)
5 forecast (quote F)

3 Do you agree with this statement from quote C?

Other people can't tell you your strengths and weaknesses; you have to work them out for yourself.

Discuss your answer with your partner.

4 What careers advice have you had, if any, at school or outside?

Speaking

Parts 2 and 4

1 Karen is 18 and is currently homeless in London. This profile of her experience at secondary school appeared in *The Big Issue*, a magazine that is put together and sold on the streets by homeless people. Read the text once only. Did you feel the same way about school?

I left my school in Newcastle at 17 with eight GCSEs. None of the kids had any respect for the teachers, though a few did deserve respect. The headmistress wouldn't allow teachers to punish the kids. We were given homework, but if you didn't do it, it didn't matter. Most people didn't get encouragement from home. When I had my exams, no one in my family asked about grades or anything. Between 11 and 16 you don't think about the future. You think you're never going to need education. If it's a choice between homework and a party, most people would choose the party. I didn't find work hard, just pointless.

"Between 11 and 16 you don't think about the future"

People from my area didn't know how to go about things like job interviews. Instead of textbooks, you need stuff about real life and things going on about you. One teacher used to say, "Face it, in ten years time, you're all going to be in council flats with kids." He wanted to get us stirred up, he was slapping the truth in our faces about where you could end up. About a third of the people in my year now do have kids, half are on the dole. Swots used to do 'A' levels and went on to university, but they used to stick in their own group.

If I got somewhere to live, I'd like to go back to college and do something different.

2 You and another student are each going to look at a different picture. Take turns to describe your picture. Talk about two things that are similar and two things that are different. After doing this, look at the two pictures side by side.

Student A, look at picture **7A** on page 201.
Student B, look at picture **7B** on page 203.

6.4 page 194

3 Do you think there is a lot of pressure on young people nowadays? What kind of pressure comes from:

- parents?
- friends?
- school?

Listening

Part 1

1 Do you know anything about the pop personality pictured below?

2 Read the sentences below about her, then look at the gaps and decide what type of information you have to listen for. For example, in the first gap you have to listen for details about Mariah's brother and sister.

3 Listen to the tape and try to complete the twelve gaps, using no more than three words in each case.

4 Compare your answers with those of another student. Then listen again and check your answers.

5 Now listen to the final part of the tape. What is Mariah's advice for success? Do you agree?

Star gazing

AFTER her parents separated, Mariah grew up with her mother, and her brother and sister, who are (1)_____ her.

Mariah's mother was (2)_____ and taught voice lessons.

Mariah was influenced at an early age by her mother and her mother's (3)_____, who visited a lot.

As a child, Mariah (4)_____ at least thirteen times.

Mariah started (5)_____ when she was thirteen.

After graduating from high school, Mariah went to live in Manhattan with (6)_____.

She did different jobs to pay the rent, including being a (7)_____.

Then she began to get (8)_____ and sang back-up at other singers' concerts.

Mariah has always been (9)_____ promote herself.

Her lucky break came at a party, where she met a CBS executive and gave him her (10)_____.

In 1990, she won two Grammy Awards, for (11)_____ and Best Pop Female Vocalist.

She is completely devoted to (12)_____.

English in Use

Part 3

Exam tip ▼

One of the proofreading tasks in Paper 3, Part 3 involves finding a word that is spelt incorrectly, or a sentence that is punctuated incorrectly. Take extra care with spelling mistakes. Mother-tongue interference can often make these difficult to spot.

Graham Rawle's **LOST CONSONANTS**

(178) **The director was auditioning a young aspirin actor**

Lost Consonants © Graham Rawle

1 The cartoon shows how spelling errors or slips can sometimes result in a different meaning from the one you intended. Which word has a missing letter and what word should it be?

2 The following paragraph is about how to become a careers officer. In most lines there is a spelling error. Proofread the numbered lines carefully, underline any incorrectly spelt words and write the correct spelling in the space provided. If you think a line is correct, put a tick in the right-hand margin. The exercise begins with two examples.

Opportunities

Graham Wade
explores a career as a careers officer

Our education <u>systeme</u> has never been strong on giving good	0 _system_
careers advice and guidance to its consumers. The vast majority	0 ✓
of careers teachers in schools are untrained in there subject and	1_____
many handle it part-time. It falls on careers officers employed	2_____
by local authoritys to provide most qualified advice to school	3_____
leavers, and the main root to becoming a careers officer is a	4_____
one-year course, followed by a probationery year, leading to	5_____
the Diploma in Careers Guidance (DCG). There are fifteen	6_____
institutions in Britain offerring the course, five on a part-time	7_____
or distance learning basis. Applicants are generaly expected to	8_____
have a degree or equivalent qualification, although exeptions may	9_____
be made for those over 25 showing "evidence they can cope	10_____
with the academic part of the course". Anyone contemplating an	11_____
apliccation to a DCG course should visit a careers office to learn	12_____
more about the work or alternatively contact The Institut of Careers	13_____
Officers for further informations.	14_____

3   Some of the spelling errors you have picked out in **2** are very commonly made. For example, nouns ending in a consonant followed by *y* change to *ies* in the plural, as in *activity – activities*.

Do you know the rules for double consonants at the end of verbs?
Compare *offer – offering, occur – occurring, run – running,* and *quarrel – quarrelling.*

4   Other errors, such as the one in the first example, may occur because of interference from your own language. When you check your written work, think twice about the spelling of English words that are similar to words in your language.

5   The error in line 3 is an example of a wrongly used homophone. Homophones are two or more words that sound the same but each have a different meaning, according to how they are spelt.

Can you think of a word with the same sound but a different meaning for 1–11 below? The first one has been done for you as an example.

1	pain / *pane*	5	heel /	9	key /
2	weight /	6	bare /	10	story /
3	poll /	7	sell /	11	draft /
4	steak /	8	great /		

Check you know the meaning(s) of each word in your dictionary.

Reading   *The World of Work*

Introduction

1   What are the jobs in this picture? In pairs, comment on the benefits and drawbacks of each job, using some of these adjectives.

absorbing	tedious	challenging	predictable	sociable
solitary	secure	stressful	high-profile	conventional
creative	mundane		menial	intellectual

2   Do you know of anyone who has an 'unusual' job? What is it?

Reading

Part 2

1 In the gapped article below, someone talks about the jobs he has had, from starting out in his career to the present time. Skim read the paragraphs below and note down in chronological order the jobs he describes.

the arts

Dominic McGonigal
on the

UPS and DOWNS of the music business

I got my first job by asking the Music Administrator of South East Arts if she knew of any vacancies. She said, "Come and work here for a week for nothing and if you're any good we'll employ you as a temporary secretary."

1

The most high-profile job I've had was as arts development officer for a borough council. I promoted concerts, assisted amateur societies with administrative and financial support, promoted the arts generally through marketing and PR activities and organised their very first festival. I'm not sure how I managed it all!

2

Most of the tasks in organising an event are easy in themselves. The difficulty is making sure that they all happen at the right time and that everything is completed before curtain-up – you can't postpone the deadline!

3

The next stage is publicising the series. This involves having leaflets printed, organising distribution (more stuffing envelopes), putting adverts in the local papers, sending out a press release and talking to the local arts reporter.

4

My present job as administrator at the Incorporated Society of Musicians (ISM) offers a similar variety. Organising seminars and conferences is in many ways like organising a concert or festival, although less stressful. The other parts of the job though are quite different.

5

I also have a more general role in promoting the music profession and I regularly send out media releases – one side of A4 paper publicising conferences or new publications. I've produced a mobile display for use by members at festivals and careers conventions.

6

On the plus side, though, it is intellectually challenging and can be very creative. It's a lively and stimulating career and I have no intention of changing.

JAZZ WARRIORS

'HOMMAGE TO JOE HARRIOT'
BY HARRY BECKETT
AND HERMAN WILSON.
FEATURING
COURTNEY PINE
HARRY BECKETT
CLEVELAND
WATKISS

MAYFLOWER THEATRE
SUNDAY 9 OCTOBER AT 8.00 PM
TICKETS £6, £5, CONCESSIONS £1 OFF, FROM MAYFLOWER THEATRE,
TEL: 229771. CREDIT CARDS ACCEPTED.
PART OF SOUTHAMPTON JAZZ FESTIVAL.

Dominic McGonigal, *Working in Music*

2 Now skim read paragraphs A–G and decide which job each paragraph relates to. Six of these paragraphs fit the gaps in the article. There is an additional paragraph that does not fit anywhere.

A Arts administration is a wonderful career but it has its drawbacks. Competition is fierce so you have to be very committed and dedicated to succeed. It is a relatively insecure existence because sometimes the finance dries up and the job or organisation is wound up. The pay is usually low and, since arts organisations are small and understaffed, you have to be able to work on your own, sometimes under considerable pressure.

B While I was there, I also started a series of lunch-time concerts. The first stage involved drawing up a budget, booking the venue, finding a sponsor, booking the musicians, and finding caterers to provide lunch. Ideally, these are sorted out at the same time since they affect each other. However, in practice, each takes some time to organise so you are constantly juggling different options.

C My typing speed was 15 words per minute! It is now about 55 wpm. The job itself actually involved compiling mailing lists, packing and sending out large numbers of leaflets, photocopying, answering routine correspondence, checking booking arrangements for rehearsal time and concerts, liaising with the printer and stuffing envelopes.

D I advise our members on contracts for recordings or publishing agreements and provide information on the level of fees to charge. If things go wrong and an engagement is cancelled, then I advise members what approach to take, and I represent them when a promoter does not pay.

E Finally, on the day itself, you hope that everything goes as planned. Last minute hitches can and do happen, but you just hope the audience won't notice. Mine came on the second concert of the series when 150 people turned up. We were expecting 60–120.

F I have a very full musical life playing the piano, singing and conducting, but I didn't want to perform professionally and although you could call me a "music administrator", my work actually has little to do with music.

G The festival included a rock showcase, jazz festival, brass band festival, youth festival, music festival in the parish church, a big open day at the docks, street entertainment and a big finale in the leisure centre with an ice-skating show, various bands, films and a trombonist!

3 Now look back at the paragraphs on page 92 and note any connections in content with paragraphs A–G. Underline the words or phrases that provide links between the paragraphs. Remember to look out for:

- references to people, things and events earlier on or later in the text.
- linking words which indicate a sequence of events or train of thought.

For example,

I got my first job by asking the Music Administrator of South East Arts if she knew of any vacancies. She said, "Come and work here for a week for nothing and if you're any good we'll employ you as a temporary secretary."

Complete the gapped reading task.

4 Look at these phrases taken from the article. What do the phrasal verbs in *italics* mean?

1 the finance *dries up* (paragraph A)
2 the job or organisation is *wound up* (paragraph A)
3 *drawing up* a budget (paragraph B)
4 150 people *turned up* (paragraph E)
5 these are *sorted out* at the same time (paragraph B)
6 *sending out* … leaflets (paragraph C)

5 Would you like to have Dominic's current job? Discuss the pluses and minuses with another student. Think of phrases you could use. Here is an example from the article:

On the plus side … it is intellectually challenging …

Writing   *Taking Time Out* ▼

Introduction

1 If you had the opportunity to work abroad, which country would you like to work in? What type of work would you like to do?

  2 Listen to the recording of someone who decided to take a year out between school and university. Why did she do this? Was the year a success? Give reasons for your answers.

Writing

Understanding the task

Part 1, letters

1 a Look at the following adverts for work abroad, which appeared in a magazine for young people. Study the three adverts carefully and decide what exactly is being advertised in each case. Which of the three adverts would you be most interested in? Note down what other information you would need to know about the jobs that are described.

b Now look at this writing task.

> Some friends of yours in England have just sent you some adverts they have found in a magazine, as they know you are keen to find a job abroad. Read the letter from your friends and study the adverts carefully.

How are you? Bill and I are OK, though we do need to cut down on our workloads a bit—we're both working flat out and coming home utterly exhausted. Heading for burnout, I reckon! Still, we've got a well-earned break coming up at the end of this month—can't wait.

You said when we last spoke on the phone that you wanted to work abroad. Well, Bill has come up with the enclosed ads, from a magazine called 19. They might give you some leads.

A word of advice, though—make sure you get as much information as possible, and if any jobs are eventually offered to you, get a written contract in advance! Otherwise, you could end up slaving away for peanuts. You must have some free time and enough money to enjoy a new country.

Good luck, anyway. Keep us posted.

We'd love to hear what you're up to at the moment!

Yours

Kathy and Bill

WORKING ABROAD

We provide you with addresses of foreign firms which look for employees in Europe, USA, Canada, Australia, the West Indies and the Far East. Vacancies for au pairs, touring guides, as well as personnel for hotels and restaurants, luxury cruisers, steel, metal and oil industries, etc.

For detailed information, please send an addressed envelope to:

New Future, Linnesväg 1, 191 47 Gotëborg, SWEDEN

PLEASE ENCLOSE INTERNATIONAL REPLY COUPON OBTAINED FROM YOUR LOCAL POST OFFICE

NB We are not an employment exchange!

SPEND A YEAR IN AMERICA
YOU'LL REMEMBER THE REST OF YOUR LIFE!

Join the hundreds of young people who are taking advantage of the first and largest 12-month au-pair programme to the USA.

We provide:
★Free London to New York return ticket, ★Legal J-1 Visa, ★Medical Insurance, ★$100 per week pocket money, ★Plus many other exciting benefits.

If you're aged 18–25 with childcare experience and a driving licence, call: 0171-584 2274 or 0171-581 2730 (24 hrs) for full details and an application form or write to Au Pair in America, 7 Kings Gate, London SW9 5HR.

au in pair AMERICA

A YEAR ABROAD, A LIFETIME OF MEMORIES

▶▶

FUN & EXCITEMENT
WORK ON CRUISE SHIPS

Thrills, adventure and great rewards. Meet interesting people; visit exotic places. My 'Cruise Ship Job Guide' explains everything you need to know. Send S.A.E. for FREE details to: Harp Publications, Thames House, Swan Street, Old Isleworth, TW7 6RG.

Now write:

a   a letter to one of the organizations, asking for further information (100 words).

b   an appropriate reply to your friends, telling them what action you have taken (150 words).

Selecting ideas

2   For letter a, decide what specific information you require. Are there any points in your friends' letter that it would be useful to include? Be careful not to 'lift' phrases from their letter. You should not only reword what they say, but also change the style of what you write to a formal register.

For letter b, decide how to reply to your friends' letter. You should include an appropriate opening greeting and brief comments in reply to their letter.

Make sure you follow instructions carefully – CAE examiners will penalize irrelevance and omissions.

Focusing on the reader

3   a   Look at these sentence openings and suggest suitable completions in relation to letter a.

• Introduction	*With reference to …* *I am writing to inquire …*
• Request for information	*I would like to receive …* *Please could you send me …*
• Additional question	*I am a little unsure about …* *I do not fully understand what …* *Could you possibly explain …*
• Ending	*I would be grateful if …* *Thank you in anticipation for …*

8.3 page 195

b   Look back at your friends' letter and find examples of each of these informal features. Then suggest relevant phrases or sentences containing the same features to use in letter b:

• phrasal verbs   • ellipsis   • informal punctuation
• contractions   • imperatives   • abbreviated forms.

Planning your answer

4   For letter a, use the outline in 3a above.

As you plan letter b, decide how many paragraphs you need and work up your own outline. In what order should you deal with the points in your friends' letter? Don't forget to mention the job you are considering and say what action you have taken.

Writing

page 184

5   Now write the two letters, using no more than 100 words for letter a and around 150 words for letter b. When you have finished check your answer carefully. Remember **WRITE** .

Structure   *The Rat Race*

Introduction

If you didn't have to work or go to school or college, how would you spend your time?

Prioritize the activities below according to which you think would be the most / least worthwhile. Give reasons for your opinions.

- Spending money.
- Going to museums or art galleries.
- Helping other people.
- Travelling.
- Looking after a garden.
- Taking care of a pet.

English in Use
Part 2

A Read the newspaper article below, ignoring the spaces, and complete the headline.

B Supply the missing words for the article by writing *one* word in spaces 1–15. The first one has been done for you as an example.

Vocabulary

Read the article again and find words or phrases which mean the same as the following:

1   reputable, esteemed or respected
2   unskilled or ordinary
3   being no longer needed at work
4   admitting defeat
5   leave or abandon
6   a member of the legal profession who draws up wills, advises clients, etc.
7   giving in her notice at work
8   producing a preliminary written version of
9   starting again
10   a place where the pace of life is frantic.

REAL LIVES

THE PROFESSIONAL WHO

Sue Webster reports

SURELY nobody in the real world gives up a well-paid and prestigious job (0) _____*in*_____ favour of a menial one (1)_____, by necessity,
5 they are forced to? Ambition has always (2)_____ considered a desirable quality; salary and professional status are advantages (3)_____ be courted. And yet, in these alarming
10 days of executive stress, burnout and compulsory redundancy, the idea (4)_____ throwing in the towel holds a strange appeal. We interviewed someone who has quit the rat race.
15 Gillian, 37, was a solicitor in a city law firm (5)_____ earlier this year. She worked long hours and weekends

and (6)_____ come to the conclusion that her highly paid, high
20 status job was just a 'living death'. She found the isolation of the job difficult and wished she could have more contact with people, rather (7)_____ dealing with her
25 clients only by phone or fax. When she left, her clients were surprised. When she told (8)_____ she was going to work behind the counter of a supermarket, they were, she laughs,
30 'flabbergasted'.
She now works a 39-hour week, at a very modest hourly rate of pay. Gillian doesn't regret resigning (9)_____ the law firm or having
35 less money. 'If only I'd done it sooner,'

she says. 'I absolutely love the new job! (10)_____ is a part of me that I'm not using; your brain feels (11)_____ I call 'stretched'
40 when you're drafting legal documents. But I don't miss that at all. I'm (12)_____ busy to feel bored.' Any lack of intellectual stimulation has yet to prove frustrating, and,
45 in the evenings, she now reads (13)_____ those books that she wishes she had had time to read before. Not (14)_____ Gillian has closed the door entirely to resuming her
50 law career. A period (15)_____ of the fast lane does not render professionals unemployable and some do manage to make a comeback. ∎

Sue Webster, *Independent on Sunday*

310 words

Wishes and regrets

A The following information about Gillian is implied in the article.

1 She didn't have much contact with people.
2 She resigned from the law firm.
3 She doesn't have so much money now.
4 She didn't resign when she should have done.
5 She is quite happy not drafting legal documents.
6 She never had time to read books before.

Find examples of wishes and regrets in the article which confirm the information above. Your examples should include:

a miss   c wish
b regret   d if only …

B Which of the words and expressions in a–d above:

1 is a strong or an emphatic expression of disappointment or desire?
2 means 'to feel or express sorrow or distress over an action'?
3 expresses unhappiness at the loss or absence of a person or thing?
4 means 'to desire or hope for'?

C Which word or expression in a–d can be followed by:

1 the infinitive with *to*?
2 the conjunction *that*?
3 a clause with or without the conjunction *that*?
4 a clause without the conjunction *that*?
5 … *ing*?

Miss

Decide what the speakers might be missing in the following sentences.

1 I hate the humidity here.
2 I can't stand travelling on public transport.
3 I feel miserable.
4 I'm bored at home.
5 Holidays are all right, but only for a few weeks at a time.
6 The countryside is so flat here!
7 I find hotel bedrooms so uncomfortable!

What do you miss most when you are away from your home, school or job?

Regret

A What is the difference in meaning between these two sentences?

1 I regret leaving / having left the firm.
2 I regret to say she has left the firm.

Regret can also be followed by *that*. How would you rephrase sentences 1 and 2 using *regret that*?

B Rephrase these sentences using *regret*. More than one answer may be correct.

1 Peter's sorry he didn't put more effort into the work.
2 I know I shouldn't have told her.
3 Unfortunately, we have to inform you that we are not able to deal with your enquiry.
4 Sally feels awful about the mistake she made!
5 I'm sorry I didn't show more enthusiasm about your idea.
6 I don't want to say this but we are unable to enter into any correspondence regarding the situation.

Wish

A Look at these examples of sentences with *wish*:

a I wish the children wouldn't play football in the house!
b I wish I could see you more often!
c I wish he didn't spend so much money!
d I wish the company hadn't gone bankrupt!
e I wish my friends wouldn't phone me when I'm in the middle of eating a meal!

Which sentences express a wish for:

1 something you would like to be different now?
2 something you would have liked to have been different in the past?
3 something you find irritating or unsatisfactory and would like to be different in future?

B Match the time references for expressing wishes on the left to the modals and tenses on the right. For example, a wish about the past could be expressed by using the past perfect.

Wishes for:
- now
- the past
- the future

Modals / Tenses
past perfect
would
simple past
could
could (*have done*)
past continuous
past perfect continuous

C Rephrase these sentences using a suitable form of *wish*.

1 Sadly, I didn't have time to visit them in New York.
2 Why don't you stop asking me such personal questions?
3 My spoken French is really dreadful!
4 He would rather be a million miles away from here!
5 It's a shame John can't find a decent job.
6 Sorry I wasn't able to make it to the party.
7 Do you have to leave so early?
8 For goodness' sake! Why don't you turn the volume down? I can't hear myself think!

If only …

This more emphatic form of *wish* can be used in a short form to refer back to something already mentioned. For example,

I didn't resign when I wanted to. If only *I had*!

Angela didn't fill the car up with petrol before she set out. If only *she had*!

Use suitable short forms to complete the sentences below. More than one answer might be possible.

1 My brother didn't remember to bring the travellers' cheques with him.
   If only _____.
2 Susan keeps forgetting things.
   If only _____.
3 The children won't tell me their secret.
   If only _____.
4 Unfortunately, I accepted the job.
   If only _____.
5 I won't be able to come to your party after all.
   If only _____.
6 We aren't having a holiday this year.
   If only _____.

Practice

Make sentences expressing wishes and regrets with *miss, regret, wish* and *if only*, where appropriate, using the ideas suggested in the pictures below.

8 Going Places

Listening and Speaking *Travelling Hopefully* ▼

Introduction **1** Listen to four people talking about different ways of getting around.
As you listen, match each speaker to one of the pictures. How does each speaker feel?

2 How do you usually get from one place to another? Think about the different types of transport you use on short journeys (for example, going to work / college) and on long journeys (for example, travelling abroad). Are there any types of transport you would not use? Give reasons for your answer.

English in Use

Part 4

1 Read the extract from an article below, ignoring the gaps. What four things are mentioned which may have a negative effect on the environment?

2 Fit the correct form of the word in capital letters into each of the gaps.

0	RESPONSIBLE
1	VANDAL
2	ACCIDENT
3	PLEASE
4	DIRECT
5	BEAUTIFUL
6	ENVIRONMENT
7	MINIMAL

"SEE IT BEFORE IT'S SPOILED," the travel agents (0) *irresponsibly* used to urge their clients. The development of tourism can certainly spoil a place in many ways. One way is by (1)_____ : enough pocketed fragments can kill a coral reef. More likely, the damage is (2)_____ , as when too
5 many feet grind away at the Great Wall of China. Crowds can themselves be (3)_____ : it is hard to enjoy the paintings of the Ufizzi with elbows in your ribs. Some (4)_____ effects can be equally damaging. The infrastructure put in to accommodate tourists has blighted (5)_____ spots in Spain and Thailand. Following the Earth Summit in 1992 a checklist of
10 (6)_____ questions was drawn up to consider when developing and running a tourist business. These were worthy generalities: (7)_____ waste, re-use and re-cycle, be energy efficient, manage water carefully and so on.

Listening

Part 3

1 What do you know about the tunnel under the channel which links Britain and France? Some people in both countries were worried about the effect the tunnel might have on the areas below. Decide what they might say about each one.

cost   environment   rabies

accidents   ferry services

 2 You are going to listen to a radio interview about the Channel Tunnel. Choose the best answer to questions 1–5 below.

> **Exam tip ▼**
>
> In Paper 4, Part 3, you may have to answer multiple-choice questions. As time is short in the exam, one way to approach this type of question is to:
> • read the questions before you listen.
> • after listening for the first time, read the options and select your answer.
> • listen the second time for confirmation of your answers.

1   Why did Mrs Jamieson first start campaigning against the tunnel?

    A   She realized at the start that the tunnel was unsafe.
    B   She knew the tunnel would disrupt village life.
    C   She thinks it is important to fight for what is right.
    D   The construction work was interfering with normal life.

2   Why was it difficult to choose a suitable route for the tunnel link?

    A   The first route selected was considered too unsafe.
    B   Most possible routes were inconvenient to passengers.
    C   Much of the south-east is covered by dense forest.
    D   All possible routes passed through residential areas.

3   Why are there still problems with the tunnel, according to Mrs Jamieson?

    A   The construction work was never properly finished.
    B   The construction company became short of money.
    C   The normal safety checks were never carried out.
    D   The operators did not spend enough money on the tunnel.

4   What does Mr Ashton say about the problems reported in newspapers?

    A   They were problems that have already been solved.
    B   Those responsible for the problems have been dismissed.
    C   The reports do not affect his confidence in the tunnel.
    D   The reports were untrue and designed to scare people.

5   Why does Mr Ashton find the idea of a rabies epidemic in Britain "silly"?

    A   It would be impossible for a rabid animal to enter the tunnel.
    B   It is unlikely that a rabid animal could get to Britain via the tunnel.
    C   No rabid animals have ever crossed the River Seine in France.
    D   It would be impossible for one animal to cause an epidemic.

 3 Now listen again. In particular, listen for the questions you are not certain about. If you are still not sure, stay with the answer you first thought was right.

Speaking

Part 3

3 page 193

Exam tip ▼

Remember there is no 'right' answer in Part 3. It's important to take time to think about what you are going to say and organize your contributions as far as you can. Be flexible and let the discussion develop naturally, but don't wander off the subject.

1 Look at the five pictures. With a partner, select three which you think will be most suitable for a travel brochure specializing in safari holidays in Africa. Try to use some of these words and phrases:

Wouldn't it be better if …?   *on the one / other hand*
I don't think …, do you?   *in the same way*
Wouldn't you agree that …?   *not / just as … as*
Don't you think it would be useful to …?   *much better than …*
What about …?

2 Imagine you are going on one of the safari holidays in **1**. You've packed your suitcase and only have room for five more things. Look at the list below and with a partner decide which would be the most useful items to take with you, putting them in order of importance. In each case, say why you think the item should be included. Use the expressions above to help you.

mosquito net	binoculars	map	tent
walking shoes	compass	sun-tan cream	hat
matches	water bottle	salt tablets	

Introduction

Do you prefer going on holidays to relax or do you like to take part in sports or other activities? With a partner, discuss the activity holidays below and say whether you would enjoy them or not.

climbing
studying a foreign language
scuba diving
working as an au pair
learning to paint

picking grapes
white-water rafting
helping on an archaeological site
working as a lifeguard

Reading

Multiple matching

1 Skim through this extract from a guide to activity holidays. What kinds of holidays are mentioned?

Go for it!

1
Anyone who thinks they would like to get a job, acquire a skill or take up a new sport, learn about the world's archaeological heritage or go on an expedition by land or sea will find the contacts in this Guide.
10 **Whoever you are and whatever your interests, you will find something to get you started. At last there is no excuse for wasting your vacation when you can be improving your skills: practical, academic or social; go for it!**

2
15 With the busy lives many people live, forward thinking does not always get the consideration it should. Some holidays clearly require early booking and with some archaeological camps, expeditions and anything involving a trip to a distant part of the world, it is
20 essential to do something as early as possible. However, it is sometimes possible to apply late and get on a waiting list.

3
Many embarking on such a venture for the first time consider taking someone with them. However,
25 thousands of people go it alone for a variety of reasons, not least that they can't find anyone to go with them. You will have more chance to take in your surroundings and receive the full benefit of the experience. Going on your own is likely to be more
30 interesting and will bring out your individuality and develop self-confidence.

4
For almost any trip, you will need to take clothing, washing kit and swimming gear, and as you'll certainly want to take photographs, don't forget the
35 camera. Most people overpack, quite forgetting that they will have to carry their luggage for themselves for fairly long distances at ferry ports and other termini, or that there may be things to bring back which they have bought or been given on the trip.

5
Before leaving, it is important to check on the vaccination requirements. For hot climates, be prepared to suffer from minor ailments such as sunburn and stomach upsets. Take precautionary measures. Try to avoid mosquito bites but take your anti-malaria treatments anyway.

6
The choice of where to go and what to do is endless
50 and strict discipline is required to narrow down the options and come to a decision! If excavating is your idea of fun, then consider a one-or two-week stay at the Arbeia Roman Fort site in South Shields in the North-East of England. Costs are heavy on the
55 volunteers, as the work is unpaid and bed and breakfast at a nearby guest house is at the special rate of £60 per week. Working hours are from 8.45am to 4.45pm and tasks include trowelling, work with heavy tools, making context drawings and measuring
60 finds. Not for those of you who do not like exercise.

2 Choose suitable headings for the first *five* numbered sections in the extract on page 102. There are more headings than sections.

A Minor Ailments	D Planning Ahead	G Escorted Travel
B Health Hazards	E Travelling Light	H Getting Started
C Be Independent	F Late Applications	

3 Now look at paragraphs 6–11. Match the statements on the left with the holidays on the right. You will find that some choices are needed more than once.

You may stay with local people.   1_____ 2_____

You may be able to stay for free.   3_____ 4_____

You will be paid for your work.   5_____

You will need to be physically fit.   6_____ 7_____

A Archaeological Dig
B Nature Conservation
C Teaching English
D Sailing and Mountaineering
E Homestays and Exchanges
F Learning Esperanto

Where to go and what to do – the choice is yours

7

Less physically demanding, but nevertheless a holiday with a serious work focus, would be a couple of weeks with Natuur 2000 in Belgium. This organization, founded in 1967, aims to create an awareness in
65 young people of their environment and to take an active part in nature conservation. The work includes assisting in the upkeep of nature reserves, maintaining wetlands in Oude Landen and helping to look after bats at Oelegem, near Antwerp. The accommodation
70 is basic but cheap and volunteers should bring their own sleeping bag and eating utensils.

8

You may prefer to avoid physical work of all kinds and plump for teaching English at a summer camp in Hungary. The Central Bureau in London is a non-profit-
75 making organization which offers you the opportunity to help local participants improve their English. The pay is minimal, but you don't have to pay for board and lodging in local homes, and visits to Budapest and other places of interest are included in your
80 month's stay.

9

The Brathay Exploration Group organizes expeditions all over the world. The programmes vary from year to year and have included a three-week trip to Norway for sailing and mountaineering. The group is based at
85 a 300-acre estate near Lake Windermere, and clients can gain experience on basic expeditions in the Lake District and Scotland. You will be required to have a fitness test before embarking on any trip.

10

Also on offer are a variety of homestay holidays which
90 offer you the opportunity to live in a country of your choice at minimal cost. The Aquitaine Service Linguistique will organize exchanges and homestay programmes in 15 countries. The duration can vary from 1 week in Hawaii to a full year in the USA. Costs
95 vary but are reasonable, and airport pick-ups are often included.

11

The Young Esperantists is another non-profit-making organization based in the USA, which runs an unusual range of holidays to promote Esperanto,
100 the international language of friendship. Activities include congresses, seminars and activity holidays all the year round. Beginners are welcome
105 and can learn Esperanto on courses held in the States. The Passporta Servo provides accommodation free of charge for backpackers and interrailers
110 who speak Esperanto. ■

 825 words

Style

This text covers different activity holidays and could have been written as a series of isolated paragraphs. However, the writer has linked the information so that it reads as one continuous piece of text.

Look at these cohesive devices, which have been used at the beginning of paragraphs. Identify the information in the text that they refer to.

- *Many embarking on such a venture for the first time ...* (3)
- *Less physically demanding, but nevertheless a holiday with a serious work focus, ...* (7)
- *You may prefer to avoid physical work of all kinds ...* (8)
- *The Young Esperantists is another non-profit-making organization ...* (11)

Now match these paragraph openings to the descriptions in a–d below.

- *With the busy lives many people live ...* (2)
- *For almost any trip, you will need ...* (4)
- *The Brathay Exploration Group organizes expeditions all over the world.* (9)
- *Also on offer ...* (10)

a	focusing on a specific topic	c	linking with the previous paragraph
b	adding context and colour	d	making a general statement

Remember to use cohesive devices like these to link your own writing.

Vocabulary

Collocations

1 Match the verbs on the left with the nouns on the right. Which of the verbs can be used with more than one noun? How many of these collocations can you find in the text?

take up	a holiday
develop	self-confidence
gain	photos
make	an outing
take	a swim
go on	experience
go for	sport
do	the surroundings
take in	a skill
	plans

2 Complete the gaps in the following sentences with one of the collocations above. Make sure that you use the correct form of the verb.

1. Michael is looking so fit and healthy. He _____ a swim every day since the start of the holiday.
2. 'Don't _____ photos of me. Liz is much more photogenic.'
3. You really should _____ a holiday. It will do wonders for you.
4. People who work for a year between leaving school and going to university tend to _____ self-confidence and become far more aware of the real world.
5. It's never too late to _____ a new sport such as skiing.
6. The holiday was a great success. The children _____ numerous outings and visited the best-known landmarks.
7. It's well worth _____ careful plans before embarking on an activity holiday.
8. Sue _____ a considerable amount of experience in her two years as a teacher in Italy.

3 With a partner discuss the sort of activity holiday that appeals to you. Use some of the expressions in **1**.

Writing *Travelogue* ▼

Introduction

1 Look at the pictures of different kinds of holiday. What type of holiday-makers do you think they would appeal to? Would you consider going on any of these holidays?

2 If you could spend one day anywhere in the world, where would you go? What would you do while you were there?

Vocabulary

Confusable words

In 1–9 below, there are sets of words which are easily confused with each other. Complete the passage by choosing one option from each set.

1	strangers	foreigners	aliens
2	historic	historical	
3	coast	beaches	shore
4	many	much	
5	sympathetic	friendly	
6	fewer	less	
7	trip	journey	voyage
8	hire	rent	
9	spend	pass	

Not many (1)_____ are unfamiliar with **MALLORCA.** Thousands of them have been flocking there over the last twenty years for
5 their holidays.

It isn't usually the (2)_____ monuments which attract them, but the sandy (3)_____ and hot Mediterranean sun. (4)_____ never venture beyond their
10 hotel and the (5)_____ bar at the end of the street. Even (6)_____ pay the extra pesetas to take a boat (7)_____ around the island or visit an ancient archaeological site.

15 The young and the more adventurous probably (8)_____ a motorcycle and set off for the less frequented beaches. As long as the sun shines, the exhausted city workers are more than happy to (9)_____ a couple
20 of weeks improving their tans and sipping the local wine!

Writing

Sample descriptions

Part 2, guidebook entry

1 a Read the three descriptions of the city of Venice given below. Decide where each piece could have come from, its purpose and the target reader.

b What are the main differences in style in each passage? Think about formality and the balance of fact and opinion, as well as verb tenses and the vocabulary used.

> **Exam tip** ▼
>
> In Paper 2, Part 2, you may be required to write a description of a place you know for a tourist guidebook. You will have to consider carefully the reader you are writing for, what you want to describe, and what suggestions and recommendations you want to make.

A

I dropped in on Venice to see an old friend on the way back from a business trip to Rome. It was January, cold and misty, and I was expecting to be met at the airport. My friend didn't show up but Venice, looming mysteriously through the fog as
5 the vaporetto glided over the water towards the shore, more than made up for it.

I was shown round the city by Matilda's aunt – Matilda had a cold and wasn't feeling up to it – a very knowledgeable old lady who spoke reasonable English very fast. She had lived
10 in Venice all her life and took me to secret beauty spots and undiscovered canals where tourists seldom went. Or so it seemed to me. The experience was magical and unforgettable.

B

No tour of Europe would be complete without seeing

VENICE, City of Water.

Situated on the Gulf of Venice, the city is
5 *a spectacular marriage of sea, sky and impressive architecture.*

If you are spending a day in Venice, we recommend that you go from **Piazzale Roma** or the **Santa Lucia** station to the
10 **San Zaccaria** landing station by vaporetto. This will take you along the **Grand Canal** to the **lagoon**, where you can view the **Campanile**, the **Basilica of San Marco** and the **Palace of the Doges**. From here
15 you can walk through the Piazza and see the Basilica, before continuing to the **Rialto** by way of the **Mercerie**.

Later on, you may want to look around the **Peggy Guggenheim Museum**, which
20 has an extensive collection of modern art. Or, if you prefer, you could go to one of the numerous nearby cafés which serve excellent coffee.

C

VENICE is the chief city of Venetia, a region in the North-East of Italy. It was built on a group of islets within the lagoon in the Gulf of Venice, at the head of the Adriatic. It has
5 splendid architecture and is rich in art treasures and historic associations. The intensive use of its canal network, including the Grand Canal, has led to the erosion of buildings. At present, the city is gradually
10 sinking into the Adriatic, and large-scale projects have been set up to preserve it.

Understanding the task   **2**   Now read this writing task.

Looking back at the extracts in **1**, which style would be most appropriate for this task?

The publishers of a guidebook on your country have asked you to write an entry for a town you know well. The guidebook is called ***All in a day*** and gives tourists information and practical details about what to see within one day.

Brainstorming ideas   **3**   Now think about a town, and add your own ideas to the diagram below.

It's a good idea to include some unusual characteristics of the place you are describing, which may not be immediately obvious to the tourist passing through. Practical details such as cost and times will also be useful.

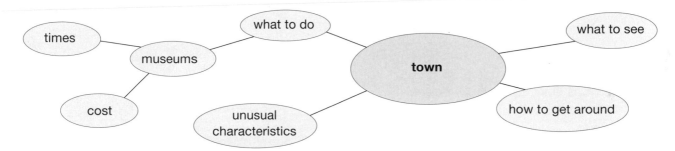

Remember that your description should be no more than 250 words, so be selective about what you include.

Planning your answer   **4**   Use the framework below to plan what you are going to write. You may like to use some of the suggestions given in each part.

- Introduction
  If you are spending a day …
  No tour would be complete without a trip to …
  Situated on the coast / near the mountains …

- Paragraph two: where to stay / how to get around

- Paragraph three: things to see and do
  Why not visit …
  You may want to try + ing / noun
  In contrast …

- Conclusion: include any unusual characteristics
  Don't forget to …
  If you want to experience something slightly different …

6.3 page 194
8.1 page 195

Writing   **5**   Now write your description in about 250 words. Don't forget to name the town and describe its location. When you have finished check your answer carefully.
Remember **WRITE** ✎.

page 188

Introduction

Most people can tell a story about an interesting or unusual thing that happened to them while travelling. Some people even make a living doing it! Tell a partner about something that happened to you while travelling.

Reading

Quickly read the magazine article below, then answer these questions:

1   What is a freighter?
2   Why did the author travel on a freighter in his youth?
3   What effect did this experience have on him?

● **Travel:** Trader Horn

All aboard!

If in your youth you read stories about the sea, the idea of sailing on a freighter might appeal to you. You might think that, in the prolonged
5 intimacy of the confines of the ship, your fellow travellers will confide stories which will bring you fame and fortune as a writer yourself.

What you soon discover when you
10 ask the Passenger Shipping Association for freighter sailing dates, is that a cabin on a cargo ship is more expensive than one on the QE2, and your voyage could last a couple of
15 months or more.

So you'll probably find a cabin full of experienced voyagers, despising package travel and liable to suggest suddenly that everybody should have
20 dinner on board the first evening of entering port, rather than go ashore.

Then there are the people who join the crew.

When I was a teenager, I was so
25 short of ready cash that I decided to work my passage from Buenos Aires to London on an old ship. In the huge Atlantic waves, she sometimes pointed her bow at the moon, as if she were a
30 rocket about to take off! One of my jobs was to lug food from the ship's kitchen to the crew's quarters, along slippery decks, while incoming waves threatened to deliver the cans of stew
35 straight into the sea below. As long as I didn't spill any, the crew were understanding!

The trip took six weeks, partly because freighters have changes of
40 plan and partly because we made an unscheduled stop in a Brazilian port so that we could have the ship's engine repaired. Despite the fact that two members of the crew failed to return
45 to the ship before we sailed, we were not delayed further, as our numbers were made up by two stowaways wanting to go and work in Portugal, which was not on our route!
50 This experience may have soured my view of entering the freighter business, although I was tempted after I'd spent a day with a dynamic Dane, who owned those ships in which tourists
55 travel along the shores of Barbados. He expounded on his sideline: buying freighters from bankrupt stock. But he insisted that he would never carry cargo, nor sell the ships for scrap. He
60 explained enthusiastically that he would redesign the super-structure, do them up and anchor them where they would make him a fortune, all around the Gulf of Mexico as floating fun
65 palaces! Though the project intrigued me, it remained a pipe dream! **G**

Relative clauses

A Look at the sentences below. What information do relative clauses add to a sentence?

1 The passengers who checked in early had a long wait at the airport.
2 The passengers, who checked in early, had a long wait at the airport.

Which clause is defining and which non-defining? What is the difference in meaning between them?

B
1 In the article, there are four examples of relative clauses. What are they and what are they describing?
2 Which clauses are defining and which non-defining, and how does this affect the meaning?
3 In which type of clause, or after what kind of word, can you not use the relative pronoun *that*?
4 What is the difference between the relative pronouns *who*, *which* and *whose*?

C Using the information below, write five sentences containing either a defining or a non-defining relative clause with a suitable relative pronoun. In some cases, there are two different ways of organizing the information.

1 Fifty people came on the trip and they thoroughly enjoyed themselves.
2 The Captain was a charming man. His name was Worthington.
   (Be careful with the relative pronoun!)
3 The sea-crossing was rough. It took several weeks.
4 Some of the students had a young person's railcard, so they paid considerably less for their tickets.
5 Mr and Mrs Evans boarded the boat in Cairo. They had made an unscheduled overnight stop there.

In which of the sentences you have written could you substitute the word *that* for the relative pronoun? Could you omit the relative pronouns in these sentences? Why? Why not?

Noun clauses

A Here are two sentences from the article which contain examples of noun clauses:

1 *You might think that … your fellow travellers will confide stories …*
2 *What you soon discover … is that a cabin on a cargo ship is more expensive than one on the QE2, and your voyage could last a couple of months or more.*

There are four noun clauses in the two previous sentences; three are used as the object of a verb and one is used as the subject of a verb. What are they?

B Find other examples of noun clauses in the article by answering these questions:

1 What might the experienced voyagers suddenly suggest?
2 What did the *dynamic Dane* insist he would never do?
3 What did he explain he would do with the bankrupt stock?

Are the noun clauses the subjects or the objects of the main verb?

C Use the following information to produce sentences containing a noun clause which is either the subject or the object of the main verb. You may have to change the order of the words and some of the words themselves in the sentences. For example,

You said something. It is true.
What you said is true.
(noun clause – subject of the verb *is*)

I know something. The company has kept no proper accounts.
I know that the company has kept no proper accounts.
(noun clause – object of the verb *know*)

1 You said something. It made sense.
2 You did something. It wasn't very sensible.
3 He made a suggestion. He wanted me to become an associate member of the company.
4 She said something to me. I agreed with it.
5 He explained something to me. He wanted to take me on a world cruise.
6 We discovered something. They had tried to deceive us!

Adverb clauses

A The article contains several different types of adverb clauses. For example, *If in your youth you read stories about the sea* is an adverb clause of condition.

How do adverb clauses make a piece of writing more interesting?

B These examples of adverb clauses appear in the article.

1 *… when you ask the Passenger Shipping Association for freighter sailing dates …*
2 *(I was) so short of ready cash that I decided to work my passage from Buenos Aires to London on an old ship.*
3 *… as if she were a rocket about to take off!*

4 *As long as I didn't spill any, …*
5 *… partly because freighters have changes of plan …*
6 *… so that we could have the ship's engine repaired …*
7 *Despite the fact that two members of the crew failed to return to the ship …*
8 *… where they would make him a fortune …*

Can you match them to the types of adverb clause below?

a condition
b time
c result
d manner
e reason
f concession, ie a clause which might be expected to interfere in some way with the action in the main clause, but does not!
g place
h purpose

Can you find any other examples of adverb clauses in the text?

[C] Using appropriate conjunctions in the correct part of the sentence, combine the information on the left with that on the right. Produce your own examples of adverb clauses like those in **B** above, then say which type they are.

1 is very rich and successful   a do the homework
2 went abroad   b needed it
3 is so difficult   c hurt his leg
4 bought the dictionary   d will phone you
5 get home   e isn't happy
6 have time   f can't do it
7 was walking strangely   g find a job
8 was going home   h the ground looked flat
9 set up the tent   i met Martha

Practice

Combine the information in the following sentences to write a mini-article similar to the one on page 108. In addition to the main clause, use a relative, noun or adverb clause where appropriate. For example,

You are interested in aeroplanes.
You might enjoy a trip in a hot air balloon.

If you are interested in aeroplanes, you might enjoy a trip in a hot air balloon.

I read an advertisement in a Sunday newspaper for trips in hot air balloons.
I phoned the company.
I wanted some more information about the trip.

After I read an advertisement in a Sunday newspaper for trips in hot air balloons, I phoned the company so that I could find out more information about the trip.

1 You discover something.
It's more expensive than a plane ticket!

2 You'll find out something next.
Your fellow travellers are not your type.

• You can combine this information by using a noun clause as the subject of the verb.

3 Some of them are frightened.
They seem to be ready to jump out of the basket!

4 The 90-minute trip was interesting.
I prefer to have my feet firmly on the ground.

• You can combine this information by using an adverb clause of concession.

5 We arrived back safely.
The passengers were relieved.
I can't mention the passengers' names.
They all disappeared for a drink in the club house.

• You can combine this information by using:
a an adverb clause of time.
b a defining relative clause describing the passengers.
c an adverb clause of result.

Rites and Rituals

Reading *Rooting for Tradition*

Peking is in China
As Kingston is in Jamaica
As Delhi is in India
As nowhere do we belong
You and I.

And should we ever run away
Where shall we run to?
And should we ever fight a war,
Who shall we fight for
You and I?

At the end of the rainbow
Is a country of goodness
If we form an alliance
Will we ever be free
To belong?

Or shall we always be carrying
Our ancestors' coffins in a bag?
Searching the globe
For a place to belong
You and I.

Meiling Jin

Introduction

1 Read the poem and discuss what you think it is saying.

2 What is it about a place that makes you feel 'at home'? With a partner, make a list of the things you would miss most about your own culture if you lived in a country which was very different from your own.

Would you find it hard to do without certain things?

Reading

Multiple matching

Exam tip ▼

In some multiple matching tasks, you have to scan a text and match sections of it to particular topics. As you scan, look out for vocabulary that is relevant to these topic areas.

1 Quickly read the article opposite. Can you name two of the difficulties that people experience when they live in a foreign culture?

2 Now look at the topics below. Scan the text and identify which sections (A–H) refer to which topics. Some sections may be chosen more than once. Which section refers to the following?

Asian attitudes to love and marriage.   1_____
Experiences at school.   2_____   3_____
The influence of conservatism.   4_____
Remaining on the outside of society.   5_____
Re-evaluating and accepting Asian culture.   6_____   7_____   8_____
The advantages of Asian customs.   9_____   10_____

3 What views and attitudes to western life are mentioned in the article? In your opinion, how important is it for people to retain their own customs and traditions when they settle in a new country?

Vocabulary

Forceful language

1 Forceful language is used in this article, both by the writer and the people who are quoted. What does it add to the article? Here are some examples:

1 leaving *acrimoniously* (paragraph A)
2 her family was *devastated* (paragraph A)
3 a *passionate* advocate (paragraph E)
4 feelings … are further *exacerbated* (paragraph G)
5 his culture is often *denigrated* (paragraph G)
6 you are a *distorted* image of yourself (paragraph H).

Look at the words in *italics*. What do you think they mean? Check your answers in a dictionary.

2 Now match the words from the article to words with the opposite meaning on the right.

1 acrimoniously   a improved
2 devastated   b indifferent
3 passionate   c delighted
4 exacerbated   d truthful
5 denigrated   e amicably
6 distorted   f acclaimed

3 Use one of the words in **2** to complete sentences 1–8.

1 For years, Naima was _____ towards her family, until her life went wrong and they were there to support her.
2 Despite previous bad relations, pay negotiations between management and the union were _____ resolved. Both parties felt they had secured a good deal.
3 Although he has some liberal views, generally Simon is a _____ believer in conservative family values.
4 The play was an amazing box office success, as well as being highly _____ by the critics.
5 The earthquake struck with such force that it completely _____ the city and the surrounding area.
6 During the protest, crowd violence was _____ by heavy-handed police tactics.
7 Sensationalism in the popular press often results in a _____ impression of what's going on in the world.
8 Emma was both surprised and _____ when she won her Academy award for Best Actress.

Going back to their roots

Yasmin Alibhai-Brown explores changing attitudes in Asian society.

A

Naima hurries along excitedly, bumping into people as she goes. Trailing behind her, her mother, two aunts and a grandmother, who tease her in Gujarati as they visit the glorious Asian shops in Wembley, north London. There are two reasons for celebration. Naima, a 28-year-old biochemist, is marrying a solicitor – a man her parents suggested. But, more importantly, Naima has come home after leaving acrimoniously six years previously. Her family was devastated. She was indifferent. Then six months ago she turned up, emaciated and shaking. 'I used to think Asians were stupid and boring,' she says, 'but when my life went wrong, I felt such a plastic person. I had to come back, my heart's here.'

B

The rewards for this reinstatement are plentiful. Her aunts, after some intense haggling, buy her 12 pure gold bracelets costing £2,000. Grandmother, not to be outdone, splashes out on a diamond necklace and nose stud. Jewels for her feet, hands and forehead are set aside. In the next shop, assistants unroll acres of wonderful wedding cloth. Naima is just one example of how Asians are rethinking their identity in this country.

C

Although the expectations of the community are that second and third generation immigrants will readily assimilate, more complex processes take place. The young from many ethnic communities long to link up with their heritage and history. This rethinking usually follows a period of denial, as it did for Naima. There was a time when many Asians felt ashamed of their backgrounds. I remember cringing with embarrassment if my mother was out with me, or if I saw a group of Asians at a bus stop. To be part of the brave new modern world, you had to cast off these people who were 'backward' and 'uncivilised'.

D

'We are old-fashioned about marriage,' says Amina, a middle-class Muslim from Birmingham, 'but English friends who want to be liked by boys are prisoners of love games. It is so degrading. The boys we know are family friends, there is respect between us. We need our parents, who have wisdom, who love us, to do proper market research before we give our lives to somebody. With romance, you start at the top and come down. We have to work up to love. You then treat it with some respect.'

E

Other aspects of traditional life are also becoming popular again. Kamla Jalota, a dentist, is a passionate advocate of the extended family. 'I want my in-laws to live with me. I think that having three generations of women will be a real education for my daughter. I want them to tell me what to do with my children, so I don't treat them with indifference or thoughtlessness; my children will then learn that, in our community, to get old is to gain respect – not to lose it as in this utilitarian society.' These attitudes have become more commonplace because many parents have come halfway to bridging gaps.

F

Perhaps these changes are also due to the fact that the younger generation is a product of the 80s, the decade of conservative values. 'Yes,' agrees Jafar Kareem, an Asian psychologist who runs a clinic for ethnic minorities. But he warns that something else is going on: 'There is a difference between a healthy return to roots – a positive expression of pride in who you are – and a retreat into a meaningless past which comes from a sense of loss and confusion in who you are.'

G

These feelings, says Jafar, are further exacerbated by rejections by the host community. 'When an Asian child goes to school, his culture is often denigrated. The child feels a sense of annihilation and time makes this worse. So he reacts either by being ashamed of himself or by becoming vociferously Indian, hating whites or whatever.'

H

Arvind Sharma, a lecturer with two sons, says, 'I sometimes want to cry when they go to school. All the experiences our children have there are about wiping out their heritage.' These pressures continue through life, says Arvind, so you 'begin to chip bits off yourself to make yourself more acceptable, until one day you realise you are a distorted image of yourself and you are still on the fringes of society. It hurts because you expected to belong because you did all the right things.'

Yasmin Alibhai-Brown, *She*

710 words

Style

There are clues in this article which show that it comes from a magazine or newspaper. Typical features of this style of writing include:

- views of the writer on a particular issue.
- actual examples which stress these views.
- views of people referred to.
- actual quotes from these people.
- short descriptions of events or people referred to in the article.

Look at each paragraph and decide which of the above are included. See if you can work out the organization of the article by looking at what links each sentence and paragraph. The first paragraph has been done for you as an example.

Paragraph A   **description** of Naima's shopping trip
                            example of Naima's previous unhappy experiences
                            quote from Naima about what happened to her

Listening and Speaking   *Manners Maketh Man?* ▼

Introduction

1   Read the short story below.

● Urban myths

Votes is votes

A friend of a friend, a parliamentary candidate, was canvassing at the last election, and came to a house with a slavering, stud-collared pit bull-
5 terrier outside. He hated dogs, but 'votes is votes', and he hesitantly rang the doorbell.
    Apparently, he was given a warm welcome by the householders, who
10 always voted for him and invited him in for a cuppa. The candidate edged past the growling mutt, and it followed him inside, baring its teeth at him from the middle of the floor.

15   The nervous politician and the smiling family discussed local issues over their tea for a while, and the dog kept snarling, until it suddenly caught hold of his trouser leg and ripped a
20 hole in it. The politician looked at the dog, then the family; they smiled back as if nothing had happened. Taken aback at their reaction (and the kind of supporter he was attracting), he
25 decided to leave. So, finishing his tea, he made a polite excuse and said his good-byes.
    He'd only taken a few steps out of the door when one of his hosts asked:
30 'Aren't you going to take your dog?' ●

Healey and Glanville The Guardian

2   This story may or may not be true, but what does it say about the importance of being polite? Are manners just a matter of being correct, or are they about making other people feel comfortable?

Speaking
Parts 3 and 4

1 What do you consider polite behaviour? What kinds of behaviour do you consider to be impolite?

2 Each of the following situations is set in a different country where there is an acceptable code of behaviour for the situation described. In pairs, decide which is the most likely response in each culture and explain your decision.

Remember that in the speaking section of the examination the examiners will be listening very carefully to see if you are able to interact effectively with your partner.

One way of approaching this is as follows:

Stage one

Open up the discussion by:

- making a comment.
- asking a question.
- making a suggestion.

Stage two

Develop the discussion further by looking at the options one by one. Remember to take it in turns to speak and don't force your point of view on your partner. You don't have to agree.

Your body language can show you are aware of your partner, so try to maintain eye contact and face each other during the conversation.

Now read through the following situations and discuss which option you think is best.

CULTURE SHOCK

'When in Rome, do as the Romans do' – but in a different country, where you are unaware of its particular customs, what would you do?

1 United States of America

A friend has invited you to dinner at a nice restaurant. You dine well, and at the end the waiter brings the bill and puts it in the middle of the table. You don't expect to have to pay for the meal, but your friend shows no signs of doing so. You wait and the conversation grows slow, and still nothing happens. You are getting very tired and are beginning to think that you are expected to pay for the meal. What would you do?

A Grit your teeth and wait some more.
B Pick up the bill and pay it.
C Pick up the bill and say, 'Shall we split it?'

2 South Africa

You and some other rugby fans have been in a pub or someone's home watching the last match in a rugby test series on TV. The South Africans have just lost to the Australian Wallabies by 16 to 12. Would you:

A cheer loudly because you really are a Wallaby supporter, having just come from that side of the world?
B commiserate with your hosts or pub mates, but give reasons for why you feel the Australians deserved to win?
C keep your feelings to yourself and just discuss the good and bad moments of the match?

3 Thailand

You are sitting with a Thai friend and his 7-year-old child on a crowded bus, when an old man gets on. Would you:

A do nothing?
B ask the child to give up his seat to allow the old man to sit?
C give up your seat for the old man?

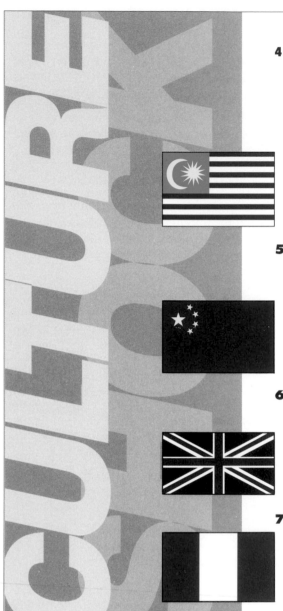

4 Malaysia

You are talking to a valued client in your office. Certain papers are needed. You ring your office boy to bring them. He brings a wrong file; you reject it and ask him to look for the right one. He brings another wrong file, and then a third.
Would you:

A stomp out of the room to get the correct file, which you show to the office boy as you bring it. You tell him what you think of his lazy, careless behaviour, etc.?

B call your secretary on the intercom and ask her to locate the file, then send the office boy to go and get it?

C excuse yourself and leave the room to go and get the file; after the guest has left, you say a few words to the office boy?

5 China

You have been invited by a Chinese family to share a special meal and the dishes appear one after the other. The hostess presents the final, large and ornate dish and when she tastes it, she makes a face and says it is 'not salty enough'.
What would you say?

A 'Never mind, I'll just add some salt.'
B 'Oh no, it's absolutely delicious, the best I've ever tasted!'
C 'I'm not very hungry, anyway.'

6 Britain

You are in a crowded lift and someone gets in and steps on your foot.
Would you:

A stare at the floor and bear the pain silently until they have moved off it of their own accord?
B glare at them angrily and tell them to 'Get off!'?
C say 'Sorry'?

7 France

You are visiting some friends who have invited you to dinner.
Would you take:

A some flowers?
B a bottle of wine?
C nothing?

3 Now check your answers with the key on page 196. Would people in your country react in a similar way? If not, how would their reactions differ?

Vocabulary
Confusable words

1 These pairs of words are often confused with each other. This may be because they are similar in meaning or they look or sound the same. Check you know their meanings in a dictionary.

gentle / polite
customs / habits
ashamed / embarrassed
birthday / anniversary

nervous / irritable
dependent / dependant
discussion / quarrel

2 Now choose the correct word for each space in sentences 1–7.

1 gentle / polite
Paul was very _____, and thanked his hosts for a delicious meal.

2 embarrassed / ashamed
When Naima was a student she used to feel _____ of her Asian origins.

3 dependent / dependant
Recent work done by the EU found that over 40% of men looked after _____ elderly people.

4 customs / habits
The local community actively encourages different ethnic groups to maintain their _____ and religious beliefs.

5 anniversary / birthday
The Nixon family always celebrated their son's _____ with a meal out at MacDonald's.

6 discussion / quarrel
The _____ was extremely productive and both companies left the meeting feeling positive about the merger.

7 nervous / irritable
Beth was so _____ during the interview that she could hardly string two words together.

Listening

Part 3

1 Listen to an extract from a radio phone-in programme in which the importance of manners is being discussed. You will hear three people, May Parnell, Geoffrey Brownlow, and a presenter, expressing their views. Indicate which comments are made by May Parnell (*M*) and which are made by Geoffrey Brownlow (*B*). Write both initials, or one initial, or neither (*N*) next to 1–10. You will hear the extract twice.

Before you listen, read the statements carefully.

1 Many young people are not ill-mannered.

2 Young people should use a different style of language to address their elders.

3 Adults can't always understand what young people are saying.

4 Adults should be more tolerant of young people.

5 The way people dress does not mean they are showing disrespect.

6 Unconventional dress sense can mean greater imagination.

7 Adults set a bad example to the younger generation.

8 Young people are more materialistic these days.

9 Young people think any kind of behaviour is acceptable these days.

10 Young people have an unhealthy lifestyle.

2 Do you agree with any of the views expressed? How important do you think it is to dress or speak in a particular way?

Writing *Celebrations* ▼

Introduction 🖭 **1** Listen to the following extract from a radio phone-in about Christmas presents. Make a note of the gifts people received and what they thought about them.

2 Have you ever been in a similar situation? Describe what happened and how you reacted.

English in Use
Part 6

1 Skim read this magazine article ignoring the spaces. What does the writer feel about gift-giving?

Gift-giving

*I*f you have ever lied about some horrendous offering until your face was puce, or lain awake worrying about what to buy the one you love, you will know that the giving and receiving of Christmas
5 gifts is fraught with political significance. (0) ___*J*___, pretending you like something is merely prudent damage limitation, designed to save the feelings of someone you love. Women, incidentally, are far better at this – like George Washington, men cannot tell a
10 lie (well, not about presents anyway) and fail to see why pretending to adore a polyester tie is better than reducing an elderly relative to tears.

(1)_____, however, at which Christmas presents are bearers of hidden messages: all the things a
15 person wants to say, yet cannot put into words. If this means undying worship, expressed with a large diamond, well and good. But it could also be an opportunity for someone to put you down – a criticism

of your entire lifestyle. (2)_____, a friend of mine who move into student digs against her mother's wishes, got a box of cleaning materials when she went home for Christmas.

(3)_____, Christmas is a great time to play power
30 games. Sandy, 23, claims she comes out in a rash when it's time to select a gift for her mother. 'It's unbelievably political. I have two brothers and a sister and our mother uses our presents to play us off against each other. (4)_____ and the others cast aside. Her
35 approval becomes the focus of the whole day.'

(5)_____ about buying presents – provided you have a moderate degree of sensitivity and a genuine affection for the recipient. But if you are presented with a daintily wrapped insult on Christmas morning,
40 just keep smiling. (6)_____ to start planning next year's revenge.

Kate Saunders, *Cosmopolitan*

2 Now complete the extract by choosing the best phrases from A–J to fill spaces 1–6. Remember there are more phrases to choose from than there are spaces. One answer has been given as an example.

A If this suggests
B There is nothing particularly difficult
C Some of us will be offended
D One present will be admired
E For instance
F On a less anguished note
G There is a more complicated level
H It's never too early
I For some parents
J At its simplest

Vocabulary

Phrasal verbs

In the listening and the article, you came across the verbs *spark off* and *put down*. Here are some other verbs which combine with *off* and *down*. Choose an appropriate form of one of the verbs to complete the sentences below.

pass   break

off
down

go   put

1 Due to bad weather, the village carnival had to be _____ until the weekend.
2 Sometimes it's healthy _____ and cry, as it releases all those suppressed emotions.
3 Ever since his promotion, Adrian has become unbearably arrogant – he just loves _____ people _____.
4 The spy gained access to the secret files by _____ himself _____ as a government official.
5 After much family interference, the young couple were forced _____ their engagement.
6 As the fireworks _____ over Hyde Park, the crowd began to cheer.
7 The family owns a valuable Vermeer painting, which _____ from generation to generation.
8 The meal in an expensive restaurant _____ well with our business clients.

Writing

Sample article

Part 2, article

1 a Read the article and choose the most appropriate title from the list below.

Festive weddings in two parts of the world
A personal account of my marriage
Differences in the weddings of two countries

It has to be said that our wedding ceremonies are pretty relaxed compared to British ones I have attended. For example, where I live you can always hear the wedding party coming because they make so much noise, hooting their horns and shouting. It's a very joyous affair. Once inside the church, the couple walk up to the priest and kneel down. Then the closest relatives, the best men and women, walk up to the bride and groom and exchange their crowns.

This can take quite a long time because there is often more than one round of crowns. The priest does this as well and then takes the couple by the hands and leads them round the church. And then the guests throw dried rice at them! It can hurt a lot.

Incidentally, none of the guests sits down in church – it's all very relaxed and informal.

On the other hand, the registry office weddings I have been to in Britain have all been very brief and rather grey occasions, sometimes lasting as little as ten minutes!

Turn up a little late and you will have missed the whole thing. I'm not too familiar with British church weddings, although one big one that I did go to was an extremely formal occasion. None of the guests seemed to be enjoying it very much, let alone the 'happy' couple, who both looked completely tense throughout the event. So there you have it, many contrasts and a very different atmosphere. I know which type of wedding I would prefer if I ever get married!

b Do you think the article has been suitably paragraphed? Summarize the content of each paragraph and suggest any changes in paragraphing which might improve the article.

Understanding the task   **2**   Look at the writing task. What style and register would be appropriate for the article?

You have seen the following announcement in an English language magazine aimed at young people around the world.

How **Special** is **your birthday?**

Tell us how you and your family have celebrated your birthday over the years. What makes it such a **special** day?

Compare your own experience with that of a friend of yours. What makes your birthday more – or less – **special** than your friend's?

The six best articles will be printed in our Spring issue!

Brainstorming ideas   **3**   **a**   Which two of your previous birthdays do you remember best? What made them special? Consider these aspects:

- how old you were
- who was with you
- what you did
- the presents you received.

Talk about these birthdays with another student.

b   Having listened to your partner's description, in what ways have you celebrated your birthdays differently? Do you think your own experience is more or less special?

Planning your answer   **4**   Look back at the sample article on page 119 and at the article on gift-giving on page 118. Underline the phrases which:

- introduce the topic.
- give examples.
- introduce contrasting information.
- introduce a conclusion.

Can you think of any other phrases that could be used in a similar way in your own article?

Writing   **5**   Now write your article in about 250 words. When you have finished check your answer
Ꞛ page 186   carefully. Remember **WRITE** ✎.

Introduction

Imagine that you are late for a dinner at the house of someone you do not know very well. Which of the following would you do?

- Phone to say you will be arriving late.
- Pretend you didn't know what time you were expected.
- Invent a good excuse for being late.
- Take your hosts a present as an apology.
- Write a letter afterwards to apologize for being late.
- Not turn up at all.

What would be the polite thing to do in your country?

Reading

A Quickly read the magazine article and give it a title.

B In the second and third paragraphs of the article, the writer paints a detailed portrait of what the life of a latecomer is like. List three things the writer suggests that you, the reader, have probably seen latecomers doing.

Patrick Marber *on...*

I WAS BORN premature and have been late ever since. Those of you who are punctual will not know about us, the other half of the world, the latecomers. You'll have waited for
5 us; the chances are that you've been kept waiting by us many a time, but you won't understand. In fact, if the truth be told, you're the enemy.

Doubtless, you've seen us. We're quite a
10 spectacle: a vast tribe of electrified anxiety. We glance at our watches and see despair. You've probably noticed us leaping in and out of taxi cabs throwing notes (no time for change!). We dodge you on the street,
15 jumping in puddles, weaving through the traffic. We are the strange, scuttling creatures bursting with wild eyes into restaurants, in the hope that you've waited for us.
20 You'll have observed us hovering nervously in every lobby and entrance hall in the world. In theatres and cinemas you stand up as we creep along the row trying so hard not to knock your knees or tread on your
25 toes. And you, what do you do? You 'tut' in

the dark. You don't need to do that, we know what we've done.

But here's a curious thing: in these moments we hate ourselves so much that we
30 have no alternative but to transfer our hatred to you, the punctilious, instead.

Here we see this aggressive lateness in action:
'I'm really sorry I'm late.'
35 'Yes, but why are you late?'
'I just am.'
'But why? Where have you been? What've you been doing? Do you realise how long I've been here? I've been waiting for over an hour!'
40 'Does it matter?'
'Yes. You should respect me enough to turn up on time.'
'But I'm not late on purpose. Look, I'll go.'
'But you've only just arrived!'
45 'So you want the truth?'
'Yes.'
'Well, I'm late because I've made a choice – a choice to be myself. I'm the kind of person who has never been on time yet and never
50 will be. That's what I'm like. Sorry!' ●

Patrick Marber, *The Observer Life Magazine*

340 words

Present perfect vs simple past

The first sentence in the article contains an example of both the simple past and the present perfect simple. Why are these tenses used in this sentence? What information do they convey about the period of time they are referring to?

Present perfect simple vs continuous

A Look at these two sentences:

1 I've tried to fix this hairdryer for ages.
2 I've been trying to fix this hairdryer for ages.

Which sentence sounds more natural and why?

B Look at these examples of the present perfect simple and continuous which appeared in the article.

1 ... *you've been kept waiting by us* ...
2 ... *you've seen us.*
3 *You've probably noticed us leaping in and out of taxi cabs* ...
4 ... *you've waited for us.*
5 ... *we know what we've done.*
6 *Where have you been?*
7 *What've you been doing?*
8 *Do you realise how long I've been here?*
9 *I've been waiting for over an hour!*
10 *But you've only just arrived!*
11 ... *because I've made a choice* ...
12 ... *who has never been on time yet.*

Which of these examples:

a   suggest that something is still going on?
b   refer to something which happened in the past, but we do not know exactly when?
c   refer to something which happened in the past, is now over, but still has a direct impact on what is happening now?
d   contain a time reference?
e   emphasize the length of time the action takes?
f   are in the passive form?

For and since

A Look at these examples from the article:

1 *I ... have been late ever since.*
2 *'I've been waiting for over an hour!'*

What is the difference in usage between *for* and *since*? Do you need to use *for* or *since* in the sentences below?

3   They've been up with the baby all night.
4   The doctor has been on call all day.

B Expand the notes below to make sentences using *for* or *since* and the present perfect continuous. For example,

try to contact / ages

I've been trying to contact this client for ages.

1   stand / 20 minutes   4   discuss / the meeting began
2   work / 1989   5   write / six o'clock
3   study / 3 years   6   wait to see / a very long time

C Complete the following sentences by supplying a suitable form of the verb: the present perfect simple, the present perfect continuous and *for* or (*ever*) *since* if they are needed.

1   I _____ (not / see) my aunt _____ ages.
2   It _____ (be) ages _____ I saw my uncle.
3   Our accountant _____ (be) off work _____ all week.
4   Tom _____ (be) a teacher _____ the last twenty years or more.
5   My grandfather _____ (not / get) enough exercise _____ his last operation.
6   Our granddaughter _____ (apply) for jobs _____ she left school last summer.
7   What _____ (you / do) _____ we last met?
8   The owners _____ (threaten) to sell the shop _____ years.
9   Please be quiet! Your father _____ (work) _____ all night and needs some sleep.
10   I can't stand it any longer! Those children _____ (scream) at the top of their voices _____ they woke up early this morning.
11   He inherited a huge sum of money unexpectedly last year and _____ (spend) it _____.
12   I _____ (wonder) a while now what _____ (become) of them.

In which sentence could you not use *since* without *ever*?

Long

This example of the present perfect simple appeared in the article:

'*Do you realise how long I've been here?*'

In which of the following examples could you not insert *long*? Why not? What could you use instead?

1   I haven't been here.
2   Have you been here?
3   I have been here.

Yet and still

A   Look at this example from the article:

… who has never been on time yet …

not / never … yet are used in negative and interrogative sentences to link the action to the present moment in time. Can you rephrase the sentence below using *still*?

He hasn't finished yet!

B   Rephrase these sentences in different ways using *still* or *yet*.

1   My husband hasn't booked a table for dinner on Saturday night.
2   The children have not told us their plans for the weekend.
3   The employment agency hasn't contacted me.
4   Hasn't the post come?
5   I haven't told you the best part of the story.
6   Hasn't your sister started her new job at the Central Hospital?
7   The committee has not decided on a possible course of action.
8   The police have not made the news of the arrest public.

Future perfect simple and continuous

A

1   The future perfect simple is formed by using *shall* or *will* plus the perfect infinitive without *to*. For example,

   I'*ll have finished* the work by three o'clock.

2   What is the difference between the use of the future perfect in 1 and in its use in the following sentence?

   By next year, I'*ll have been working* here for five years.

3   What is the difference between the use of the future perfect in the examples above and these two sentences from the article?

   You'll have waited for us …

   You'll have observed us …

B   Complete these sentences using a verb from the list below in either the future perfect simple or continuous. Decide whether the sentences are like those in A 1, 2 or 3 above.

write   finish   come   marry   reach
realize   organize   work

1   The students _____ (not) across this word before, I'm sure!
2   By next summer, the construction company _____ on the sports complex for two years.
3   _____ (the coach) its destination by midday?
4   Our next-door neighbours _____ (not) their holiday yet, I'm certain.
5   You _____ (not) that report by this evening, _____ you?
6   It's John and Julia's anniversary next month. They _____ for two years.
7   I'm convinced that the assistant manager _____ (not) anything like this conference before.
8   The teacher thinks that the students _____ the book by the end of the term.
9   Surely the insurance company _____ their mistake in paying out so much compensation by now?
10 Just imagine! On the first of next month, I _____ articles for this newspaper for five years.

Talking about someone else

Imagine you are appearing on a radio programme. You have been asked to prepare a short one-minute talk about someone you know well and admire. It could be someone famous, or a friend or member of your family. Use the tenses you have studied in this part of the unit to talk about the person you have chosen.

You might include what they:

*   have done (for example, experience, qualifications and when they did it).
*   still haven't done / haven't done yet.
*   have been doing up to now and how long they have been doing it (use *for* or *since*).
*   hope they will have done by a certain time in the future.
*   will have been doing (and for how long) by the end of the year.
*   have decided to do in the future.

When you have finished, tell a partner about the person you have chosen.

10

Who Cares ?

Reading *The Care Label* ▼

Introduction

In groups, discuss these views:

People should not have to depend on charities for their health and welfare – the state should provide.

Giving to charity makes you a better person.

Our society is suffering from 'compassion fatigue', ie people are fed up with giving to charitable causes.

Reading

Part 2

1 In the article below, the writer talks about *fashion compassion*. Skim read the article, ignoring the missing paragraphs and explain what she means.

Fashion*Compassion*

COVER STORY

Margarette Driscoll on the stars of the compassion industry

HOTEL ROOMS were at a premium in town 10 days ago, but that proved no impediment to Bianca Jagger as she sailed into the middle of the war zone. "Dark eyes sparkling with fury" (*Mail on Sunday*), "not afraid to get her hands dirty" (*Daily Express*), Bianca unleashed a major Latin charm offensive on the assembled officers of the UN, commandeering satellite phones, helicopters, armoured cars and a room at the hotel, which had been so overcrowded that seasoned relief workers and journalists were sleeping in corridors and, more dangerously, in their cars.

 1
Not so long ago, we were treated to the sight of Iman, the dark, glittering model, in Africa – swathed in peasant robes for one photograph, sporting jeans and casual shirt for another. The catwalk's "Angel of Africa" wandered around a dusty town looking soulfully at the destitute, spending eight days making a documentary for the BBC.

2
"They" are the Ladies Bountiful of the global village – beautiful, monied, internationally mobile, photogenically caring. There's glamorous Cher, just off to distribute supplies. There's the lovely Marie Helvin, who sponsors "foster children". Cindy Crawford worries her gorgeous head about political oppression. Yasmin Le Bon is concerned about the rain forests.

3
In parts of South America, you can barely move for beautiful people chipping their nail polish on endangered hardwoods, and, in Africa, cuddling up to wild animals. Tracy Ward, the actress and now Marchioness of Worcester, started trying to save the tropical rain forest after a stint on a detective TV series. As she tellingly explained, "I had never really had the time or the knowledge, and suddenly when I had no work I realised there was a problem."

4
It was another man, Bob Geldof, who, after the heroic efforts of Live Aid, coined the phrase "compassion fatigue". As far as the more stoical female celebrities are concerned, designer fatigues are much more to the point …

5
But there is a fine line between helping the aid agencies which are already up and running – and simply getting in the way. "Very often, when celebrities go into the field, they focus the attention on one area, maybe at the expense of others which are just as needy but don't get the publicity," said David Grubb, executive director of Feed the Children.

6
Fashion compassion has its place, and perhaps it is no bad thing that some of the ladies who lunch have become the ladies who learn. Perhaps if we were more sure – go on, call me a cynic – that their concern was entirely for the cause, and in no way for the cameras, that oddly disturbing feeling would just fade away.

2 Now read paragraphs A–G. Six of these paragraphs fit into the gaps in the article. There is also one extra paragraph which does not fit anywhere. Insert the paragraphs into gaps 1–6. Remember to look out for references to people and things, as well as linking words.

A But the women, to give them their due, appear to have more staying power than men. Sting, it was reported last week, was suffering from disillusion – fed up with trying to save the rain forest. (The story was quickly and firmly denied in a statement from Sting's office.)

B In between giving world-wide news networks snappy sound bites of her views from the hotel roof ("the most evil and cruel war I have ever seen"), Bianca Jagger toured a hospital, comforting child victims, acquired a top-security pass from the UN to enable her to meet the city's mayor and delivered 38 tons of aid. After 36 hours, she flew out.

C Nobody can doubt the sincerity of both these women; Bianca Jagger, for example, has, through years of work, more than proved her commitment to human rights. So why is it so oddly disturbing to see such women – and they are legion – carrying out their charitable work? Are we guilty of cynicism? Or is it something about them?

D All this might sound like carping; it is impossible to deny that celebrity involvement does draw public attention to terrible situations. Charities large and small have been quick to perceive the importance of television and newspapers in getting the funds rolling in, and therefore of snapping up the most influential faces. Models and actresses, usually seen stepping out of San Lorenzo or Mortimer's in Manhattan, translate perfectly – suitably togged up in battlefield chic – on to the pages of the tabloids.

E Two hundred years ago, all these women might have been trudging down the lane from the manor house bearing a basket of goodies for the poor. These days, they can jet to their particular good cause and – who would deny them this? – pick up more than a little caring *cachet* en route.

F By all accounts, professional aid workers often have to bite their lips. I know how it feels. Two years ago, reporting on a refugee crisis, I stood paralysed with embarrassment as the aid operation was temporarily suspended to allow a minister for overseas development to fly on to a mountain for a photo-call, armed with a carrier bag full of chocolate bars. Day after day, minor league ministers from other countries were also helicoptered to and fro. They *did* have an important job to do in supervising government aid. But did they have to have their photos taken?

G Another way celebrities can help raise the profile of a cause is by involving famous friends. Koo Stark is currently organising a photographic exhibition to fund a study centre for a monastery. She has collected photographs by such luminaries as Annie Leibowitz and Don McCullin, which will be sold at £250 each.

Fashion *Compassion*

3 Underline the words and phrases which helped you to put the paragraphs in the correct places.

4 Look again at the extra paragraph which did not fit into any of the gaps. Why is this paragraph inappropriate for gaps 1–6?

5 Look at the phrases below which are taken from the article. Can you explain what they mean? Using your dictionary, look up the words underlined in 1 and 2. Now underline the words you need to look up in 3–8.

1   were at a <u>premium</u> (paragraph 1)
2   <u>coined</u> the phrase "compassion fatigue" (paragraph 5)
3   But the women, to give them their due (paragraph A)
4   and they are legion (paragraph C)
5   All this might sound like carping (paragraph D)
6   suitably togged up in battlefield chic (paragraph D)
7   trudging down the lane (paragraph E)
8   by such luminaries (paragraph G)

Style

1 Which adjectives would you use to describe the writer's attitude?

a ironic   b humorous   c unconcerned   d angry

Consider the following extracts from the text:

… she sailed into the middle of the war zone …

The use of the word *sailed* suggests her grace and beauty (like a ship) but this is at odds with the ugliness of the war going on around her.

Bianca unleashed a major Latin charm offensive on the assembled officers of the UN, commandeering satellite phones, helicopters …

The language used to describe Bianca's effect on the UN officers is also the language of war – she uses the weapon of her charm to conquer the resistance of the officers. There is an unwritten suggestion that Bianca, because of her looks and personality, gets what she wants at the expense of the perhaps more justifiable needs of the relief workers and even journalists.

2 Look at the sentences below and decide what the writer intends you to understand by them. Pay particular attention to the underlined words and phrases.

1 *Not so long ago, we were <u>treated</u> to the sight of Iman, the dark, glittering model, in Africa – <u>swathed in peasant robes</u> for one photograph …*

2 *The catwalk's "Angel of Africa" wandered around a dusty town <u>looking soulfully at the destitute</u> …*

3 *"They" are the <u>Ladies Bountiful of the global village</u> – beautiful, monied, internationally mobile, <u>photogenically caring</u>.*

3 What do you think about famous people being involved in charity work? Do you agree with the views expressed by the writer?

Writing *Cruelty or Conservation?*

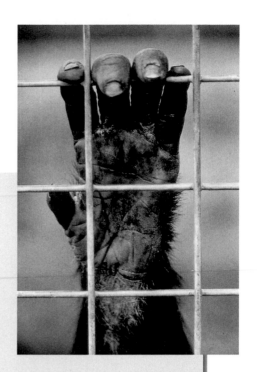

Introduction

1 Complete the following questionnaire. Then compare your results with another student.

THE ZOO INQUIRY:

do **ZOOS** have a **future** ?

1 When did you last visit a zoo?
- ❑ during the past year
- ❑ within the last five years
- ❑ more than five years ago
- ❑ never

2 What was your reason for visiting?
- ❑ for a day out
- ❑ to entertain children
- ❑ to find out more about animals
- ❑ other (specify)

3 What did you like best about your visit?
- ❑ being able to see the animals at close quarters?
- ❑ learning more about the animals?
- ❑ going to special events, eg film shows, feeding times
- ❑ other (specify)

4 Did anything annoy you on this visit?
For example,
- ❑ not enough space for the animals
- ❑ too high an entrance fee
- ❑ animals seemed unhappy or disturbed
- ❑ not enough information given
- ❑ other (specify)

5 What is the most important function of a zoo?
- ❑ conservation of endangered species
- ❑ education about how animals live
- ❑ entertainment
- ❑ other (specify)

6 How do TV wildlife programmes compare with visiting a zoo?
- ❑ they make zoo visits unnecessary
- ❑ they don't replace seeing live animals
- ❑ they enhance a zoo visit
- ❑ other (specify)

Please return to **The Zoo Inquiry**, Freepost, Manchester MC20 6YZ.

2 On the basis of your discussion, do you think that zoos should be abolished? Why? Why not?

Understanding the task

1 Read this writing task and the extracts. Who is in favour of closing the zoo?

> You are currently living in England and a friend of yours is working at a small zoo in the area. You recently read an article in the local paper about the likely closure of the zoo. You have asked your friend for some information, so that you can write a letter to the editor of the paper.
>
> Read the advertisement for the zoo, the newspaper article, and your friend's letter. Then, using the information, write a letter to the editor, stating why you think the zoo *should* be closed.

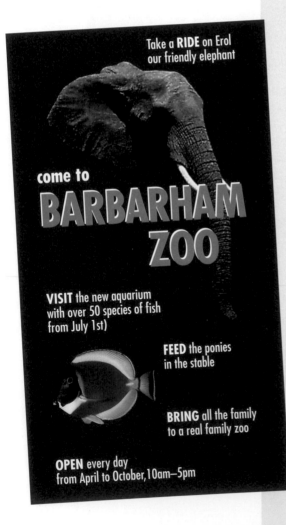

Take a **RIDE** on Erol our friendly elephant

come to

BARBARHAM ZOO

VISIT the new aquarium with over 50 species of fish from July 1st)

FEED the ponies in the stable

BRING all the family to a real family zoo

OPEN every day from April to October,10am–5pm

It's a howling shame!

It seems that the spoilsports amongst us are having their way again. Barbarham Zoo, which first opened its doors **54 years ago**, has been visited by inspectors and council staff and looks likely to close within the next two months.

Those of you who can remember the happy childhood hours you spent gazing at Erol the elephant (still going strong) will be sad to learn of the zoo's probable demise. No more will it provide hours of pleasure for the young and old alike.

The council says that Barbarham no longer serves a useful purpose and that conditions for the animals are unsatisfactory. According to a tearful Mrs Parkinson, who has acted as animal feeder, ticket collector and car-park attendant for the last fifteen years, many of these animals will now have to be put down, as no other zoo can take them.

In these days of conservation when there has been an upsurge of interest in creatures of the wild, it is astounding that small zoos like Barbarham are being threatened with closure. We would like to hear from our readers on this issue.

So you want to write a reply to the paper about Barbarham? Good for you! I couldn't believe the article in last week's paper — my experience is completely different. Although I'll be out of a job, I'm sure closure is the best thing. It's really depressing working here and seeing how miserable some of the animals are — the cages are so cramped. None of the animals are very healthy either. Between you and me, Erol is in a bad way and seems in a lot of pain. The latest disaster is the building of the new aquarium, which has had to be abandoned — water leakage.

So much for a memorable day out — my advice to the public is: Don't waste your money!

I hope you include this info in your letter. Don't mention me by name though, because I'll get into trouble!

Selecting ideas

2 a Match the negative points in your friend's letter to relevant parts of the newspaper article and the advertisement.

   b Highlight any other points in the newspaper article that you want to take issue with. Note down your arguments.

   c Remember not to 'lift' actual phrases from any of the extracts.

   d Don't forget you can add points of your own, as long as you have covered the required content. Go back to the reasons you discussed in the Introduction, for why zoos should or shouldn't be abolished. But remember that you have to support the closure of Barbarham Zoo!

Focusing on the reader

3 You are writing to the editor of the paper, so a formal register will be required. What would be a suitable opening?

Planning your answer

2 page 193
9.3, 11 page 195

4 a Decide on the order of the points you wish to make. You should give your strongest arguments first.

   b Think about how to introduce your friend's observations. Some of these phrases might be useful:

    an unnamed source
    a personal contact at the zoo
    off-the-record comments
    to leak information
    to reveal a source.

   c Remember to include a specific reference to the original newspaper article.

Writing

5 Now write your letter in about 250 words. When you have finished check your answer carefully. Remember **WRITE** ✎.

Listening and Speaking   *Are you a Good Citizen?*

Introduction

What social issues are a significant problem in your country? In groups of three, make a list and choose two problems to discuss. If you were in a position of power, what would you do to change things for the better?

Listening

Part 2

1 Read the sentences below about Charles Dickens, the English novelist, who wrote about the poor and ill-treated people of his time. As you read, think about what sort of information is missing. Remember that no more than three words will be necessary for each gap.

Hard Times

Charles Dickens made use of his unhappy
(1)_____ in his novels.

His father was sent to jail for (2)_____.

When Charles was fifteen, he earned his living as a
(3)_____ in the House of Commons.

His ability to describe characters as well as his feelings
about (4)_____ soon became apparent.

As a result of his novels, some boarding schools were
forced (5) _____.

Many characters were based on family and friends.
In *David Copperfield,* his (6)_____ was the
model for Mr Micawber.

Charles Dickens died from a stroke in 1870 at the age
of (7)_____.

2 Now listen to the tape and complete the information about him in gaps 1–7. You will hear the tape once only.

Vocabulary

Phrasal verbs

1 In the listening extract, the following phrasal verb with *on* was used.

Dickens *went on* to write such powerful stories …

What is the meaning of *went on* in the above context? How does it differ from the following sentences?

1   'I like Tom a lot, but he really does *go on* at times!'
2   The fund-raising meeting *went on* for three hours.
3   'Oh, *go on*! Come with us to the concert.'

2 In pairs, look at the following sentences and decide what the verbs in *italics* mean.

1 Well, I can't stand around chatting all day. I *must be getting on*.
2 Grandad isn't as lively as he used to be. I suppose he *is getting on* a bit now.
3 It took a while for the idea *to catch on*.
4 The game is quite complicated, but some people *catch on* very quickly.
5 The airport authority *laid on* extra flights to cope with the summer rush.
6 What *brought on* this change of mind so suddenly?
7 Rachel *took on* more work than she could cope with.
8 The charity *has taken on* 200 new volunteers over the last three months.

English in Use

Part 4

> **Exam tip** ▼
>
> In Paper 3, Part 4, you are given two texts on different topics. Remember to read through the completed texts checking that the words you have used make sense and fit the gaps grammatically.

1 Quickly read through the first article ignoring the gaps. What is Manuel Elizalde's connections with the Tasaday tribe?

2 Read through the article again, carefully, and decide what part of speech you will need in each gap.

3 Fit the correct form of the word in capital letters in each of the gaps.

Manuel Elizalde and the Tasaday tribe

When Manuel Elizalde announced the discovery of a tribe in the Philippines (0) *uncorrupted* by civilisation, he touched a (1)_____ chord among the ordinary millions who muse on the appeal of the simple life. Immediately there was skepticism from experts (2)_____ about any surviving human 'dodos'. How could the Tasaday have remained (3)_____ until 1971 in a country of 40 million people? Elizalde came under deep suspicion. He was from a rich family and had gained (4)_____ as a playboy. Were the Tasaday an elaborate hoax? It would be tidy to close the story there, as one more example of a (5)_____ anthropological joke, comparable to the Piltdown man, which was not exposed as a (6)_____ until 1953. However, the Tasaday discovery is not a Piltdown. Elizalde did not invent the tribe. He was personally interested in (7)_____ and in fact he and his wife had adopted fifty orphaned children from such families.

0	CORRUPT
1	SYMPATHY
2	DOUBT
3	DISCOVER
4	NOTORIOUS
5	MISCHIEF
6	FORGE
7	MINOR

4 Now complete the following task in the same way.

Shortage of Nurses ●●●●●●●●●●●●●●●●●●●●●●●●●●●●

The average working life of a nurse is 7.1 years and 30,000 leave every year. There has always been the (8)_____ that those leaving could be replaced by an (9)_____ supply of 18-year-olds. Nowadays, however, such keen 18-year-olds are (10)_____ thin on the ground and the profession is facing a (11)_____ crisis. Nurses who take a break to have children and then wish to return find that (12)_____ shifts do not fit in with school hours and holidays. Many may (13)_____ have severe gaps in their working knowledge, often lacking (14)_____ as a result. Until these issues are adequately addressed, staff (15)_____ will continue to threaten the successful running of many hospitals. ●

8	ASSUME
9	END
10	COMPARE
11	RECRUIT
12	FLEXIBLE
13	ADD
14	CONFIDENT
15	SHORT

Speaking

Parts 3 and 4

1 In pairs, look at the following dilemmas. In each case, decide what you think you would do.

What would YOU do?

1? On a motorway, you see a car parked on the hard shoulder with two children in the back seat and the driver looking distressed. Do you:

A stop at the next opportunity and alert the police?
B stop and help them?
C take no action?

2? Your neighbour, whom you hardly know, has been widowed. Do you:

A drop by to say you're available if any help is needed?
B make a real effort to develop a relationship with her?
C leave things as they are: someone else will deal with it?

3? You answer the door to a caller campaigning against the building of an airport near your town. Do you:

A sign the petition offered?
B make an excuse and shut the door?
C ask for more details before deciding to sign?

4? Hurrying to catch a train for an important interview, you see an elderly person fall to the pavement. Other pedestrians are within sight. Do you:

A stop and assist?
B carry on to the station?
C stop a little further up the road, looking back to check that someone has reacted?

5? You see a group of children tormenting a dog. Do you:

A attempt to stop them?
B decide to report them to an animal protection society?
C give them a hard look and walk on?

2 Discuss your decisions with another pair, giving your reasons. Decide which you think is the most difficult dilemma before reporting back to the class.

3 Now look at the pictures for a competition promoting caring within society. In groups of two or three, discuss which ones illustrate caring most effectively.

Decide which picture should be the winner, which should receive 2nd and 3rd prize, and which should receive a runner's-up prize. Suggest a title for the winning picture.

4, page 193

Remember to give reasons for your decisions. Now tell another group what led you to make your selection.

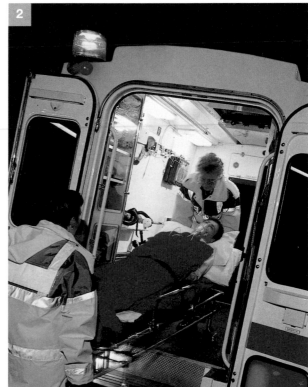

Structure *A Caring Image* ▼

Introduction

Imagine that you are organizing a sponsored sporting event. Discuss the following ideas, and decide which you think would be the most or the least successful in helping to advertise the event and raise money. Give reasons for your answers.

- Putting leaflets through people's letter boxes to advertise the event.
- Collecting sponsorship money door-to-door.
- Holding another competition during the event, for example, the funniest hat.
- Making a charge for entry.
- Selling raffle tickets for prizes.
- Playing music in the streets.
- Including different kinds of sporting events.

Can you add any ideas of your own to the list?

Reading

The advertisement below is for the photographic competition you discussed in the speaking section of this unit. Skim read the advertisement and find out:

- how the photographs will raise money.
- what the prizes are.
- how to enter.

PHOTOGRAPHIC COMPETITION

If you are keen on photography, or simply like messing about with cameras and enjoy taking impromptu photographs, your hobby might win you a fabulous Caribbean cruise for two, a flight on a
5 supersonic aeroplane, or the latest photographic equipment.

caring

The focus of our photographic competition is on caring. We'd like you to focus your camera lens on the caring world around you. Entering our exciting competition
10 could win you one of these amazing prizes, as well as help raise money for four deserving charities whose task is to provide essential caring support, despite ever-rising costs. Ten runners-up will receive a travel alarm clock / calculator.

15 Anyone can enter as our competition is strictly for amateurs, so you don't need to buy expensive equipment. What we're looking for is a very special image which succeeds in capturing a caring situation. It might be of the elderly, the very young, someone
20 who is sick or disabled, or even a pet, but it must be eye-catching!

Your photographs can be black and white or colour, and the competition is open to both adults and children. So, if you decide to enter, between now and
25 the end of next month, try to find an image that illustrates for you the essence of caring and send us your photograph(s).

If you can send a donation with your entry, the proceeds will directly benefit four designated charities
30 that work with people with disabilities and their carers.

The distinguished panel of judges will include a famous TV presenter and an acclaimed international photographer.

We look forward to receiving your entries.

When sending your photograph(s), remember to write your name and address clearly on the back. We regret to inform you that we are unable to return entries.

250 words

Gerunds

A Which words in the three sentences below are gerunds and how are they used differently?

1 Raising money is one of the most difficult things in the world!
2 Some organizations are very good at persuading people to part with their money!
3 Few people like collecting money for charity on street corners.

B Can you find examples of each use of the gerund in the advertisement opposite?

Present participles

A Present participles can be used as adjectives. For example,

a caring image
an amusing story
the situation is worrying.

Can you find other examples of present participles used as adjectives in the advertisement?

B Present participles can also be used after a connecting word or phrase instead of using the complete continuous tense. For example,

When you are posting a letter, remember to check that you have put a stamp on it.

When posting a letter, remember to check that you have put a stamp on it.

Find a similar example in the advertisement.

C Now rewrite these sentences using a present participle.

1 He was living in Africa when he wrote his most successful books.
2 If you are trying to start a car engine from cold, you may need to pull out the choke.
3 He was studying at university when he decided that he wanted to become a politician.
4 When you are watching TV, you are advised not to have the volume turned up too loud.
5 While we were staying in Rome, we came across some old friends we hadn't seen for ages.

Infinitive or present participle?

A What is the difference in meaning between these two sentences?

1 We saw him skate.
2 We saw him skating.

B Complete the following sentences using either an infinitive without *to* or a present participle, as appropriate.

1 A spellbound audience heard Pavarotti (sing) at La Scala in Milan.
2 The teacher noticed some of his students from the college (dance) and (sing) on the street corner.
3 Through the open window, the children saw the actors (rehearse) for their play.
4 The Thompsons heard their neighbours (argue) as they passed their front door.
5 The nurse noticed the patient (stare) blankly out of the room.
6 The drama students watched the famous theatre company (give) their acclaimed performance of Macbeth.

Verbs followed by a gerund or infinitive with no difference in meaning

A Certain verbs are followed by either a gerund or an infinitive with *to*, with little or no difference in meaning (for example, *begin, continue, like, love, hate, prefer, start*).

However, why can't you use the gerund in this sentence?

We'd like you to focus your camera lens on …

B Which form would you use in this sentence and why?

He was beginning (have) doubts about the decision he had made.

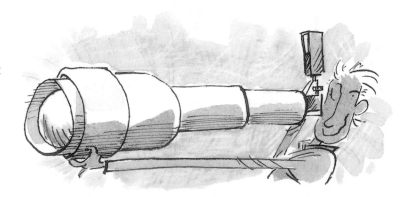

Verbs followed only by a gerund or only by an infinitive

In the advertisement, you came across:

… enjoy taking impromptu photographs …

… if you decide to enter …

Enjoy can only be followed by a gerund, and *decide* only by an infinitive. Here are some other verbs which behave in the same way. Which verbs can be followed by a gerund, and which by an infinitive?

afford	agree	avoid	consider
deny	dislike	expect	finish
keep	learn	mind	miss
practise	pretend	promise	refuse
seem	suggest	threaten	wish

Verbs followed by either a gerund or an infinitive depending on their meaning

Some verbs can be followed either by the gerund or the infinitive, depending on their meaning or context.

A   Need

The advertisement stated that:

… you don't need to buy expensive equipment …

Would it be possible to say *you don't need buying expensive equipment*?

What is the difference in form and meaning between these three sentences?

1   You need to buy special equipment for this type of photography.
2   This camera lens needs cleaning.
3   This camera lens needs to be cleaned.

How would you make these sentences negative?

B   Try

For the photographic competition, you had to:

… try to find an image that illustrates … caring …

What is the difference in meaning between the first parts of these two sentences and how could you complete them?

1   I tried writing to them but I received …
2   I tried to write to them but I couldn't …

C   Remember

When sending in your entries for the competition, you had to:

… remember to write your name and address clearly on the back.

What is the difference in meaning between these sentences?

1   I always remember to put the postcode on a letter.
2   I remember putting the postcode on the letter.

Can you think of any other verbs like *remember* which are followed by either the gerund or the infinitive with a comparable difference in meaning?

D   Complete the sentences below with a suitable form of the verbs in brackets.

1   My father (remember / spend) long happy hours on the beach when he was a child.
2   We (regret / say) that you have not won a prize in our competition.
3   Your football boots (need / clean) before the next match!
4   You (not need / explain) the situation to me because I understand perfectly.
5   John (try / remember) his aunt's address, but it had completely gone out of his mind.
6   (Try / not / make) elementary grammar mistakes when you are writing a composition.
7   Please (remember / phone) home and tell them I'll be late.
8   My sister (regret / not / work) harder when she started university.
9   The technician (try / fiddle) with knobs, but the machine still wouldn't work.
10 The matter (need / look) into.

Practice

In pairs, find out from your partners:

*   what they enjoy doing most.
*   what they would like to do in the future.
*   what they can remember doing when they were very young.
*   if they have ever seen anyone famous act, sing or dance.
*   if they have ever tried to do something but not been able to.
*   if there is anything they regret doing.
*   what they think they need to do in order to improve their English.

When you have finished, tell the class the most interesting thing you have found out about your partner.

Today's World

Reading *The Beauty Myth*

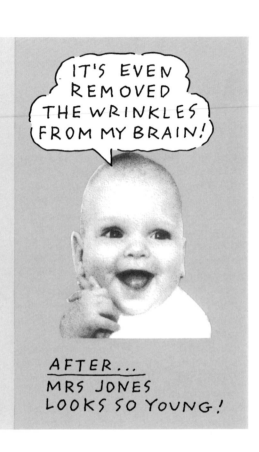

Introduction

1 What do you think the message of this picture might be?

2 Read these statements from the article on page 138.
Do you agree with what is being said?

Our ability to believe what we want to has … made life easy for the beauty industry.

… youth and beauty have become the currency of our society, buying popularity and opportunity.

The value of age and experience is denied …

Reading

Part 3

1 Read the article on page 138 quickly.

What does the writer think about contemporary attitudes towards ageing?

Youth and beauty have become the currency of our society. The value of age and experience is denied.

The true value of age

Patricia MacNair, *The Guardian*

When I casually mentioned to a colleague that I was looking into cosmetics that claimed to beat back the ravages of ageing, her worries poured out. A month ago, she told me, she had suddenly noticed wrinkles all over her face. Fingering her beautiful but finely-lined features, she explained that, although she knew that her discovery had more to do with the abrupt ending of a six-year relationship than premature ageing, she just had to do something about it.

Giving her the painful facts on her possible salvation, I poured scorn on the miracle cures. Despite my damning remarks, however, she begged to know where she could get the treatments I had mentioned. When it comes to beauty who wants to know the truth?

Our ability to believe what we want to has, in the past, made life easy for the beauty industry. Fuelled by the immense value attached to youth, it has made millions out of vacant promises of renewing faces and bodies. To give skin care scientific credibility, beauty counters have now stolen a veneer of respectability from the hospital clinic. Sales staff in white coats "diagnose" skin types on "computers" and blind customers with the science of free radical damage and DNA replication. Providing the "drugs" for this game, the marketeers have created the 'cosmeceutical' – a real term coined to describe new cosmetic therapies which, they say, don't just sit on the surface but actually interact with the cells.

Is this really just a harmless game, though? The increasingly extravagant claims made by the cosmetics manufacturers about their products' ability to get rid of wrinkles have worried doctors and toxicologists. The promotional blurbs declare that active ingredients such as extracts of human placenta or animal spleen stimulate cells deep in the skin's layers to divide, so replacing old cells and effectively renewing the skin.

If these claims are true, could the effects be harmful? If normal cells can be stimulated to divide, then abnormal ones could also be triggered to multiply, so causing or accelerating skin cancer. A new arrival on the anti-wrinkle front claims to be a more natural way to avoid the dreaded lines. As a pill rather than a potion, Imedeen works from the inside out, providing the skin with nutritional and biochemical support to encourage the body's own self-repairing process.

First developed in Scandinavia, it contains extracts of fish cartilage, marine plants, and the chitin from shrimp shells which provide a formula including proteins, amino acids, minerals, and vitamins. According to a published study, visible improvements appear in the skin texture after two or three months of treatment. The skin is softer, smoother, wrinkling decreases but is not eliminated, and blemishes and fine brown lines disappear.

Leslie Kenton admits she was sceptical until she tried Imedeen herself. Women, she believes, should take responsibility for the natural balance of their biochemistry – a principle she calls "body ecology". Careful body ecology, she says, not only improves looks but also enhances energy processes and even expands awareness. Imedeen fits this concept by providing for the skin's needs. But can shrimp shells really do the trick with wrinkles?

Offering a more scientific interpretation, Brian Newman, a British surgeon who has studied Imedeen, explains that the compound has a specific action in the gut, preventing the breakdown of essential proteins in the diet and allowing their absorption in a state more easily utilised by the skin.

Dr White, a Consultant Dermatologist, is unimpressed by the data and questions the methodology. In addition, the medical journal in which the study of Imedeen is published is a "pay" journal – one in which any studies can be published for a fee. According to Dr White, any attempt to play by the medical world's rules of credibility has backfired.

Such controversy is familiar ground to Brian Newman, who used oil of evening primrose years before it was generally accepted. Undeterred, he insists the most important point to establish is that Imedeen actually works.

Ultimately, however, the real issue is why we are so terrified of wrinkles in the first place. Sadly, youth and beauty have become the currency of our society, buying popularity and opportunity. The value of age and experience is denied, and women in particular feel the threat that the visible changes of ageing bring. According to Pamela Ashurst, Consultant Psychotherapist at the Royal South Hants Hospital, when men gain a little grey hair, their appeal often increases because, for them, age implies power, success, wealth, and position. But as a woman's power is still strongly perceived to be tied up with fertility, ageing demonstrates to the world her decline, her redundancy for her primary function. Wrinkles are symbolic of the shrivelling of the reproductive system.

Until we appreciate the true value of age, it is difficult to be anything but panicky when the signs of it emerge. While the media continues to portray men of all ages alongside young, smooth-skinned women as a vision of success, women will go on investing in pots of worthless goop. Let's see more mature, wrinkled women in attractive, successful, happy roles and let's see men fighting to be with them. ■

> **Ultimately, however, the real issue is why we are so terrified of wrinkles in the first place.**

845 *words*

2 Look at the first multiple-choice question. The parts of the article which relate to this question have been underlined. Which is the correct option?

1 What does the writer's colleague want to find out?
  A the truth about beauty creams
  B how to save a relationship
  C how to prevent premature ageing
  D where to get hold of the products

3 Now look at these other questions. Use the technique of underlining the parts of the text to help you decide on the correct options.

2 The beauty industry attracts customers by
  A producing creams that interact with cells.
  B giving its sales staff a professional image.
  C emphasizing the use of natural ingredients.
  D linking beauty with youthful looks.

3 Leslie Kenton and Brian Newman believe that Imedeen may work because it
  A nourishes the skin.
  B increases energy levels.
  C dissolves in the gut.
  D contains vital proteins.

4 Why is doubt cast on the journal which published the study of Imedeen?
  A The articles are not based on accurate data.
  B The journal is not widely read by doctors.
  C Any article is published if the author pays a fee.
  D The journal is funded by pharmaceutical companies.

5 What does the writer think about anti-ageing creams?
  A They cannot reduce the effects of old age.
  B Research has not been rigorous enough.
  C On the whole they are worth using.
  D Both men and women should use them.

4 At the end of the article, the writer expresses her views about age and its different effects on men and women. Say whether or not you agree with the writer. Give reasons for your answer.

Style

An article such as this is similar in many ways to a report but is written in a more informal way to make it interesting for the general reader. Find more examples from the text of the following.

- Giving an opinion.
  Sadly, youth and beauty have become the currency of our society, buying popularity and opportunity.

- Speculating.
  If these claims are true, could the effects be harmful?

- Reporting what someone said.
  Leslie Kenton admits she was sceptical until she tried Imedeen herself.

1 Read the advertisement and say what the clinic claims it can do. What does the writer of the letter that follows think about it?

2 Complete the gaps in the letter, using no more than two words to fill each gap. Remember that the words you use should not be the same as the ones that appeared in the advertisement, but should have the same meaning. The first gap has been done for you as an example.

Before you start, make sure you:

- read the letter carefully and decide on the register. What kind of language is used?
- study the example given in the letter and see how it differs from the original words in the advertisement.

The Raeburn Clinic is the country's leading hospital dedicated exclusively to cosmetic surgery for men and women.

Consultations are held only with highly experienced, caring surgeons – who specialise in this very important and highly visual aspect of surgery.

Men and women of all ages benefit from Cosmetic Surgery. There is a wide range of improvement procedures – including operations to refine the shape of the nose. Each nose is different and the experienced surgeon achieves a harmonious balance with all facial features. Of course, it is only at The Raeburn Clinic that you can see on screen what improvement surgery could do for you.

Cosmetic Surgery for Women and for Men

The Raeburn Clinic

0181-371 9432

101 Kings Avenue,
West London, NW3 4CK

Stubborn areas of fat that refuse to respond to diet or exercise can be removed through liposuction. The figure is recontoured more pleasingly and the improvements are often quite dramatic. It is the logical way to complete a "trim" figure and has been performed with great success, over many years, on men and women.

I've seen an advertisement about cosmetic surgery. It says that it (1) _works well_ for men and women (2)_____ age and so I thought I would finally get something done about my nose!

Apparently, as every nose is different, they try and make the new one (3)_____ with the rest of your features. This clinic seems to be able to (4)_____ on a TV screen what you would (5)_____ after surgery.

The other thing it talks about is liposuction. Sounds dreadful but it may be the answer to getting (6)_____ of fat that won't go even when you've been (7)_____ or (8)_____ lots of exercise. It can actually improve the (9)_____ of your body (10)_____. They say it's an obvious answer to the problem of (11)_____ into shape. The success rate of the operations is supposed to be very (12)_____. So how about it, Barry?

3 In pairs, discuss the issue of cosmetic surgery. Think of examples where cosmetic surgery can improve the quality of life. Are there any situations where you think it might not be a good idea?

Listening and Speaking *Alternative Technology*

Introduction

1 Look at the paragraphs below and decide which of these 'low-tech' solutions are being described.

growing high-yield crops
alternative energy sources

biological control of pests
practical preventive measures

A

A RECENT SURVEY showed that 60% of Masai children suffer from trachoma. One way it can be spread is by the use of polluted water or communal water already
5 used by people with the disease. Flies are the main carrier, lured by the milk around a child's lips and nose. An empty tin with a small hole in the bottom is a simple way to combat the problem. A cupful of clean water is poured into
10 the tin. Children then use drops of clean, uncontaminated water to wash their eyes.

C

Agricultural experts have developed a new prolific variety of cassava, but, unlike Asia's wheat and rice, the cassava needs no fertiliser or irrigation. The plant has long roots
5 that tap soil moisture deep in the ground, helping it to survive in the droughts that have become common in Africa.

D

The technical experts and the politicians agree that the barren, windswept cliffs of Scotland are ideal sites for the
5 huge wind turbines which will help to meet Britain's growing need for power. Some even argue that the scale, shape and motion of the turbines will
10 improve the environment in the same way that a beautiful statue enhances a garden. Locals, like Jim Campbell, are not convinced: 'I can see that
15 one of these things on its own might look good to some people but when you get a hundred of them threshing away then it's just an eyesore.'

B

THE GREYBACK BEETLE is a serious threat to sugar-cane crops throughout the world. We depend on cane as the raw material from which sugar is made. Marine toads were
5 originally brought over to Puerto Rico and the West Indies in the 19th century to control the beetles and other sugar-cane pests. When the toad was introduced into Australia, it soon posed a threat to Australian wildlife. Native
10 species were displaced and lizards, snakes, koalas and even crocodiles were attacked.

2 What are the benefits and drawbacks of the 'low tech' solutions in each of the situations described?

3 Can you think of any 'high-tech' solutions, for example antibiotics, which could be used in A–D instead?

Speaking

Parts 3 and 4

2, 3 page 193

1 In pairs, look at the extracts below. Can you think of any disadvantages to the solutions described? Which solution do you think is more practical and acceptable and why?

The nuclear fuel we use is uranium, a resource which is not only plentiful but logical since there is no other day-to-day use for it. It is also extraordinarily efficient: two uranium pellets the size of sugar cubes will meet the electricity needs of one person for an entire year.

Today the Centre for Alternative Technology produces almost all the electricity it needs using the wind, the sun and water. Water supplies about 55% of the electricity, the wind supplies 25%, and 10% is from solar energy. A diesel generator provides the rest.

2 Now form groups of four and report the decisions you have reached.

3 In your groups, discuss the following questions. Make sure that you all contribute equally.

What difficulties might there be in trying to persuade people to use alternative sources of energy?

What changes would you agree to if you thought it would make a difference to the environment?

Do you think there is too much emphasis on environmental issues in the media? Explain your answer.

Vocabulary

Phrasal verbs

In extract B on page 141, you came across the expression *brought over*. Here are some other verbs which combine with *over*. Choose an appropriate form of one of the verbs to complete the sentences below.

take
hand   look
over
talk   get
pass

1 The masked man asked the passengers to _____ all their money and jewellery to his accomplice.

2 Helen was devastated when she realized she had been _____ for promotion in favour of a younger colleague.

3 We plan to _____ control of the wind turbines to the local community as soon as the necessary training has been given.

4 The senator warned his colleagues that the party was in danger of being _____ by extremists.

5 It was good to _____ the factory and I would like to thank you for inviting me to visit.

6 They _____ their ideas for several hours before putting them in writing.

7 Julia couldn't _____ how much her friend had changed since they had last met.

8 I am pleased to announce that Jonathan Evans will _____ as project manager when Brian Baker retires in June.

9 Paul had just _____ the shock of having his car stolen, when his house was burgled.

10 Would you like me to _____ the driving for a while, so that you can have a rest?

Listening

Part 2

Exam tip ▼

In Part 2 listening passages, you will find that there is often some 'recycling' of the details. This means that you may get a second chance to listen for the correct answer.

1 You are going to listen to a radio interview about a dam development. Read through the information you have to complete before listening.

Asian Dam Project

Size:	(1) _____ high	
Location:	(2) _____	
First proposed:	(3) _____	
Number of studies:	(4) _____	
Area to be flooded:	(5) _____ hectares	
Cost:	(6) _____	
Purpose:	deliver (7) _____ to Malaysia	
Sponsored by:	(8) _____	
Contractors:	(9) _____	
Life span:	(10) _____	

2 Now listen to the radio interview and fill in the missing information.

Which information did you hear more than once?

3 Without listening to the interview again, but using the completed notes on the dam to help jog your memory, decide whether you think the statements below are true or false.

1   Work on the dam began in the 1980s.

2   It will cost $600 to relocate the local inhabitants in the south.

3   Three tribes will be affected by the flooding.

4   Dr Lim believes that the project is too costly.

5   The interviewer wants to know why an Asian company is not constructing the dam.

6   Most of the electricity generated by the dam will leak out under the sea.

7   Britain will be contributing only a small amount towards the project.

8   Dr Lim complains of the lack of information about the studies.

Introduction

Which of these environmental problems would affect you most if they occurred in your local area? What action could you take as an individual to deal with the problems?

Writing

Part 2, leaflet

Part 2, leaflet

Part 2, leaflet

1 a Read this leaflet about the Cambridge Green Belt Project. Why has the leaflet been produced?

Cambridge Green Belt Project

What does the project do?

1 It improves the landscape and habitats for wildlife by
- *planting new trees and hedges*
- *restoring derelict ponds, overgrown footpaths and ancient monuments*
- *managing existing nature reserves, meadows and woodland*
- *creating new areas for wildlife, such as nature areas in schools and pocket parks**

*pocket parks are small areas of land maintained by local people for wildlife conservation and informal recreation

2 **It increases understanding and enjoyment of the local countryside by**
- *organizing guided walks and other events throughout the year*
- *producing information leaflets on local walk routes*
- *giving illustrated talks to community groups and schools*

3 **It also provides practical help and advice on conservation schemes to farmers, landowners and local councils.**

How can you help?

People of any age can help their local government.

We need volunteers to help with our practical conservation tasks.

You can come along as little or as often as you want to, for as long or short a time as you have to spare.

We also welcome volunteers to design our posters, prepare our leaflets and generally help out with office administration.

What else can you do?

Explore and enjoy your local countryside.

Come on one of our guided walks or open days, or attend a training event.

Contact us if you know of any neglected sites, overgrown ponds, or footpaths that need attention.

Invite our Project Officer to give an illustrated talk to your local society or residents' association.

Phone 01223 846363 for further information now!

b   How has the leaflet been laid out? Look at each of these organizational aspects and say why you think they have been used:

- headings
- bullet points
- a footnote
- short paragraphs.

c   Now look at the language. Which tense is used in the leaflet? Why? How does the writer use imperatives?

d   What register and tone is used in the leaflet? Why do you think it has been written in this way?

e   What impression do you have of the Green Belt Project? Is it a project that appeals to you?

Understanding the task

2   Now read this writing task. What is the purpose of the leaflet?

Your town has been short-listed with eight others for the award of best-kept town in your country. The final decision will be made in three months' time, and until then, it is crucial that the town looks at its best. The local council has asked you to prepare a leaflet aimed at residents, informing them of the award and encouraging them to participate in making the town as attractive as possible.

Brainstorming ideas

3   a   Think first of existing environmental problems in the town that could be tackled. Remember your earlier discussion in the Introduction to this section.

b   Now brainstorm ideas of ways to improve the look of the town. The things you suggest must be practical within the time period and possible for individual people to do.

c   Finally, think about how and where to mention the award. How prominent should this information be in the leaflet?

Focusing on the reader

4   Which register do you think would be most appropriate, given the purpose of the leaflet and its target readership?

Planning your answer

 **8.2, 9.3, 10** page 195

5   Look again at the overall layout of the model. Then plan the layout of your leaflet, using headings and bullet points to map out the main messages you want to get across.

Writing

✎ page 190

6   Now you are ready to write the leaflet. Remember to ensure that you write around 250 words. Check your final answer carefully. Remember **WRITE** ✎.

Structure *'Designer' Babies* ▼

Introduction

What do you understand by the term 'genetic engineering'?

Genetic Engineering

When Charles Darwin published *On the Origin of Species* in 1859, the Bishop of Worcester's wife was most distressed. "Let us hope it is not true," she remarked. "But if it is, let us pray that it does not become generally known!"

5 Supposing that we had been alive a hundred years ago, would we have been repelled by the suggestion that humans and apes may have had a common ancestor? And had our ancestors been born in modern times, would they have been
10 similarly repelled by the thought of 'designer' babies? I suspect that the answer to both questions would be in the affirmative!

I have tried (0)____to____ rationalise my own response (1)_____ genetic
15 engineering. I personally feel that (2)_____ we were supposed to be perfect, we would have (3)_____ designed that way. Surely experimenting with genes is (4)_____ invasion of the human self? On the
20 (5)_____ hand, can we honestly say that the human self is to (6)_____ found in our genes?

From the medical point (7)_____ view, genetic engineering has opened up exciting
25 possibilities for the treatment (8)_____ genetically related disorders. However, the real problem (9)_____ this new science is that it threatens to undermine the categories through (10)_____ we understand our world: our
30 moral and social codes.

(11)_____ the Bishop of Worcester's wife, the anti-science lobby wishes to shut out the facts that might upset its moral universe.

Yet, if morality had originally been based
35 (12)_____ reason, our attitudes might (13)_____ been justifiable. Unfortunately, morality has (14)_____ origin in prejudice, ritual and habit, and, (15)_____ a result, the possibilities afforded by scientific advance are increasingly constrained. ■

250 words

English in Use
Part 2

Read the article on the left, then supply the missing words by writing *one* word in spaces 1–15. The first one has been done for you as an example.

The third conditional

A Meaning

Look at these examples of the third conditional:

1 If I had lived in Darwin's time, I, too, would have been shocked by his publication.
2 If Darwin hadn't published his revolutionary theories, our ancestors wouldn't have found themselves in such a dilemma.

To understand the meaning, you need to ask these questions:

Did you live in Darwin's time?
Were you shocked by the publication?

Did Darwin publish his theories?
Did the Victorians find themselves in a dilemma?

B Form

What tenses are used in each part of the conditional sentences in A?

What could you use in the main part of each sentence instead of *would*?

C Variations in form and meaning

Look at these three examples of the third conditional from the article:

1 *Supposing that we had been alive a hundred years ago, would we have been repelled by the suggestion that …*
2 *And had our ancestors been born in modern times, would they have been similarly repelled by the thought of 'designer' babies?*
3 *Yet, if morality had originally been based on reason, our attitudes might have been justifiable.*

a Sentence 1 uses *Supposing that* instead of *If*. Does this alter the meaning? If so, how?
b Sentence 2 does not use a link word. What do you notice about the order of words in this example? Why does the writer use this form?
c Sentence 3 uses an alternative to *would* in the main part of the sentence. How does it alter the meaning?

Conditional link words

A Match the link words in 1–5 to the meanings in a–d below. Two of the link words have the same meaning.

1 *As / So long as* the students are prepared to work hard, the teacher will give them some extra lessons before the exam.
2 *Supposing (that)* you had been offered the opportunity to work abroad, would you have taken it?
3 *Provided / Providing that* the student had had the right qualifications, the university would have been prepared to consider his application.
4 *Unless* I really try hard to save some money, I'll never be able to afford to buy a car.
5 *Even if* they had offered me a huge salary, I still wouldn't have accepted the job.

a it wouldn't have / have had any effect on the outcome.
b 'except when' or 'if not'.
c on the condition or understanding, or 'only if'.
d let's assume.

B Use one of the link words above and the correct form of the verb in brackets to complete the conversation below.

Anne Just _____ you _____(be) alive a hundred years ago. Your life _____(be) very different, _____ it?

Brian Oh, yes! But _____ I _____(live) a hundred years ago, I _____(not / have) a different personality.

Anne Oh, come on! You _____(not be) able to cope in those days _____ you _____(have) a dozen servants running round after you!

Brian What do you mean? I _____(be) fine _____ I _____(be) allowed to travel and do what I wanted to do.

Anne Look, you _____(hate) every minute of it. _____ you _____(travel) half way round the world, you still _____(not have) the excitement and satisfaction we get in the modern world!

Brian Well, I disagree. I think that _____ my family _____(make) certain that I had enough to live on, I _____(have) a wonderful time.

Anne Even if I _____(be) born rich, I _____(not be) happy living in that era!

Mixed conditionals

A **Second and third**

In the article, you came across the sentence:

… if we were supposed to be perfect, we would have been designed that way.

You can often mix the second and third conditionals like this when you want to refer to a past event which would / might / could / should have had a direct result on a present situation. For example,

1 If we hadn't bought the car, we wouldn't be so short of money now.
2 If we had bought the car, we would be short of money now.

Ask yourself these questions about each sentence:
Did you buy the car? Are you short of money now?

B You can also mix the second and third conditionals when you want to refer to a present state of affairs which would / might / could / should have changed a past situation. For example,

1 If Tom weren't such a lazy person, he would have helped you.
2 If Sonya spoke English, she wouldn't have had to come to English classes.

Ask yourself these questions:
Is Tom lazy? Did he help you?

Does Sonya speak English?
Did Sonya have to come to English classes?

Practice

Make mixed conditional sentences similar to the ones above, using these ideas. Think carefully about the meaning of the sentences!

1 We read the book. That's why we are so well-informed about the matter.
2 We didn't phone the rescue service. That's why we're still stranded on the motorway.
3 I don't like the countryside so I didn't settle down there.
4 Peter doesn't like foreign films so he didn't go to the cinema.
5 The children don't need any help with their homework so they didn't ask us for it.
6 I haven't got any children so I didn't buy a big house.
7 I didn't meet the right person. That's why I'm not married now.
8 Philip doesn't have good eyesight so he didn't become a pilot.

Let's get Organized

Reading *The Customer is Always Right*

Introduction

1 Look at the cartoon strip. What is it illustrating?

2 Do you agree with the saying 'the customer is always right'? Why? Why not?

Reading
Part 2

1 Skim read the article below, ignoring the missing paragraphs. According to the writer, what is the key to running a successful business?

Small is *beautiful*

Tom Edge on how to run a business

Back in the 1970s, Edward Shumacher wrote a book called *Small is Beautiful*. In it he proposed that big businesses had cost advantages over small ones, but that any advantage was soon lost because they were too big to manage and gave impersonal service.

1

All successful companies supply products and services that the customer wants – at a fair price. They also sell in pleasant surroundings and offer unforgettable service. Their staff are trained, positive, approachable, enthusiastic and knowledgeable.

2

When you run your own business, you have decided to sell to and serve others. Unfortunately, for many British people, selling is a job that is beneath them and they regard customers as being in the way. But make no mistake, we are going to have to become much cleverer sales people and serve customers a great deal better, or we are going to lose business to competitors who already do so.

3

Our rewards in life have always been in direct proportion to the quantity and quality of the service we have given. The more people we serve and the better we serve them, the more rewards we will get. Poor service equals poor rewards, average service average rewards. Good service reaps good rewards.

Tom Edge, *Your Business*

4

If the car breaks down within a week of his garage fixing it, he sends someone out to repair it, day or night. He gives me a loan car and I leave the broken-down vehicle with the mechanic. Does he charge more? Yes, he does, but he has increased his share of the local market by 400% in the last two years.

5

My doctor has a target to see 97% of her patients on time. When you go into her surgery, the receptionist comes to you. There is a play area for the kids, a coffee machine, pay phone, up-to-date magazines, soft, relaxing music and potted plants that look healthy.

6

To find out how to give unforgettable service in your business, book yourself on a customer service training course. Some are free and many cost only a few pounds. Ask your local Training and Enterprise council for details. If you prefer, send off for a leaflet I have produced on customer care. It will outline the basics and I hope inspire you to put what you read into action.

Small is *beautiful*

2 Read paragraphs A–G. Six of these paragraphs fit the gaps in the article. There is one extra paragraph which does not fit anywhere.

Divide the paragraphs up into those which are about general principles, and those which give specific examples. This will help you to decide where each paragraph should go. Now insert the paragraphs into gaps 1–6.

A How about the petrol station that invites you out of the car with a free cup of coffee and newspaper while its staff pump the petrol, check the tyres and oil, wipe the inside and outside of your windscreen? They charge top price but pump twice as much petrol as any other station in town.

B The bosses keep tight financial control and exhibit the same attitudes as the staff – they are positive, approachable, enthusiastic and knowledgeable. The boss also has the best possible marketing tool because he listens and finds out how to serve his customer better from first-hand experience.

C To many people, the customer is a pest, to the Americans, the customer is a king, but to the Japanese, the customer is a god. Perhaps that is why the Japanese are so successful. After all, the success of every business can be found in its attitude towards selling and its attitude towards serving customers.

D In the 1990s, small businesses still have lots of advantages over larger ones. For a start, they are slimmer with no head office absorbing money. But they are also lighter on their feet, responding to customers' demands.

E Take my mechanic, for example. He cleans my car inside and out and cleans my engine. He puts my seat back to my leg size. He offers an overnight service where he picks up the car from the drive and delivers it back ready for work the next day.

F Moreover, it is happening. Day in day out, despite the focus on customer care, there are similar incidents occurring all over the land: ultimately orders are lost because of them. Big businesses are more likely to fall foul of this than smaller ones.

G When we get there, she gives the kids a sweet, stands up, comes to my side of the desk, smiles, shakes my hand and says, convincingly, "It's nice to see you, Tom". If she's been running late, she apologises and you know she's done her best.

3 Look at the extra paragraph and decide why it does not fit into the article.

Vocabulary
Prefixes

In the article, you came across the words *impersonal* and *unforgettable*. Below are other adjectives which can combine with some of the prefixes on the left.

in -	dis -	experienced	valuable
im -	mis -	perfect	mature
ir-	sub -	conscious	rational
il -	under -	judged	loaded
un -	over-	valued	honest
		normal	legible

1   Which words combine with *in-*, *im-*, *ir-* and *il-*? Which consonants usually follow *im-*, *ir-* and *il-*? What is *in-* usually followed by?

2   Which words combine with *un-*, *dis-* and *mis-*? What is the difference in meaning between these prefixes?

3   Which words combine with *sub-*, *under-* and *over-*? How does the prefix change the meaning of the new word?

4   Now complete the text below by inserting the word in brackets with its correct prefix.

> *The job advertisement had asked for a self-motivated individual with good social skills. I remember thinking that the salary wasn't brilliant, but the job didn't seem too (1) _____ (paid) for what was required. However, I soon found out that what they wanted was a workaholic!*
>
> 5 *The factory was dirty, noisy, and the work was incredibly tiring. The place was seriously (2) _____ (staffed) – ten people doing the work of fifteen – and the management was lazy and (3) _____ (efficient). It soon became clear that anything the factory produced was (4) _____ (standard) as quality control was minimal. Not* 10 *surprisingly, relations within the workforce were poor and it was impossible to get anybody to co-operate on projects. People were either irritable and (5) _____ (patient) or just couldn't be bothered.*
>
> *I remember the day I finally handed in my resignation. I tried to explain some of the problems I'd experienced to senior* 15 *management, and implied that some of their working practices were quite frankly (6) _____ (legal). But, true to form, they were completely (7) _____ (communicative) and (8) _____ (interested). I was faced with a wall of silence, then more or less thrown out of the factory gates!*

English in Use
Part 2

1   Running a successful business can be extremely stressful, so the ability to unwind is crucial. Read the following extract from a magazine article, ignoring the spaces. What is the typical executive's attitude to 'leisure' activities?

2   Now read the article again and supply the missing words by writing *one* word in spaces 1–15. The first one has been done for you as an example.

Easy does it

WILLIAM DAVIS
tries to relax

RELAXING ISN'T EASY. I know – I have tried it. I can see, (0) _therefore_ , why Japan's Ministry of International Trade and Industry want corporations to have full-time 'leisure advisers'.

5 It seems (1)_____ idea worth copying. A start should be made (2)_____ the very top. Captains of industry often find it hardest (3)_____ all to relax.

Workers (4)_____ least have the excuse
10 that they need to protect their job and pay (5)_____ the loan on their house. Many tycoons already possess (6)_____ the money they could ever hope to spend. So why don't they ease (7)_____?

15 Some buy a luxurious yacht, a beach house, or even an island, (8)_____ seldom make use of these expensive leisure facilities. "I don't have time for a holiday," (9)_____ insist. Some consider themselves so indispensable that they
20 think their business would collapse (10)_____ they were not there to supervise every detail.

But more often than not (11)_____ plain truth is that they don't know how to relax.
25 (12)_____ has ever told them how to do it. You can't be a frantic executive (13)_____ day and a leisurely beachcomber the next. Put a captain of industry (14)_____ a beach and he tends to (15)_____ bored and restless.
30 He misses the pace, the action.

 200 words

William Davis, *High Life*

3 Work in pairs. You are each going to read two paragraphs from further on in the article. Student A, turn to extract **12A** on page 201. Student B, turn to extract **12B** on page 203. Read your paragraphs, then decide which grammatical words you could remove to make a gapped exercise. Write out the paragraphs, omitting eight words you would like to test.

Remember to:

- space the gaps out over the paragraphs.
- select a variety of grammatical words.
- make sure there are only one or two acceptable answers.

When you have finished, try out your cloze on your partner.

4 What do you think about the idea of having a leisure adviser? Can you think of any other ways to relieve stress? Discuss your ideas with a partner.

Writing *When Things Go Wrong ...* ▼

Introduction

1 Listen to four people talking about their experiences of the same organization. Decide what kind of organization it is and what their connection is with it. In each case say what they think about the organization.

2 Think of an organization that you have had contact with, either as a customer or a member of staff. Was it efficient? With a partner, discuss the positive and negative aspects you can remember about it.

Vocabulary

The language of guarantees

1 Manufacturers often guarantee to repair or replace faulty products free of charge. Understanding the formal legal language used in guarantees can sometimes be difficult. Match the formal phrases in 1–10 with the explanations in a–j.

1	faulty workmanship	a	error in the manufacture
2	the date of purchase	b	legal
3	undertake to exchange	c	following / as a result of
4	taking further action	d	to deal with
5	consequential	e	at no cost
6	in the event that	f	doing something else
7	free of charge	g	when you bought the item
8	statutory	h	demanding money or a replacement
9	to attend to	i	if it happens
10	making a claim	j	promise to replace

2 Now complete the guarantee card below using the formal phrases in **1**. The first one has been done for you as an example.

G U A R A N T E E

This instrument is guaranteed for twelve months from (1) *the date of purchase* by the original owner against failure due to (2)_____ or component breakdown, subject to the procedure stated below. Should any component or part fail during the guarantee period it will be repaired or replaced (3)_____.

The guarantee does not cover:

1 Damage resulting from incorrect use.
2 (4)_____ damage.
3 Receivers with removed or defaced serial numbers.

Procedure: Any claim under this guarantee should be made through the dealer from whom the instrument was purchased. It is likely that your dealer will be able (5)_____ any defect quickly and efficiently, but should it be necessary the dealer will return the instrument to the company's service department for attention. (6)_____ it is not possible to return the instrument to the dealer from whom it was purchased, please contact Roberts Radio service department at the address below before (7)_____.

These statements do not affect the (8)_____ rights of a consumer.

Roberts Radio 41 Kingston Street, Manchester SW1 9RL

Writing

Part 1, formal letter and note

Sample letters

1 a Read the two letters below which are complaining about the inefficiency of a courier service. Which letter is more appropriate? Consider the following aspects:

- order in which the information is presented
- register
- quality of the information
- clarity of expression (eg what does the writer want to happen?)
- repetition of information
- layout.

Letter A

Transaction ref: FR6104 Star

Dear Sir / Madam

On the 25 May 1994 your courier service agreed to send a package of confidential materials to Monsieur Lebleu, a colleague of mine in France. I was assured that, if I took advantage of your 'Star' express service, the materials were guaranteed to arrive within 24 hours and would be delivered personally to the addressee. However, the materials did not arrive until a week later, by which time my colleague had left the country. The parcel was left on the doorstep and was eventually taken in by a neighbour.

Needless to say, this caused great inconvenience. I had expected a more efficient and reliable service, especially considering the higher charges for 'Star' delivery.

Although I have contacted your office by phone on two occasions and explained the circumstances, I am still awaiting a response to my complaint. I would appreciate it if you could arrange for the package to be collected and returned to me as soon as possible. The address where the package can be collected is at the bottom of this letter.

I look forward to receiving your reply.

Yours faithfully
    Kenneth Thompson

Please collect the parcel from: Madame Tournier
Rue Saint Denis 651, Vernosc-les-Annonay
France. Tel: 4477 9340

Dear Sir / Madam

I have phoned you twice already about a parcel of confidential materials which was sent to a colleague of mine. Although I was told that your 'Star' express service (which costs twice as much as the normal service!) would get it there by Wednesday, it didn't actually arrive until last Friday. Monsieur Lebleu had gone on holiday by then and the parcel was taken in by Madame Tournier who lives next door. You can imagine that I am very angry, especially as I asked for the 'Star' service and paid a lot of money for the privilege. I really didn't expect such inefficiency and incompetence!

So please let me know what you are going to do about it. Although I have phoned your office twice, I still don't know what you are going to do about it. Can you get the parcel back to me as soon as possible? The next-door neighbour's name is Madame Tournier. Please let me know what is happening.

Best wishes
    Kenneth Thompson

Letter B

b In what circumstances would it be better to complain in writing about faulty goods or services? When is it better to complain face to face?

Understanding the task **2** Now read this writing task. If you were really in this situation, what would you hope to achieve by writing such a letter?

You are currently studying at a college in Britain and you have recently bought a CD player. You did not buy it in the town where you are studying and since it has stopped working, you have had to contact the manufacturer direct.

Read the manufacturer's letter to you (on which you have made some comments), the original receipt and guarantee, and the note from your friend Jill.

STL ELECTRONICS LTD

Industrial Unit B
Tewkesbury Road London SW4 3AF

STL Compact Disc Player

Cost:	**£149.50**
Model No:	**RCD-990H**
Serial No:	**IHHB400485**
Date of purchase:	**06.6.96**
User's name/address:	**M. Brown**
Receipt No:	**7650**

GUARANTEE

This **STL Compact Disc Player model no. RCD-990H** is guaranteed against all faults due to poor workmanship during manufacture.
If a fault should arise collection is guaranteed within 5 working days. If the CD player cannot be repaired within one week of collection a replacement of the same model will be provided free of charge.
These conditions will hold only if the player is subject to normal wear and tear, and do not extend to damage through abnormal use or breakages. The customer's statutory rights will not be affected.

No way!
Too busy anyway

STL ELECTRONICS LTD

Industrial Unit B
Tewkesbury Road
London SW4 3AF

12 June 1996

45 Thorne Avenue
Oxford
OX4 2HL

Dear Customer

With reference to your telephone call, would you please take your CD player RCD-990H back to our showroom in London for repair. We estimate that the player should be ready for collection within four weeks and we will notify you of this in due course.

Yours faithfully   *NB guarantee*

Thanks for the offer of your CD player for James's party next week. I could pick it up on Friday and it would be great if you can let us have some CDs as well. I'm going to be out of town for a few days so can you leave a note for me at college if this is OK? By the way, are you coming and if so do you want a lift?

Cheers!
Jill

Now write:

a   a letter of complaint to the manufacturer (about 200 words).
b   a relevant note to your friend (about 50 words).

Planning your answer **3** In your letter of complaint, don't forget to include the following:

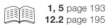

1, 5 page 193
12.2 page 195

1   the circumstances and details of the original transaction, ie the name of the item (with model number if this exists)
2   when you bought it

3   the invoice or receipt number
4   how much it cost
5   the reasons for your complaint
6   what action you wish them to take.

4 In your note to Jill be careful not to repeat the words used in the main task. Don't forget to:

- be concise.
- choose an appropriate style.
- explain why you can't lend her the CD player.
- answer her other requests.

Writing

✎ page 184

5 Now you are ready to write your letter and note. Once you have completed the task, check your work thoroughly. Remember **WRITE** ✎.

Listening and Speaking *A Room with a View* ▼

Introduction

1 Look at the words and phrases below. Do any of them describe the place where you work or study?

austere	cheap and cheerful	functional	luxurious
open-plan	spacious	light and airy	cluttered
cramped	oppressive	messy	neat and tidy
up-to-the-minute			

What type of improvements would you like to make to the place where you work or study?

2 Look at the five pictures. Try and match them with statements a–h. You may find that some phrases will fit more than one picture.

a 'It could be very claustrophobic …'
b 'It's bare and functional but it serves its purpose.'
c 'It's the noise level that gets to me …'
d 'All this luxury just leaves me cold …'
e 'I'd feel better if it wasn't so untidy.'
f 'Spacious, quiet areas make me feel relaxed …'
g 'I think I'd just feel trapped …'
h 'It seems old-fashioned but I think it's more sociable …'

3 With a partner, discuss whether you would like to work in each of these environments.

Listening

Part 3

 1 You are going to hear two people, Jane and Martin, discussing the places they have worked in and whether they were happy there. They will be expressing different views and you must put a *Y* (yes) or *N* (no) according to whether you have heard the view expressed or not.

1 Buildings with air-conditioning can make you ill.
2 Office life is dull and boring.
3 Working in old buildings can be bad for your health.
4 Fresh air is preferable to air-conditioned air.
5 Artificial light can make you tired.
6 Outside views can be distracting.
7 The layout of an office can't influence how you feel.
8 People who work in the same office should only make necessary phone calls.
9 Quiet offices are not necessary for creative work.
10 Busy offices are exciting places to work.

2 Now listen to the tape again, and look at the sentences you marked with a *Y*. Which of these views are expressed by:

a Jane?   b Martin?   c both of them?

Speaking

Part 3

6.3   page 194

1 Look at the picture and discuss it with a partner. Talk about:

• what it would be like to work in this type of environment.
• the responsibilities the job entails.
• the most important qualities needed for a job like this.
• the advantages and disadvantages of the job.

3   page 193
7.1 page 194

2 Below are conditions you may want in an ideal job. In pairs, list the conditions in order of importance. Take about four minutes to do this, giving reasons for your answers.

• a comfortable office or workspace
• career opportunities
• cheerful colleagues
• flexitime (being able to decide your working hours within a basic framework)
• good pay
• staff development (training courses, etc.)
• a reliable, encouraging boss
• subsidized canteen
• generous holidays
• stimulating work

Structure *Personal Organizer* ▼

Introduction

Would you describe yourself as an efficient person?
Why? Why not?
Which of the following helps you remember all the
things you have to do in your everyday life?

- Writing lists.
- Making notes in your diary.
- Asking someone to remind you to do things.
- Keeping a filing system.
- Repeating things in your head before you go to sleep.

Can you add any other ideas to the list?

Reading

Read the following article which appeared in the news
section of a business magazine, and choose the heading
which you feel best sums up the point the writer is
making.

Managing systems	*Ruled by the Filofax*
Leave it to electronics	*Small is beautiful*
Organizing the organizer	*Price it right*
A notable notepad	

IN THE EIGHTIES OUR LIVES WERE RULED BY
THE FILOFAX. NOW SMALL ELECTRONIC
ORGANIZERS ARE BEING HERALDED AS THE
PERFECT ANSWER TO PERSONAL EFFICIENCY.

If you are attracted by the thought of a compact and
rather impressive-looking corporate planner, Management
Projects have come up with the Personal Electronic
Organizer Series 3.

5   Said by Management Projects to be the ultimate
'advanced management system', its sections have been
designed to include the obvious, like monthly and daily
diaries, as well as pages marked for planning, delegating
and finances.

10   It claims, impressively perhaps for a notebook
measuring fourteen by twenty-one centimetres, to be able
to give you the power to manage people and projects
more effectively, thereby increasing productivity.

   So, if you are not an organizer by nature, and would
15 like to have your office managed for you, this could be
the answer to all your problems!

The passive

A   Form

1   What changes need to be made to put the verbs in
italics into the passive?

    The computer *does* the work for you.
    The computer *can do* the work for you.
    The computer *could have done* the work for you.

2   Now put these sentences into the passive form.

   a   People are writing fewer letters by hand
      nowadays.
   b   We have ordered a new printer for the computer.
   c   The workmen were installing central heating
      when the fire broke out.
   d   Fortunately, the fire had not damaged the office
      equipment.
   e   They printed the manual in Taiwan.
   f   The company might recruit several hundred
      new workers over the next few months.
   g   The committee ought to finish the report by next
      week.
   h   They would have finished the report sooner if
      they hadn't been so busy.

3   Look at the article again. Find examples of the
following used in the passive form:

   a   simple past
   b   present continuous
   c   simple present (two examples)
   d   present perfect
   e   passive infinitive without *to*.

THE PERSONAL ELECTRONIC ORGANIZER SERIES 3

- comes in vinyl, leather-like sewn vinyl or full-grain
leather (the difference being reflected in the prices!).
- has added extras. The vinyl version has a solar-
20 powered calculator, while the other two have a pull-
out panel, incorporating a calculator and useful
notepad.
- can be ordered by phone or fax from Office World
or other office equipment retailers.

 210 words

B Function

The passive is used for several different reasons. Match the passive sentences in 1–4 with explanations a–c below.

1 The cars are assembled by robots and quality control is carried out by computers.
2 A pedestrian has been injured in a hit and run accident near the airport.
3 Steps have been taken by the committee to ensure that this does not happen again.
4 The speech at the board meeting was given by a very prominent member of the government.

The passive is used when:

a the action is more important than who or what does it, although who or what does it is still mentioned.
b who or what does the action is as important or noteworthy as the action itself, and is placed at the end of the sentence for special emphasis.
c who or what does the action is not mentioned, because it is unknown, obvious or unimportant.

Why are some verbs in the article used in the passive and not the active form? Match the examples you found in the article with the explanations in a–c above.

Practice

Rewrite the following sentences in the passive and, referring to explanations a–c above, explain why you would use this form in each rewritten sentence. One sentence cannot be changed.

1 You insert the paper into the printer with the smoother side facing up.
2 The managing director from the head office in Halifax briefed the staff about company reorganization.
3 The new company secretary has made a very serious error.
4 We are going to update all the office equipment early next year.
5 The local inhabitants on a remote island in the Pacific make this jewellery.
6 The college authorities awarded every student a certificate on completion of the course.
7 Someone has attended to the matter.
8 I taught myself how to use a computer.
9 A computer marks the exam papers.
10 They say the company is on the verge of bankruptcy.

Have something done

A What is the difference in form and meaning between these sentences?

I installed the new computer yesterday.
The new computer was installed yesterday.
I had the new computer installed yesterday.

The article stated:

… *if you … would like to have your office managed for you, this could be the answer to all your problems!*

Why does the writer use the causative use of *have* in this sentence?

B What is the difference in the meaning of *had* in these two sentences?

I had the car serviced yesterday.
I had the car stolen yesterday.

Practice

A Complete the following sentences with an appropriate form of *have* (*something done*) and the words in brackets. For example,

The curtains look shabby. I really must (clean).
The curtains look shabby. I really must have them cleaned.

1 I went to the dentist's (tooth / fill).
2 The car looks filthy already! I (just / clean yesterday).
3 Could you make an appointment at the hairdresser's for me (hair / perm)?
4 The heel's come off my shoe. I'll have (repair).
5 The grass is getting long again. We should (cut).
6 While I was travelling on the underground, I (handbag / steal).
7 This skirt was too long when I bought it so I had (take up).
8 They've just moved into an old house. It's in a terrible condition so they (decorate).
9 The office is always freezing cold but next week the management (central heating / install).
10 While they were away on holiday they (house / break into).

B In spoken English, you can use *get* instead of *have something done*, but you do not usually say who or what does the action. In which of the sentences in A would *get* sound odd, and why?

C List two things you have had done recently, two you had done (or used to have done!) when you were younger, and two you would like to have done if you had the time or the money. Compare your list with that of another student.

13 Law and Order

Reading *Fine Young Criminals*

Introduction

1 Read the following headlines from a selection of newspapers. Match each one to the most appropriate extract.

Little Caesars Blamed for Terrorizing Northumbria

Houdini Kid does it again

It's time to Crack Down on Crime Babies

A

A government report on the increase in crime amongst juveniles has made recommendations to schools and parents to supervise
5 children more carefully, especially during holidays and after school. The report suggests that many children are left to their own devices at these times and some find
10 themselves involved in illegal or dangerous activities. It recently came to light that a group of children from a primary school had tied up a seven-year-old boy in his
15 bedroom and proceeded to ransack the house. The report also recommends that it is time the police got tough with the parents of youngsters who break the law.

B

For the third time this year, a ten-year-old child in the care of the local authority has absconded from a secure unit by wriggling under an electrified fence. The child, who
5 cannot be named for legal reasons, was placed in a secure unit in Northumbria after running away from a local children's home on six occasions over the last two years. A spokesperson for the authority told a news
10 conference that there was no satisfactory way of detaining children against their will other than sending them to adult prisons.

C

A gang of children aged between six and eleven have been accused of making the lives of old-age pensioners a misery. Residents in
5 housing estates on the outskirts of Newcastle and Sunderland have complained that gangs of young children have been tormenting the old folk by throwing rubbish in their
10 gardens, banging on their doors and windows at night and generally making a nuisance of themselves. Northumbrian District Council has announced plans to send police into
15 the area to talk to parents and teachers in a bid to stop further escalation of the problem.

2 Is crime committed by children a problem in your country? What methods are used to deter young criminals or punish them for their offences?

Little Joey's Lost Childhood

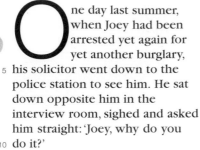

One day last summer, when Joey had been arrested yet again for yet another burglary, his solicitor went down to the police station to see him. He sat down opposite him in the interview room, sighed and asked him straight: 'Joey, why do you do it?'

And Joey looked straight back and told him, 'I dunno. I gotta buy fags, drink. There's drugs and things. I gotta girl. It's money you know …' Joey shrugged, like any man with a weight on his mind. Joey was then eleven years old.

Soon afterwards, he became famous when, in October last year, he was locked away in a secure unit outside Leeds where he was three years younger than any other inmate, so young that his incarceration required the personal authority of the Home Secretary. As he was led away from court, he hurled insults at the press and then disappeared in a cloud of publicity.

He became a caricature – 'the Artful Dodger', 'Britain's most notorious young crook', 'Crime baby', 'the Houdini Kid'. He made all the papers. Soon his case was being used as ammunition in a sustained assault which has seen the Home Secretary, the Police Federation, the Daily Express and various Chief Constables campaigning to lock up more children.

They pointed not only to Joey but to a rash of other adolescent delinquents: the eleven-year-old brother and sister whose attempted arrest caused a riot at a wedding party; the six 'Little Caesars' from Northumbria who were blamed for 550 offences; the thirteen-year-old armed robber from Cheshire. Their solution was simple: these children had to be punished; the courts needed more powers to put them behind bars.

Joey grew up with his father, Gerry, a Southern Irish labourer who has not worked regularly for years; and his mother, Maureen, also Irish and barely literate, who was only eighteen when she married Gerry, fifteen years her senior. The neighbours remember Joey playing with his go-cart in the street, running around with his two smaller brothers, banging on the door to scrounge cigarettes for Gerry. They say he was a nice kid. They remember

Reading

Part 3

Exam tip ▼

In Part 3 of Paper 1, the multiple-choice questions will follow the order of the text. Remember that there may be a summary question at the end.

1 Read through the article and say if you think the title is appropriate.

2 Now answer these multiple-choice questions.

1 Joey became famous because
   A he had committed so many burglaries.
   B he was always being arrested.
   C he was the youngest inmate in the secure unit.
   D he swore at the press photographers.

2 How did the Home Secretary and the police respond to the rise in juvenile crime?
   A They wanted to see more young criminals put in prison.
   B They believed that there should be a return to corporal punishment.
   C They thought that the courts had too much power.
   D They thought that the police force should be strengthened.

3 What can the neighbours recall about Joey?
   A He smoked cigarettes.
   B He was a bully.
   C He started stealing when he was four.
   D He played truant from school.

4 Why was it decided that Joey should go to a secure unit?
   A He refused to give up thieving.
   B He kept running away from the homes.
   C He behaved better in a secure unit.
   D He was too old for the children's home.

5 What does the writer think is the main cause of Joey's behaviour?
   A He is a victim of his own circumstances.
   B He is unable to sort himself out.
   C He has been forced to behave in an anti-social way.
   D He has been badly treated by the police.

'Throw a child into the sea, it will drown. If you throw it into a ghetto, it will grow up like Joey'

70 him skiving off school, too, and thieving, but they don't remember it well. Almost every-
75 body's kids skive off school, and a lot of them go thieving.

Gerry says he's
80 not too sure when Joey first broke the law. He thinks he stole some crisps for dinner
85 when he was four. In Gerry's family, there has often been trouble with the law: petty crimes, handling, the occasional
90 fight, a succession of brothers and uncles behind bars.

By the time he was 10, thieving was the only game Joey knew. He had 35 arrests behind him and the
95 social workers decided he had to be locked up. They had tried

taking him into care but he had simply walked out of the homes where they put him so, in
100 December 1990, he was sent to the secure unit at East Moor outside Leeds.

He liked it there. Everyone at East Moor agrees that Joey liked
105 it. It is not like a prison: there are no peaked caps or truncheons. It is more like a school with extra keys. Tucked away there, far from the mean crescents of the
110 housing estate, he was a child again. He played with lego. He practised joined-up writing. He woke up feeling ill in the night and cried on the principal's
115 shoulder.

Joey is due to be released from the secure unit in February. Everyone who has dealt with him is sure that he will go straight
120 back to his old ways. They say they have given up on him. They have two options: lock him up or let him go. Everyone in social

services knows the danger of
125 locking up a child: it breaks up the family, it stigmatises the child, it floats him in a pool with older criminals.

Yet letting him go is no better,
130 not when it means returning to the battered streets of the city. Joey is not the only child like this. Every English city has them. Joey just happens to be the famous
135 one. He's bright and he's brave and the psychiatrists agree he is not disturbed. He is, by nature, anxious to please. In the secure unit now, he conforms with
140 everything around him.

If you throw a child into the sea, it will drown. If you throw it into an English ghetto, it will grow up like Joey.

The names of Joey and his family have been changed for legal reasons.

750 words 🕑

Nick Davies, *The Guardian Weekend*

3 Underline the phrases which helped you choose the correct answer. Compare your underlined phrases with those of another student.

Now look at the incorrect options. On which parts of the article are they based? Why are they incorrect?

4 Find words or phrases in the text which are similar in meaning to the words in *italics*.

1 Amy looked as if she had *a lot to worry about*.
2 The prison staff found it difficult to keep the *prisoners* in their cells.
3 The young man's *imprisonment* in a small, windowless cell was cruel and unnecessary.
4 Kevin has been breaking the law all his life; he's a *criminal* and nothing is going to change him.
5 Most people would prefer to see convicted criminals *in jail* rather than doing community service.
6 When the prison governor stopped the prisoners from watching TV, they *went on the rampage*, causing hundreds of pounds worth of damage.
7 Many people commit *minor offences* when they are young.
8 I don't think he's likely to improve – we *have no hope* for him.

Listening and Speaking *Let the Punishment Fit the Crime?* ▼

Introduction

Read the following newspaper extract. Does the punishment fit the crime?

> # Three strikes and you're out
>
> CALIFORNIA'S new 'three strikes' law, which was introduced with overwhelming public support, requires people with a serious criminal conviction to receive twice the normal sentence when convicted of a second felony – and 25 years to life for any third offence. In one recent case, this resulted in a jail sentence of 25 years for a man found guilty of stealing pizza from a group of children.

Why do you think this law was introduced? What effects could it have? Is it a sensible law, in your opinion? Give reasons for your answer.

Listening

Part 4

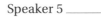

1 Listen to five people talking about how they were treated by others when they had done something wrong. Match the speakers to the pictures.

Speaker 1 _____   Speaker 3 _____   Speaker 5 _____

Speaker 2 _____   Speaker 4 _____

2 Discuss which of these situations you regard as the most serious. Which of them amounts to breaking the law?

3 Listen again to the speakers. Decide what they feel about the punishment they received. Match the speakers to the reactions below.

a   unfairly treated
b   surprised by the severity
c   terrified by the suddenness
d   extremely upset
e   worried about what might have happened
f   tough but just
g   unconcerned about the outcome
h   relieved but annoyed

4 Check your answers with the key on page 196, and then decide why certain answers are correct. Is it what the people say, or how they say it, or a combination?

Vocabulary

Expressions with 'get'

The sentence below is taken from one of the listening extracts. What does the phrase in *italics* mean?

… if I'd left the moped outside the pub, it would probably have *got nicked*!

Now look at these other expressions with *get*. Can you fit a suitable expression into sentences 1–8 below? Don't forget to choose an appropriate tense.

get one's own back	get over	make one's getaway
get the sack	get off	get down
get away with	get at	

1   It's outrageous! Those two crooks _____ very lightly! Their sentences were reduced to six months.
2   Colin will never _____ the shock of losing all his money on the stock market.
3   Have you seen the way John lets his little daughter _____ murder? It's amazing when you think how inflexible he is at work!
4   When Tom left Sally, she _____ by telling everyone how selfish he was.
5   The never-ending string of family problems has really _____ Simon _____ recently.
6   Stop _____ me! I've just about had enough of your accusations.
7   Have you heard about Mike? He _____. It's incredible after all these years with the company.
8   The thieves _____ from the scene of the crime in a stolen car.

Speaking

Part 2

📖 **3** page 193
6.4 page 194

1 You should do this task in a group of three. You are each going to look at a different picture. Student A, describe your picture in detail. Students B and C, listen carefully. Talk about two things which are the same and two which are different in your pictures.

Student A, look at picture **13A** on page 201.
Student B, look at picture **13B** on page 203. Student C, look at picture **13C** on page 204.

Part 3

2 Look at this picture. What kind of situation does it represent?

Read through this list of punishments which are used in various countries for different types of crime. Discuss what sort of crimes you think they are most appropriate for. Are there any that should never be used? You should all try to contribute equally.

- solitary confinement
- community service
- imprisonment
- hard labour
- fines
- corporal punishment
- death penalty
- life imprisonment
- suspended sentence
- probation

Report back to the class on your decisions.

3 What do you think is the effect of punishment on people who have committed crimes?

What do you think is the most appropriate way for society to encourage good behaviour?

Writing *Character Assessment* ▼

Introduction

1 Listen to the recording about Bampfylde Moore Carew, an 18th-century con man. Why do you think he chose to live as he did?

2 Here are some of the character qualities and defects referred to in the recording.
Can you supply any related verbs or adjectives, for example, *trickster – to trick – tricky*?

invention	deceit	boastfulness
dedication	audacity	ingenuity

English in Use
Part 5

1 Read this informal note about a college lecturer. What aspects of his character are described?

> ### BILL YOUNG – SACKED!
>
> The news about Bill Young's sudden dismissal is horrendous. As his students, we should let the Principal know just how shocked and angry we feel. Bill is taking action against the college to get them to back down. We must help him all we can.
>
> 5 He's been at the college for ages. He's a really kind, sensitive guy and you can always count on him to listen when you've got a problem. What's more, he's usually been on our side – remember the student strike last year, when he persuaded the Principal to agree to some of our demands for necessary
> 10 changes to the college rules? Bill didn't let us down then, did he? Now it's our turn to support him.
>
> They say he's been ripping off the college funds, which is quite ludicrous. Who could you trust more than Bill? Perhaps someone in authority dreamed up this scandal as an excuse to
> 15 fire him? Anyway, they can't prove he's done anything wrong.
>
> He's a great teacher and we want him back in his job now!

2 Using the information contained in the note, complete this formal statement to the Principal. You should use no more than two words in each gap.

> Exam tip ▼
>
> In Paper 3, Part 5, remember to check the register of the text you must complete; make sure that the words you use do not occur in the first text; read your completed text to check that the style is consistent.

TO THE PRINCIPAL

We would formally like to (1)_____ our outrage at the way Bill Young has been treated by this college. We understand that he is appealing against the charges and we hope that the college will (2)_____ its allegations. Bill Young has our full (3)_____.

   He is a (4)_____ member of this college. His (5)_____ and sensitivity have always been appreciated by his students. In addition, he is totally (6)_____ when it comes to giving our problems a hearing. Throughout the unfortunate strike last year he was very (7)_____ to our cause and helped to bring about changes to college regulations that were much (8)_____.

   Now he stands (9)_____ embezzling college funds, which we cannot accept as being true. In our view, Bill Young is utterly (10)_____. Moreover, there is no (11)_____ of his alleged wrongdoing.

   We hereby request that he (12)_____ immediately in his post.

3 Which of your answers in 1–12 above could be used to describe positive character qualities?

Vocabulary

Confusable words

Sensible, sensitive

Look back at both texts and find the words *sensitive* and *sensitivity*.

The word *sensible* is often confused with *sensitive*. Decide which of the two is appropriate in sentences 1–5.

1   She's very _____ to critical remarks since she made that unfortunate error.

2   Theatre directors cannot allow themselves to be too _____ to bad press.

3   How _____ you are! I wasn't nearly as organized at your age.

4   People should be much more _____ to the needs of the disabled.

5   It's _____ to limit your exposure to the sun, particularly if you have _____ skin.

Writing

Sample reference

Exam tip ▼

In Paper 2, Part 2, you may be asked to write a character reference about someone. This is most likely to be a work-oriented task and you should take this into account by using the appropriate register.

Part 2, character reference

1 a Read this character reference. Would this person be an asset to a company, in your opinion? Which words and phrases in the text support your view?

To whom it may concern

Hilary Randle

I have known Hilary Randle for seven years and have collaborated with her on several projects during that time. My most recent association with her has been the Elwood Arts Festival, where she and I co-ordinated the publicity and marketing of the event.

Hilary brings two fundamental qualities to her work – single-mindedness and thoroughness. She always has a clear view of objectives and a flair for prioritizing. She shows dedication in willingly putting in extra hours if the need arises, so as not to compromise the quality of her work.

Her level-headed approach to problems is a positive and creative one. She is never daunted when things go wrong and generally remains self-possessed. In fact, I would go so far as to say that she is virtually unflappable under pressure.

As a team member, Hilary is sensitive to the views of other people, though she is undeniably a dominant individual. She usually takes on the role of team leader unasked, in order to fulfil her objectives as she sees them and to get things done. Her determination is in this sense both a strength and a weakness.

On a social level, Hilary has an outgoing personality and contributes a great deal to any occasion. Her unique sense of humour appeals to most people. I have always enjoyed being in her company.

For all the reasons I have given above, I am pleased to recommend Hilary Randle for a position in your organization.

b In a character reference, it is important to give a balanced picture of the person. No prospective employer would believe a description that was totally positive! At the same time, weaknesses are often played down, both in terms of how they are described and at what stage in the reference they occur. Find examples of this in the model.

c What is the structure of this piece of writing? Write down the main point of each paragraph.

Understanding the task

2 Now read this writing task.

> A close friend has applied for a job as a tourist guide in your country and you have been asked to write a character reference to support this application. You should focus on qualities and experience that are appropriate to the job and add any other comments that you think are relevant.

Decide first on the likely scope of the job of the tourist guide. This will help you to define the qualities and experience you need to write about. Don't forget to include a weakness as well.

Planning your answer

3 Note down the main points that you want to include in your reference, organizing them into paragraphs. Finish with a suitable recommendation. Exchange your plan with another student and compare what you have done.

Focusing on the reader

4 a It is important to keep your comments to the point. Don't be side-tracked by the fact that you are writing a reference about a close friend. A brief explanation of your relationship is sufficient. If you describe your friendship in detail, you will be penalized for including irrelevant material.

Bearing this advice in mind, which of these statements would you describe as irrelevant to the task?

I have known X since 1985.

X and I shared a flat at university and spent a lot of time together.

After university, X got a job in an office at much the same time as I did.

X and I are still good friends and we see each other regularly.

Recently we have been studying English together at the same evening school.

b Now consider the register of your piece of writing. Look back at the formal statement in the English in Use exercise and at the model for useful expressions.

Writing

page 187

6.1 page 194
9.2, 12.1 page 195

5 Write your character reference in about 250 words. Remember **WRITE** ✎.

"What makes you think you'd be suitable for this job?"

WE BELIEVE IN EQUAL OPPORTUNITIES

Introduction

What steps can you take to protect your property from being stolen? Look at the list below and choose two items which you think would be effective and two which you think would be useless.

- Mark your property with an electronic pen.
- Keep a guard dog.
- Lock everything of value in a safe.
- Leave a light on in the house when you go out.
- Fit a burglar alarm to your house or car.
- Put shutters across the windows in your house.
- Buy a house next to the police station.
- Never leave valuables in a conspicuous place.
- Go out as little as possible.

English in Use

Part 2

A Read the following article about a burglar alarm, ignoring the spaces, then describe briefly what the alarm does and how it works.

B Read the article again and supply the missing words by writing *one* word in spaces 1–15. The first one has been done for you as an example.

Inversions

A The article states that:

1 life has never been more difficult for an intruder.
2 present-day alarms indicate movement only when a burglar is busy breaking in.
3 you will no longer need to emerge in dressing gown and slippers – only to find the neighbourhood cat rummaging in the dustbin!
4 they can reliably distinguish footsteps from other movements only by carefully programming Footfall to recognize data patterns.

Find the relevant information in the article and note down how the writer expresses it.

Which words now begin the sentences?
How does putting these words at the beginning change the word order of the sentences?

What do these initial words have in common?
When would you use sentences like these?

Walk on the wild side

Innovations

NEVER has life been more difficult for a would-be intruder! Burglars now have to, quite literally, watch their step. Dutch engineers (0) _____are_____ hard on the heels of
5 poachers and prowlers with a footstep detector that can identify anything (1)_____ the heaviest of hob-nailed boots to the daintiest of tiptoes.
　　Developed by the Physics and Electronics
10 Laboratory in the Hague, the novel device, (2)_____ as Footfall, outdoes current alarms. Only when a burglar is busy breaking in do present-day alarms indicate that someone or (3)_____ has moved. Footfall, on
15 the (4)_____ hand, can react specifically to human footsteps well (5)_____ they have reached the house. No longer will you need (6)_____ emerge in dressing gown
20 and slippers – only to find the neighbourhood cat rummaging in the dustbin!
　　The surveillance system attempts to exploit the fact that, just (7)_____ fingerprints, footprints are unique. Not only
25 does this difference manifest itself in shape but (8)_____ in the noises we make when tramping, trudging, pacing or plodding, which (9)_____ characterized by certain acoustic patterns. Applying seismo-
30 graphic techniques, the tell-tale patterns show on a graph (10)_____ a jagged dance of frequency waves fluctuating in intensity.
　　'Only by carefully programming Footfall to recognize patterns (11)_____ data
35 can we now reliably make a distinction (12)_____ footsteps and other movements,' says electrical engineer Huub van Hoof.
　　'But (13)_____ this, we can't
40 differentiate between the footsteps of intruders and those of family members or neighbours. Although, (14)_____ people always walked in the (15)_____ way, at the same speed, in
45 the same shoes, we would even be able to do that!'

⏱ **250** words

B Now rewrite these sentences putting the words in *italics* at the beginning. You may have to omit words, change words, or alter the word order within the sentences.

1 Peter was *not only* a well-known detective but he became a successful writer as well.
2 Parliament had *never* made such dramatic changes to the legal system *before*.
3 It was *only when* the intruders had forced their way into the house that they came across the huge Alsatian dog.
4 It was *only by* mounting a full-scale investigation that the police discovered who the murderer was.
5 Organizations should *no longer* expect people to work unsociable hours without being paid overtime.
6 Heads of State *seldom* seem to learn any lessons from history.
7 James was *in no way* responsible for the theft of the painting.
8 The bank employees did *not* discover the robbery *until* they opened the night safe.
9 The emergency services can *no longer* cope with the huge amount of calls they receive.
10 We *rarely* hear about what happens to prisoners after they are released into the outside world.

Concessions

A The article states that:

1 we can distinguish footsteps from other movements.
2 we cannot differentiate between different people's footsteps.
3 if a person always walked in exactly the same way, we could differentiate between different people's footsteps.

How does the writer combine these pieces of information?

Which words are used to introduce contrasting information ?

B Combine the information in 1–8 with that in a–l, using the following expressions at least once:

in spite of   although   despite
not that   even though

1 the snow was heavy
2 the hotel was extremely expensive
3 many modern alarm systems are highly effective
4 a nationwide search was mounted by the police
5 fewer prisons are being built

6 this is a no-parking zone
7 we are making every effort to despatch your order as soon as possible
8 more motorways are being built

a we are having problems with our suppliers
b this doesn't solve the traffic problems
c it appears that the number of inmates is increasing
d you wouldn't think so looking at the number of vehicles parked here
e the escaped prisoner was not found
f the roads are always congested
g we decided to book in
h they fail to deter intruders
i we had no intention of staying there
j you are allowed to load and unload vehicles
k we managed to make it home safely
l this makes no difference to some would-be intruders

Sentence completion

A **Inversions**

Complete sentences 1–6 with a suitable subject / verb inversion.

1 Never _____ such a terrible storm!
2 Only by trying every single key on the key-ring _____ the right one.
3 No longer _____ on the state to support them for the rest of their lives!
4 Only when the taxi driver pulled up at his destination _____ that his passenger was no longer in the back seat!
5 In no way _____ for what happened yesterday.
6 Rarely _____ such kindness and consideration in a person.

B **Concessions**

Complete these sentences in any way you think suitable.

1 Although …, I couldn't resist …
2 Despite …, he succeeded in …
3 Big cities are often dangerous places to be alone in – not that …
4 Even though …, I have decided to …
5 In spite of …, the committee managed …
6 The government …, despite the fact that …

14 Tomorrow's World Today

Listening and Speaking *Robotics* ▼

Introduction

1   Do you know these robot characters? What are they designed to do?

2   What do you know about actual robots? Decide whether the following statements are true or false.

   1   The average robot takes ten man-years to build.
   2   One robot can run at more than 30 kph.
   3   The heaviest robot weighs approximately 2 tons.
   4   The smallest robot weighs only 150 grams.
   5   Three-quarters of all robots run on batteries.

   Check your answers with the key on page 196.

Listening

Part 1

1   You are going to listen to a radio programme about an event in Scotland called the *World Robot Championships*. Look carefully at the summary on page 171 before you start, to find out what type of information you have to listen for.

2 Now complete the information in 1–12, using no more than three words in each space. When you have finished, listen again and check your answers.

World Robot Championships

Summary of events

These are the first championships to be held in Glasgow and they will return there every (1)_____. There will be more than 500 robots from about (2)_____ countries.

In IEE Micro-Mouse, robots have to discover a way through a (3)_____ in a fixed time.

Nano-Mouse is a (4)_____ of the game.

The athletics events will include two-legged and multi-legged (5)_____ and hurdling where robots need to use their (6)_____.

In the pool, there will be (7)_____ and submersible robots.

Sumo wrestling for robots will have several (8)_____.

There will even be a robotic form of (9)_____ called 'Robat'.

Robots are often used for (10)_____ clearing up.

The Championships have two events in this area: (11)_____ and (12)_____.

English in Use

Part 3

1 Most of the lines in the following text contain an unnecessary word, which is either grammatically incorrect or does not fit in with the sense of the text. Write the word in the space provided or tick the lines that are correct. Two examples have been done for you.

state-of-the-art robotics

The **World Robot Championships** are the ingenious idea of
Dr Peter Mowforth, as Director of Glasgow's Turing Institute,
one of the world's leading centres of research into the artificial
intelligence and robotics. Peter Mowforth believes there is great
demand also for an international showcase for state-of-the-art
robotics, both from industrialist companies and research bodies.
As well as for the competitions, the robots' designers are
planning a full programme of trade exhibitions, contests,
seminars, workshops and similar unusual events like a
celebration concert performed by a robot orchestra.
Behind which the razzmatazz of the Robot Championships
lies a serious purpose in promoting the advance of robot
technology, which has in recent last years perhaps not
advanced quite as rapidly as some professionals think it
should to have done. Dr Mowforth's efforts will hopefully
put this right. ■

0	✓
0	*as*
1	_____
2	_____
3	_____
4	_____
5	_____
6	_____
7	_____
8	_____
9	_____
10	_____
11	_____
12	_____
13	_____

2 Would you like to attend an event like this? Why? Why not?

Speaking

The complete Paper 5 Speaking lasts approximately 15 minutes, or more if you are in a group of three. As you will be assessed with another candidate, or possibly two candidates, it is important that you participate as fully as possible in each Part, except when your partner has his / her 'long turn'. Remember that asking your partner questions and expressing agreement or disagreement are equally valid ways of demonstrating your skills in spoken English.

Here is a complete Speaking test. Time yourselves for each part.

Part 1 (about 3 minutes)

You are going to introduce another student. Talk about where he / she is from, how long you have known this person and why he / she is learning English with you.

If you run out of hard facts to mention about the person, why not invent some!

Part 2 (about 4 minutes)

1 Futuristic factory (spot the difference)

Your pictures are very similar, but not the same. Student A, turn to picture 14A on page 201. Student B, look at picture 14B on page 204. Student A, describe your picture in detail. You will have about a minute to do this.

Student B, listen carefully. Then talk about four differences in your picture. You can check with Student A.

When you have finished, compare the two pictures side by side.

2 Automated automobiles (describe and identify)

You and another student are each going to look at a different picture. Student B, describe your picture in detail. You will have about a minute to do this.

Student A, listen carefully. Talk about two things that are the same and two things that are different in your picture. If you need more help, you can ask Student B some questions.

After doing this, compare the two pictures side by side.

 3 page 193
6.4 page 194

Student A, look at picture **14C** on page 203.
Student B, look at picture **14D** on page 204.

Part 3 (about 4 minutes)

A robotic future

7.1 page 194

Both of you should look at the four pictures of robots on page 205. Decide together what each of the robots is used for. Do you think all of the robots shown are useful aids to people? Evaluate them together, putting them in rank order according to their necessity. You may have to agree to disagree with your partner when doing this.

Try to vary the expressions you use to evaluate things. For example,

I think X is crucial / vital / invaluable / extremely important …
For me, X is the least useful / of marginal use / borderline …

What did you and your partner decide about the pictures?

Part 4 (about 4 minutes)

What are the advantages and disadvantages of using robots instead of people? What type of tasks do you think robots will be capable of doing in the future?

Reading   *Where is the Workplace?* ▼

Introduction

1 In pairs, compare and contrast the different environments depicted in the two pictures. If you had a choice, which would you prefer to live in?

2 Read this extract from a newspaper article about John Ruscoe, an employee of ICL. Find out what his job involves, where he works and where he lives.

> **ALARM BELLS** rang on Orkney when the computer system crashed in Hong Kong harbour, threatening to halt shipping movements in one of the world's busiest waterways. John Ruscoe stumbled from his bed in a farm cottage overlooking the sea and after four hours in the "broom
> 5 cupboard" housing his computers, docks traffic was under way again on the other side of the world.
>   Mr Ruscoe works for the computer company ICL, connected to its Manchester office by the sort of technology offering a radical future to the information industry. He is among those rewriting industrial history,
> 10 using advanced technology to re-create cottage industry hundreds of miles from commercial centres.

 3 Listen to a recording about working in Los Angeles. Is *telecommuting* becoming more or less important in Los Angeles? Can you explain why?

4 In pairs, discuss what you think are the benefits and problems of *telecommuting*.

Reading

Multiple matching

1 Skim read the extract from a report below. According to the writer, what are the main advantages of *teleworking*?

2 The extract is from a report by British Telecom, who have set up a project team to evaluate the development of teleworking in Britain. Look first at these section headings, which are out of order. There are three extra headings which do not belong to the report.

> A Teleworking and Social Contact
> B The Development of Teleworking
> C Current Trends in Society
> D A Definition of Teleworking
> E The Technology of Teleworking
> F The Problems of Teleworking
> G The Benefits of Teleworking
> H Career Opportunities in Teleworking
> I Teleworking and Employment Issues

Now read the report and match the headings to their correct sections.

AN OVERVIEW OF TELEWORKING
A Report by BT Research Laboratories

Introduction

This document provides an introduction to teleworking for those unfamiliar with the topic. All words that have an important meaning within the project are highlighted by the use of italics. These words are defined within the text.

1

5 Teleworking encapsulates a whole range of work activities, all of which entail working remotely from an employer, or normally expected place of work, on either a full-time or a part-time basis. The work generally involves the electronic processing of information, the results of which are 10 communicated remotely to the employer, usually by a telecommunications link.

The next section of this paper deals with the growth in work activities that can be classed as teleworking, highlighting the characteristic technology, location and 15 organisation of the work.

2

Many informal activities have always been undertaken in the home, the work of housewives being the most important area. Also, a certain amount of generally low-skilled formal employment in the home has continued. People involved 20 in this type of work are referred to as *traditional homeworkers*. There are also a number of professional jobs that have traditionally been carried out in the home, including writing and illustrating.

The advances in computer technology since the early sixties 25 has led to the rise of *new homeworkers*. These are, typically, computing professionals, such as systems analysts and programmers, who work at home. The convergence of computer technology and communications technology over the past three decades to form information technology has 30 made it possible to decentralise many types of work involving the electronic processing of information.

Remote areas of Britain are now seeing the development of teleservice centres (informally known as *telecottages*). The idea for these rural work centres comes originally from 35 Sweden, where they have been developed as community assets to overcome the problems of rural isolation. The basic aim of a teleservice centre is to provide access to computer and telecommunications equipment. British Telecom is supporting the development of such centres in Derbyshire 40 and the Highlands and Islands of Scotland.

3

Not all jobs are suitable for teleworking. Those that depend on personal 'face to face' contact or that require 'hands on' operation cannot be done by a teleworker. This includes jobs such as receptionist, counter clerk and makers of goods 45 that require complex machinery to produce.

Jobs suitable for teleworking are mostly those that are primarily concerned with the handling, processing, transforming and dissemination of information. The

3 Read the report again. Which section talks about:

a   jobs caring for other people?
b   central services in rural areas?
c   status in the workplace?

d   demographic trends?
e   low turnover of staff?
f   job satisfaction?

4 Look in detail at the sections of the report dealing with benefits and problems. Are they similar to those you discussed in the introduction?

5 Here are some statements from the conclusion of the report:

Many factors suggest that teleworking could become a major trend in employment in the late 1990s.

People are increasingly looking for a better quality of life. Work needs to become a more integrated part of an individual's life.

Teleworking is an idea whose time has come.

Do you agree or disagree with these statements? Discuss your views on the future of teleworking with another student.

---

number of people employed in this type of *information*
50 *intensive job* is growing significantly as a proportion of the workforce.

Information intensive functions can be broadly split into two types: high level and clerical. High level information intensive individuals are professional people who process
55 information as a major part of their job. Examples include systems analysts, accountants and specialist consultants. Clerical *information operatives* process information in a very simple way. Tasks include input and manipulation of information (e.g. processing forms). Desk top computers
60 and reliable data communications services have allowed the development of this type of work.

4

The future of teleworking will be dependent on two sets of forces: economic and social. Economic forces are the result of technical developments that not only make teleworking
65 possible, but also in certain circumstances make it an economic benefit to employers and the country at large.

Social forces are the result of changes in employees' lifestyles and aspirations, coupled with other changes in society. Changes in the age profile of the population will cause
70 demand for skilled workers to exceed supply. Many people unable to work in the traditional way (e.g. disabled and handicapped) will be able to take up jobs for the first time because of teleworking. This will help to overcome the skills shortage.

5

75 The chief advantage to employees is that less time, money and effort are spent on travelling to and from the workplace. For city-based workers who commute daily, this represents a major saving. Related to this is the wider choice of areas to live in once the constraint of travel is removed.

80 The flexibility that teleworking will give over hours of work will be a great advantage to parents with young children. It will also attract those who care for elderly or disabled relatives. Retired people may also use teleworking as a way of working part-time.

85 The employer can benefit from teleworking in three main ways: increased productivity, reduced costs and a wider pool of potential employees. Since people are generally happier in their jobs, it is easier for the employer to attract and retain employees.

6

90 Teleworking could give rise to a number of unwelcome complications for the employee and the employer. The impact of these has yet to be assessed but there will obviously be a trade-off between the advantages and the disadvantages of teleworking.

95 A major concern for any employee is the possibility of having a lower profile as a teleworker within an organisation. Since a teleworker is not physically present in the employing organisation, he or she may not be seen as an equal to the on-site employees. The consequences of
100 this could be lack of promotion opportunities.

Some teleworkers may miss the interaction of the workplace. The daily interaction with other people is a major reason for many in going out to work. If the interaction is removed, the job may no longer seem
105 worthwhile.

There are many financial costs associated with teleworking. These may well increase the cost of living for the teleworker, although they must be balanced against the savings that were highlighted in section 5.

British Telecom

900 words   175

Style

The BT report on pages 174 – 175 contains many features that are typical of factual reports. Look at the examples below and try to include them in your own writing when appropriate.

- Using section headings as signposts for the reader.
  The Development of Teleworking

- Using prefacing structures to highlight main advantages and disadvantages.
  The chief advantage to employees is ...

  Did you notice any other examples of prefacing structures in the report?

- Using adverbs to state the typical situation.
  The work generally involves the electronic processing of information ...
  Information intensive functions can be broadly split into two types: ...

  What other adverbs can be used in this way?

- Referencing to other parts of the report.
  The next section of this paper deals ...
  ... that were highlighted in section 5.

  The inclusion of referencing makes for a tighter and more cohesive report.

- Using *will* and *may* to make future predictions.
  Changes in the age profile of the population will cause demand for skilled workers to exceed supply. Retired people may also use teleworking as a way of working part-time.

Writing   *An Electronic Future* ▼

Introduction

1   Which of these items do you predict will no longer be used in the next century? What might replace them?

2 Read these short articles about the impact of electronics on commerce and travel. Are the innovations described a good thing, in your opinion?

Scanner 'ends checkout woes'

An electronic scanner which can read the entire contents of a supermarket trolley at a glance has just been developed. The Supertag scanner could revolutionise the way people shop, virtually eradicating supermarket queues.

5 The scanner would have a double benefit for supermarkets – removing the bottleneck which causes most customer frustration and reducing the number of checkout staff.

The face of retailing will change even more rapidly when the fibre optic networks being built by cable TV companies begin to be
10 more widely used. Customers will be able to place their orders from home, using a handset to flip through menus on their TV screens.

The day cannot be too far off when the weekly shopping ordered from home will be collected later from the supermarket, already
15 in a trolley. The customer will wheel it through a Supertag-type scanner, pay electronically using a plastic card, and be off home within minutes.

Booked for ghost train

French train passengers thought they had seen it all: reservations for the wrong train, tickets issued at the wrong price, seats double-booked or not booked at all.

5 Then this weekend Socrates, the country's computer rail booking system, surpassed even its own unenviable record for goof-ups and electronic gaffes. It booked up a train that did not exist.

10 The excessively complicated Socrates system has prompted staff strikes, passenger protests, jokes and the odd law suit. During the summer one Paris commuter was inadvertently charged the equivalent of a month's salary for a one-way
15 journey to the suburbs. On another occasion, a peak service high-speed train left Paris with just four passengers on board because Socrates had said that the service was booked out.

English in Use

Part 6

1 Look at the picture and decide what it is illustrating.

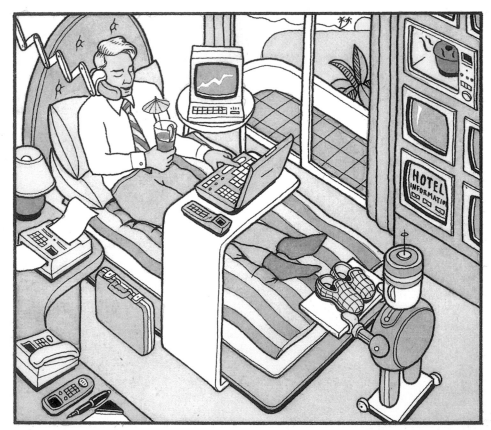

2 Now complete this article by choosing the best phrases from A–J to fill spaces 1–6. Three of the phrases do not fit at all. One answer has been given as an example.

Marian Cotter *The Guardian Weekend*

TRAVEL HOTELS

Room for revolution

Electronic gadgets have moved out of the office and into the hotel bedroom in a big way. Gone are the days when smart city-centre hotels provided mere B & B with a few in-room luxuries thrown in.

5 **T**oday's travellers are less interested in clothes hangers and hairdryers than in-room fax machines and natty TV sets that let them pay the bill, (0) _J_. Some people even predict that tomorrow's globetrotters won't waste any time in the lobby when they roll up at 10 their hotel for the night. They'll check themselves in on an in-room monitor, heat up a snack in their wall-mounted microwave and then (1)_____. While personal service will remain a premium at the top end of the market, technology will (2)_____.

15 Hotels geared to push-button living now provide personal pagers, extra phone lines for fax and computers, in-room answering machines, magnetic door keys and touch-screens which can (3)_____. Bedside remote controls enable guests to flick through a score of TV 20 channels, turn up the temperature and (4)_____. Should push-button living make guests lazy, hotels are also jacking up the high-tech content of their gyms. Videos to plug into while pumping iron are now commonplace, while staff will often (5)_____.

25 Whether microchips will ultimately replace the personal touch at tomorrow's leading hotels remains to be seen. Robots are unlikely to (6)_____. However, there's little doubt that properties with up-to-the-second communications technology will steal a march on the 30 competition.

Will tomorrow's travellers gladly swap 21st century gadgets for a helping of good old-fashioned service? The chances are they will have checked out on their TV screen and be halfway to the plane before anyone thinks to ask.

A draw the curtains without stirring from under the duvet
B hit the exit command on their display screen
C include training programmes in its charges
D decide where most of the business goes
E start steaming suits and pouring coffee
F deliver exercise bikes to the room on request
G show everything from messages to weather reports
H press a few buttons to check out next day
I offer tangible benefits to guests rather than staff
J check share prices and watch movies

3 What type of hotel would you prefer to stay in and why?

Vocabulary

Phrasal verbs

1 In the article, you came across the following phrasal verbs:

1 thrown in (line 4)
2 roll up (line 9)
3 heat up (line 11)
4 turn up (line 20)
5 checked out (line 33)

Look back at the verbs in context. Can you explain what they mean?

2 These verbs all have more than one meaning. Do you know any of the other meanings?

3 Now select one of the verbs for each of the sentences below.

1 She had the feeling that someone had been _____ her movements.
2 Could I perhaps _____ a comment here?
3 The debate on genetics started to _____ as tempers became frayed.
4 The search ended when Josie Daley, aged 12, _____ at her aunt's house last night.
5 He went to the kitchen, _____ his sleeves and got on with the cleaning.

Writing

Part 2, report

Understanding the task

1 Read the following writing task.

21st century technology
A multinational electronics company is offering to fund a student scholarship for the writer of the best report they receive on current and future technological advances. Write a report outlining the changing situation in your country, including references to work, travel and the home.

2.2 page 193
7 page 194
8.4 page 195

Look at the stylistic features highlighted in the reading section. Which of them are relevant to this task? What other stylistic points should you bear in mind here?

Brainstorming ideas

2 Now think about how technology is changing the aspects mentioned. Try to add specific examples to the diagram below. Are there any other aspects apart from those given that you could cover? Look back at the reading section for extra ideas.

> **Exam tip ▼**
>
> Examiners give credit for the inclusion of original ideas, provided that they are relevant to the topic and the task itself is completed.

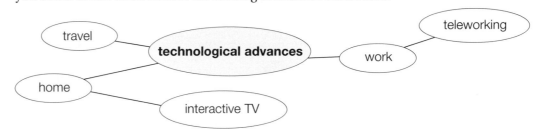

Planning your answer

3 a Decide on suitable section headings for your report, making sure that you have included all the aspects referred to in the question.

b List the main points to cover under each of your section headings. Show the plan to another student to see whether the suggested organization of your writing is clear.

c Now spend some time thinking about your introduction. Remember, in the exam you probably won't have time to go back to the beginning and redraft your opening paragraph. The development of a strong introduction is crucial.

Here is an example of an introduction to the task. What is wrong with it, and how could you improve it?

> *I am writing a report on the changing situation in my country. I would like to win the scholarship for this report. I think there have been many changes in the workplace in my country, including the growth of teleworking and the introduction of many new gadgets around the office, such as computers and fax machines, which have made communication easier. I will talk about travel and the home too.*

d Write your own introduction (about 40 words), explaining the scope of your report and indicating the sections you have chosen. Give it to another student to read through. Does your introduction meet these criteria?

- Is it clear enough?
- Is it general enough?
- Is it in an appropriate style?

Writing

4 Now write your report in about 250 words. Remember **WRITE** .

page 191

Introduction

Look at the title of the article below. What do you understand by *keyhole surgery*? Why do you think it is described as *'a kinder cut'*? Why do you think it might be an improvement on more traditional methods of surgery?

Reading

Read the following article. Then, in small groups, discuss how endoscopic surgery works and what its benefits are.

Keyhole Surgery
– A Kinder Cut

The development of so-called keyhole surgery means that the surgeon's knife may soon disappear altogether as it is replaced by miniature cameras, microscopic scissors and staplers. Instead of making
5 long cuts in the patient's body, surgeons look at the site through an 'endoscope', or operating telescope. This is passed into the body through a small hole that will barely leave a scar.

As long as the operation is carried out skilfully by
10 an experienced surgeon, keyhole surgery damages the patient far less than a conventional operation. "Minimal access surgery is a real breakthrough," says Alf Cuschieri, a leading endoscopic surgeon. "I wish we'd developed it years ago. Not only does it
15 reduce the trauma to the patient – it also means that we no longer have to make major incisions to perform major operations."

The viewing technology that allows doctors to see what is happening deep inside the human body has
20 been borrowed from the aerospace industry. Although in the 1960s flexible scopes were developed by technicians in order to check engine interiors without them having to be taken apart, today's endoscopes are not just simple tubes you
25 can see through; they are equipped with minute television cameras. An image of the operation – magnified eight times – is transmitted by the camera onto a strategically placed TV screen. Doctors and nurses needn't crowd round to peer
30 into the wound. Instead, they keep their eyes on the screen and work with straight backs and plenty of elbow room. As surgeons cannot work in the dark, light is beamed into the area of the body being operated on through optical fibres – strands
35 of special glass, each as thin as a human hair, through which light travels.

Keyhole surgeons hope that miniaturisation will make it possible for patients to have their operations performed by robots small enough to
40 crawl through the patient's body. Despite the fact that, until now, even the smallest robots have been

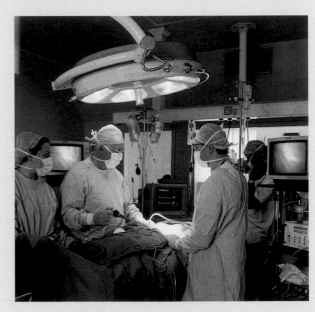

**Minimal access surgery is
a real breakthrough**

too large to be exploited in endoscopic surgery, in Massachusetts the Institute of Technology's Artificial Intelligence and Robotics Laboratory is
45 working on ever-smaller miniature and micro-robots. These robots could be used for filming, taking biopsy specimens or on-the-spot analysis.

One of the most exciting future developments involves telesurgery, where doctors will operate by
50 remote control. This means that a patient can be operated on by two surgeons who are hundreds of kilometres away from each other – and from the patient! Some believe that such techniques will have been perfected in the next ten years or so.

420 words

Grammar review

In groups of three or four, work through the revision exercises below. You may need to refer back to the relevant grammar sections in the book. Your teacher will help you if necessary.

A Modals

The following modals appear in the article:

may   will   would   could   can   needn't

What can these modals express?

Complete the following sentences, using one of the modals above. In some cases, there may be more than one possible answer.

1   Help me with this composition and I _____ be your friend for life!
2   Look, it _____ be the right decision, it _____ not. It's difficult to say.
3   You _____ take me with you if you don't want to!
4   Helen's only five, but she _____ play the piano beautifully.
5   Do you think you _____ possibly help me carry this box of books?
6   For goodness' sake! _____ you stop making that dreadful noise!
7   _____ I ask you a few personal questions?
8   _____ you mind if I used the telephone to make a long distance call?

What other modals are there and what do they express? How do modals behave differently from other verbs?

B Conditionals

The following conditional appears in the article:

As long as the operation is carried out skilfully by an experienced surgeon, keyhole surgery damages the patient far less than a conventional operation.

What type of conditional is this and why is it used?

What is the difference between the first, second, and third conditionals?

Complete the sentences below, using an appropriate form of the conditional. Two of the sentences are mixed conditionals.

1   As long as the children (not find out) about the trip to Disneyworld, they (have) a wonderful surprise.
2   I (hand in) my resignation tomorrow unless the manager (apologize) for her rudeness.
3   (I know) you were coming, I (prepare) for your visit.
4   Supposing you (be) born a century ago, what difference do you think it (make) to your life?
5   If I (work) harder when I was at school, I (be) at university now.
6   If we (have) the money we (go) abroad last year.
7   Supposing that you (can) live your life all over again, how (you change) it?
8   If she (not break) her leg last week, she (be) skiing in Switzerland now!

C Reported speech

These examples of direct speech appear in the article.

'Minimal access surgery is a real breakthrough,' says Alf Cuschieri, a leading endoscopic surgeon. 'I wish we'd developed it years ago. Not only does it reduce the trauma to the patient – it also means that we no longer have to make major incisions to perform major operations.'

Can you report what Alf Cuschieri *says*?

What changes would you make if the reporting verb were *said*?

Report the following conversation between a mother and her teenage son. Begin by using *asked*.

Sam   Mum! What are you doing with the tool box?
Maria Don't touch that electric cord!
Sam   I wish you wouldn't shout at me.
Maria Sorry! I just didn't want you to hurt yourself.
Sam   What's it for, anyway?
Maria I'm trying to mend the CD player.
Sam   What happened to it?
Maria Well, somebody knocked it off the shelf a couple of days ago and it won't work.
Sam   Look! I didn't do it! Honestly!

D Dependent clauses

1 Clauses are a group of words containing a verb, which give additional information about a main sentence.

Can you name:

a two types of noun clause?
b two types of relative clause?
c as many types of adverb clauses as possible? If you cannot remember them all, look back at Unit 8.

2 In the article, can you find examples of noun clauses which answer these questions?

a What does the development of keyhole surgery mean?
b What does Alf Cuschieri wish?
c What does *minimal access surgery* also mean?
d What do keyhole surgeons hope?
e What does *telesurgery* mean?
f What do some people believe?

Are these noun clauses the subject or the object of the main verbs in the sentences?

3 In the article, there are several examples of relative clauses. Can you find one example of a defining relative clause towards the end of the first paragraph, and one example of a non-defining relative clause towards the end of paragraph three?

Is it possible to omit the relative pronoun in the two examples you found? Give reasons for your answers.

4 Look at paragraph three of the article. Can you find examples of the following adverb clauses?

• concession
• reason

Complete the following sentence in five different ways, using the conjunctions below, and say what type of adverb clause you have used.

Sally decided to accept the job …

a because …
b so that …
c although …
d after …
e so … that …

E Verb tenses

1 The following sentences appear in the article:

a *I wish we'd developed it years ago.*
b *The viewing technology … has been borrowed from the aerospace industry.*
c *… in the 1960s flexible scopes were developed by technicians …*
d *… until now, … robots have been too large to be exploited in endoscopic surgery …*
e *Some believe that such techniques will have been perfected in the next ten years or so.*

Why is the present perfect used in b and d but not in c?

Why is the past perfect used in a? What other tenses can be used when *wish* is followed by a clause and what do they refer to?

Why is the future perfect tense used in e?

2 Complete the following sentences, using an appropriate form of the verb in brackets:

a It (be) a long time since I (taste) real Italian food

b How long (the authors write) for examinations?
c By the end of this year the builders (complete) the project.
d Until now the recreational facilities in this town (be) less than adequate.
e Your mother (have) a lot of difficult decisions to make recently.
f The manager asked me why I (not mention) the design problem before.
g Gary wishes he (pay) more attention when he (be) at school!
h I (had) no previous training before I (take) on my last job.

F Gerunds and infinitives

The following gerunds and infinitives appear in the article:

Instead of making long cuts …
… allows doctors to see …
… without them having to be taken apart …
… small enough to crawl …

Match the words on the left to those on the right, and use each combination in a sentence of your own. If more than one answer is possible, explain any difference in meaning.

1	to regret		
2	to remember		
3	without		
4	to look forward		do
5	in order	(to)	doing
6	to help		
7	to object		
8	(I) used		

G Passives – the causative use of *have*

What is the difference in form and meaning between these three sentences?

a   Small robots may perform operations.

b   Operations may be performed by small robots.

c   Patients may have their operations performed by small robots.

Rewrite the following sentences, using either a passive form or the causative use of *have*. When using the passive form, remember to omit the agent if it, or he / she is unimportant, obvious or unknown.

1   Surgeons pass the operating telescope into the body through a small hole.

2   Surgeons no longer need to make major incisions to perform major operations.

3   The medical profession borrowed the technology from other fields.

4   Technicians no longer have to take engine interiors apart to check them.

5   Technicians beam light into the area of the body which surgeons are operating on.

6   The surgeons arranged for the installation of a TV screen in the operating theatre.

7   The Institute of Technology's Artificial Intelligence and Robotics Laboratory is designing ever-smaller miniature and micro-robots.

8   In future, patients might be able to get surgeons to perform their operations by remote control.

H Inversions

Look at the following sentence.

No longer is it necessary to perform major operations by making major incisions.

Why are inversions used?
How do they change the construction of the sentence?
What kind of words are used at the beginning of the sentence in this kind of construction?

Rewrite these sentences, using a suitable word or phrase at the beginning followed by an inversion.

1   Remote control surgery is not only revolutionary but it is beneficial as well.

2   We can only improve our technology by investing in further research.

3   We can only truly benefit from these technological advances when we make them available to everybody.

4   We will not be able to take full advantage of the proposed health scheme until well into the next century.

5   Patients no longer have to put up with pain and suffering when they undergo an operation.

6   Nothing like this has been invented before.

ABINGDON COLLEGE
LEARNING CENTRE

Writing Resource

Part 1 *Letter and Note*

- Write for the specified target readership. If two tasks are required, they will probably need different registers (for example, one formal and one informal).
- Make sure you read all the material provided.
- Use only the parts of the material that are relevant – underlining key information can be helpful.
- Rephrase this information so that you do not 'lift' exact phrases from the question paper.
- Add your own ideas wherever appropriate, but be careful not to go off the point.
- If there are two tasks, make sure you complete each one in the number of words specified. Over-long answers may be penalized.
- Include suitable opening and closing formulae: e.g. *Dear Sir*.

Task

You belong to the AZED International Club, which is currently performing an English musical in your town. The local English language newspaper has just written a review of last night's opening performance.

Read the note from your club secretary and the review, on which she has made some comments. Then, using the information carefully, write the **letter** and the **note**.

I enclose the review of last night's performance – it's absolutely dreadful, I'm afraid. Poor Jan. It's so unfair, after we worked so hard for months at all those rehearsals!

We must take action immediately and ask for an apology to be printed. Otherwise, no one will come and see next weekend's performances.

Could you write a strongly-worded reply on behalf of the club? Please include my comments and add anything else you want to say. I'm sure we should complain about the general rudeness of the reviewer.

Please could you also send a note to Jan? He's terribly upset and needs our support.

Thanks

Maria

Wooden in the woods!

AZED International Club's production of the musical *Into the Woods* (opened Friday 20 November)

This amateur effort, directed by Jan van der Leeden, is not recommended for anyone who enjoys musicals. Not only did the director personally manage to ruin a wonderful musical by completely <u>re-ordering the storyline</u> but also, his entire cast of AZED members acted woodenly and the singing wasn't special either.

In short, it is a disastrous production that has clearly not been adequately rehearsed. The AZED members had great problems performing in English, too – quite frankly, why did they bother?

My ordeal lasted a very <u>long three hours,</u> on an uncomfortable seat in a cold theatre. AZED have asked me to say that there are two more performances this coming Friday and Saturday, at <u>7.30</u> <u>8.00.</u> But if you take my advice, you'll stay indoors and watch TV!

Cruel !

Not true

6 mths of hard work!

Audience enjoyed it?

2 hrs

Now write:

a   a letter to the Editor of the paper (approximately 200 words).

b   a relevant note to Jan (approximately 50 words).

Sample answer   Letter

letter format but no address needed

To the Editor

formal register

Dear Sir or Madam

clear opening: statement of who is writing and why

I am writing with regard to the review entitled 'Wooden in the Woods', which appeared in yesterday's edition. As an AZED member, I would like on behalf of the club to take issue with the review's inaccuracies and unfair remarks.

appropriate linking of points and paragraphing

Firstly, Mr van der Leeden did not re-work the script. We worked from the original version. Nor can I accept the criticism that we acted 'woodenly'. We may be amateurs but it was clear to us that our performance was well-received.

addition of own ideas

The review claims that the production has been under-rehearsed. We have in fact been rehearsing for the last six months. Our director in particular has sacrificed a great deal of his time. I therefore find the reviewer's criticism of Mr van der Leeden's work especially unfair.

rephrasing of input

As for timing, the performance is approximately two hours, not three. All performances start at 7.30.

I hope you appreciate the negative effect the review has had on our morale. Knowing your paper's reputation for balanced reporting, I am sure you will print both an apology and a correction of the facts — in particular the actual time of next weekend's performances.

persuasive ending to prompt further action

Yours faithfully

Keiko Ishiguro

Note

My dear Jan

Just a quick note to let you know that I've written to the paper — I'm sure they'll print an apology. Don't let this stupid review get you down. Remember that last night's audience thoroughly enjoyed the performance and so did we.

You're a brilliant director!

With love

Keiko

informal register

friendly tone

concise note (single paragraph)

Part 2 *Article*

Key points

- Note what type of publication the article is to appear in – for example, an international travel magazine for adults would require a neutral or formal register, whereas a college magazine aimed at teenagers could be written in a very informal register.
- Make sure the register you use is consistent throughout the article.
- Remember to include an appropriate title.
- Introduce your topic in the opening paragraph.
- Be as clear and informative as possible.
- Engage the reader's interest throughout.

Task

An international magazine is running a series of articles on the current problems being faced by young people around the world. You have been asked to write about a problem that particularly affects young people in your area. Your article should include suggestions for a solution to this problem.

Sample answer

interesting title to encourage reader to go on reading

strong opening sentence through contrast

development through one specific example

solution included

neutral / semi-formal register for 'serious' magazine and adult readers

clear outline of problem

final sentence concludes article forcefully and leaves reader with something to think about

Nowhere left to go

Growing up today should be an exciting experience, with every opportunity – but the reality is all too commonly the very opposite. In my own town, the recession has hit hard. In a shrinking job market, young people are now leaving college with little prospect of finding work. Many are on government benefit and have endless 'free time' seven days a week. But where are they supposed to go? Several local facilities which used to be available are in the process of being closed down by our council, who claim that they have insufficient funds to keep them open.

One example of this is my local library, where up until last month it was possible to go and read the newspapers, or meet a friend for a cheap cup of coffee and a chat. With the recent closure of this and other facilities, young people are forced to hang around outside, shivering on park benches, or drift through the shopping centre, without the money to buy the things they see. Or, even worse, they don't leave their rooms at all and become reclusive.

Our council must take urgent action to bring these people back into society. If necessary, working people in the community could pay higher local taxes, in order that facilities are reopened and new leisure pursuits and further training can be provided. *If nothing is done, our community will not have a safe or happy future, since this rejection will ultimately lead to crime and social unrest.*

Part 2 *Character Reference*

Key points

- Make sure the information you give is relevant.
- Write in a formal register – you are writing to an employer.
- Identify how you know the person briefly and clearly.
- Use a variety of expressions to convey positive qualities, rather than repeating the same phrase.
- Include a reference to a weakness.
- Conclude by recommending the person for the job.

Task

A colleague of yours at work has applied for a job in the export sales department of a large multinational company. Since you have known and worked with this person for over five years, you have been asked to write a character reference to support the application. You should include relevant information both about the business skills and the character of your colleague.

Sample answer

To whoever it may concern

Giuseppe Accinni

Giuseppe Accinni and I have been colleagues in the sales department of CFTD for nearly six years. During this period, we have worked closely together on a number of export campaigns, an area in which Giuseppe himself has over ten years' experience.

> brief explanation of relationship with colleague

Over the years, he has built up a number of close working relationships with key customers, who trust him completely. He gives an impression of honesty and fair-play in his business dealings, although he usually manages to get the optimum agreement for our company.

> each paragraph introduces a different point

Giuseppe is extremely dedicated to his work. For example, he has often remained at his desk late at night, in order to make vital phone calls to the other side of the world. This zealous, single-minded approach does cause exhaustion and Giuseppe can occasionally be difficult to work with. However, his brief displays of bad temper seem a small price to pay for the success that he achieves and, generally, he is a likeable colleague.

> inclusion of weakness is qualified to give positive impression overall

He has a flair for foreign languages and is fluent in English, French and Spanish. I have seen him conduct meetings in each of these languages with confidence and he is equally at ease using them in a social setting. Our clients appreciate his readiness to use their language and this has often been a significant factor in closing a deal.

For all these reasons, I believe Giuseppe would have much to contribute and I have no hesitation in supporting his application wholeheartedly.

> final recommendation

Part 2 *Guidebook Entry*

Key points

- Make the information accessible to the reader through headings and layout.
- Note any information about the guidebook, which may help to establish the register you should use. A neutral register is usually a safe choice.
- Ensure the style and register is consistent throughout the entry.
- Bring the facts to life in your description.
- Write equal amounts on each place or event that you include.
- Remember to include practical information such as times and prices, if relevant.

Task

A publisher is preparing a guidebook for foreign visitors, which will focus on historic buildings in your country. You have been asked to write a contribution to the guidebook, describing the main sites in your local area and giving practical information for visitors.

Sample answer

> self-contained section of the guidebook – no introductory material needed

> impersonal style

> plenty of facts within descriptive framework

> neutral / semi-formal register

> practical details displayed separately

Bruton and its surrounding locality

Bruton Castle

This beautiful castle dates in part from the fifteenth century and has been recently restored. Of particular interest are the twin towers and original entrance. The east wing, which contains the library, was added to the castle in the eighteenth century and is also highly recommended. Its interior has many fine examples of tapestries and wall hangings, as well as a large collection of oil paintings.

Open: Tuesday to Sunday, 10am-5pm.
£3.50 admission. Free car parking.

Wildesbury Manor House

Home of the Wildesbury family for over four hundred years, this is a house of great architectural interest, with some prime examples of Georgian features. Every room contains exquisite furniture and unusual mementoes from an earlier age. The family's collection of silverware is displayed in the dining hall. An extensive garden contains many rare species and should not be missed.

Open: Saturday 2am-5pm; Sunday 10am-4pm.
Group visits by prior arrangement with the owner.
House and garden £3.00. Garden only £1.80.

Tetchington Cottages

Built in 1760 and used until 1905 as accommodation for workers on the Tetchington Estate, this row of cottages has been restored using traditional materials and now provides a colourful illustration of rural life. There are four cottages in all, one of which houses the Living History museum, with its outstanding portrayal of past lifestyles.

Open: daily, 11am-4.30pm. Numbers in parties should not exceed ten, due to the small size of the rooms.
£5.00 charge includes museum entry.

Part 2 Informal Letter

Key points

- Ensure that you keep to an informal register.
- Cover all the points required – if there is an extract from a letter provided, read it carefully so that you can reply appropriately.
- Include your own ideas but be careful not to introduce irrelevant points.
- Use sufficient paragraphing.
- Use phrasal verbs and a range of informal expressions.
- End the letter in a friendly way.

Task

Here is part of a letter you have just received from an English pen friend:

... I really don't know what to do. Although I enjoy college life in general, I'm finding the work really difficult. I'm sure I won't pass my final exams this summer. Perhaps I should give up the course now? My parents would be furious though! What would you do if you were me?

Love Jane

Write a letter to your friend, advising her whether to continue the course or not and giving her some reassurance.

Sample answer

Dear Jane

Thanks for your letter. I was very sorry to hear that you are struggling a bit at college. Between you and me, I've felt the same way at times, but I've never considered giving up my studies. I don't think you should either!

You should keep telling yourself that it's only for another six months. That's not very long to wait, is it? You've already spent two and a half years at college – it would be such a shame to stop now. I'm sure you'd regret it at some stage in your life if you did leave, too.

Try to set aside a little more time for studying, then you won't find it all so hard. How about drawing up a weekly plan of what you need to do, in advance? And if it means missing some parties, I'm afraid that's tough! You may enjoy the social side of being at college, but once exams loom up on the horizon, you have to forget about going out with your friends for a while.

I think your parents would have every right to be 'furious' if you quit. They have paid for a lot of the course, haven't they? See it through to the end, for their sake and yours. After all, the qualification will help you to get a good job afterwards, won't it?

Jane, stick with it, okay? I'll be thinking of you over the next few months – and remember, it will soon be over. The very best of luck!

Love

Eleanor

Annotations:
- modal verbs and imperatives used to introduce advice
- phrasal verbs used
- more reassurance given at the end
- early reassurance given
- each piece of advice in new paragraph
- friendly expressions

Part 2 *Leaflet*

Key points

- Be informative.
- Ensure the register is appropriate to the readers specified in the question.
- Use headings for clarity.
- Write in short paragraphs or sections.
- You are likely to use mainly present tenses.
- Don't waste time on illustrations, which will not be assessed.
- Make sure you write the full 250 words – because leaflets are written in a concise way, you may find it possible to cover the task in fewer words. If this is the case, add another point!

Task

Your language school has recently opened an English study centre, where students can work with materials on their own. In order for new students to get the best out of the study centre, you have been asked to write a leaflet for them, describing the range of facilities offered.

Sample answer

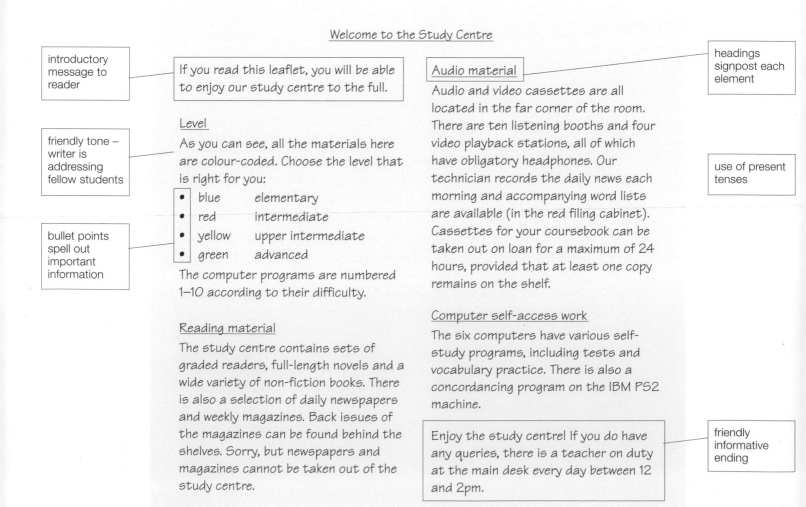

introductory message to reader

friendly tone – writer is addressing fellow students

bullet points spell out important information

headings signpost each element

use of present tenses

friendly informative ending

Welcome to the Study Centre

If you read this leaflet, you will be able to enjoy our study centre to the full.

Level

As you can see, all the materials here are colour-coded. Choose the level that is right for you:

- blue   elementary
- red   intermediate
- yellow   upper intermediate
- green   advanced

The computer programs are numbered 1–10 according to their difficulty.

Reading material

The study centre contains sets of graded readers, full-length novels and a wide variety of non-fiction books. There is also a selection of daily newspapers and weekly magazines. Back issues of the magazines can be found behind the shelves. Sorry, but newspapers and magazines cannot be taken out of the study centre.

Audio material

Audio and video cassettes are all located in the far corner of the room. There are ten listening booths and four video playback stations, all of which have obligatory headphones. Our technician records the daily news each morning and accompanying word lists are available (in the red filing cabinet). Cassettes for your coursebook can be taken out on loan for a maximum of 24 hours, provided that at least one copy remains on the shelf.

Computer self-access work

The six computers have various self-study programs, including tests and vocabulary practice. There is also a concordancing program on the IBM PS2 machine.

Enjoy the study centre! If you do have any queries, there is a teacher on duty at the main desk every day between 12 and 2pm.

Part 2 *Report*

Key points

- Remember that this is a report – do not start the piece of writing as if it were a letter.
- Decide on the level of formality according to the target reader. The report will almost always be formal, but if, for example, you are asked to write a report for your class, you can be more informal.
- Ensure that you fully understand the purpose of the report.
- Include an introduction that summarizes the content of your report.
- Use section headings for clarity.
- State any recommendation clearly in the final paragraph.

Task

To: All students returning from US exchange programme
From: The Principal

It has become increasingly costly to send our students to the US and the college is currently considering whether this programme should continue.

Would you please write a report, answering these questions:
- How did you spend your time? (main studies and any other activities)
- What were the particular benefits to you?
- Should the programme be modified at all?

> You recently spent two months studying in the United States, as part of an exchange programme. Your college principal has now sent you this memo. Write your report.

Sample answer

Report on the US exchange programme

Introduction   This report outlines my two-month stay in Seattle and highlights the various benefits I experienced. It also considers possible amendments to the programme for next year and makes a final recommendation.

[brief introduction]

My stay   Although I arrived on August 30, the college semester did not start until mid-September. I then spent six weeks attending classes in contemporary American poetry and the modern novel. I also attended lectures by visiting speakers, the most relevant one being Professor Grimes on the works of Edith Wharton. The college offered many sports facilities and I regularly took advantage of these. I played ice hockey for the college B team.

[clear section headings]

The benefits   Both courses were excellent and gave me insights into American literature that I could not have gained elsewhere. In particular, the lecture by Professor Grimes was highly informative. The college library had an extensive collection of books and enabled me to research my dissertation.

[more than one benefit mentioned]

In addition to the academic benefits, the experience of studying in another country was invaluable and I learnt a great deal about the American way of life. My spoken English has also improved immeasurably.

[main studies and additional activities both covered]

Recommendations for the future   In view of the need to economize, the timing of the stay could be shortened. A six-week period would in my opinion be sufficient. The starting date should be delayed to mid-September, to coincide with the beginning of their semester.

[recommendation relates to principal's concerns]

I urge the college to continue this programme, which is clearly so worthwhile.

Part 2 *Review*

Key points

- Write for the target readership – read the question carefully to establish this.
- Give a brief summary of the plot.
- Focus on evaluation and recommendation.
- Include both positive and negative points.
- If two or more separate reviews are required, write equal amounts on each.
- Remember to state the title(s) of what you are reviewing.

Task

A group of young British visitors is going to visit your town shortly, as part of a town-twinning initiative. An English newsletter is being prepared for their arrival and you have been asked to contribute to this. Write a review for inclusion in the newsletter of two films that will be on show during the visit. One film should be suitable for children aged 8–12 and the other for teenagers.

Sample answer

directed at younger readers

title underlined

brief description of the plot in present tense

Films on Show during your stay

For children under the age of 12 (but not younger than 8, for you'll be too scared!), I would recommend <u>The Nightmare before Christmas</u>. This innovative animation is by Tim Burton, the director of <u>Batman</u>.

The action takes place at the end of Hallowe'en, when all the ghoulish characters decide to kidnap Santa Claus and take charge of Christmas themselves. Led by the Pumpkin King, they prepare a horrific version of the event.

The story is fast-moving and will have you on the edge of your seat throughout. Burton's zany creativity has no limits – you'll love the stocking filler presents! An impressive team of animators has produced techniques that are absolutely first-class. And above all, it's an extremely funny film.

Teenagers must see <u>Star Trek Generations</u>, the latest Star Trek movie. The film brings together Captain Kirk and characters from the successful Next Generation television series, including Captain Picard, Ryker and Data. They work together to prevent Soren, an obsessed and enigmatic scientist, from destroying an entire planet. The British actor Malcolm McDowell is excellent in the role of Soren.

Although something of a disappointment in relation to previous Star Trek block-busters, this film has an unusual plot and gives reasonable value on special effects. My own personal favourites, the Klingons, were in short supply – I would have preferred to see more action from them and rather less of Captain Kirk's retrospective private life! However, all in all, it is definitely to be recommended.

These are both great films. Enjoy them during your stay!

each film given equal treatment

reservation included

appropriate ending for target readers

Vocabulary Resource

This reference tool is organized alphabetically for ease of access, both within lists and as a whole. The overall organization ties in with the language needed for Papers 2 and 5 of CAE. There are cross-references from relevant sections in the units to all these lists. The lists include vocabulary practised in the units and also bring in other related words and phrases, as well as common collocates. If you are unsure of the meaning of any word or phrase, use your dictionary.

1 Apologizing

apologize
express regret
give excuses for
take the blame
be / feel ashamed
    distressed
    embarrassed
    guilty
    sorry
    upset

2 Argument

2.1 Describing arguments and reasons

compelling
convincing
forceful   arguments / reasons
logical
powerful
sound

2.2 Introducing an argument

*It is **apparent** that people are pleased with this policy.*

apparent
clear
evident
extraordinary
important
inevitable
interesting
likely
natural
obvious
possible
probable
significant
true
unlikely

2.3 Referring to arguments and explanations

one	aspect	of
	explanation	
the	controversy	about / over
the	debate	about / on
	discussion	

angle
issue
justification
theory
viewpoint

3 Comparison and contrast

a bit	less / more than
considerably	better / worse than
far	

a good deal
a great deal
infinitely
a little
somewhat
exactly the same as
just as good / bad as
rather (too)
on the one / other hand

looks	as if
	as though
	like

4 Competition

4.1 People

competitor
entrant
judge
opposition
runner-up
winner

4.2 Things

award
prize
shortlist

5 Complaint

5.1 Linking devices

although
despite
even if
even though
in spite of
whereas
while

5.2 Mentioning shortcomings

incompetence
inefficiency
ineptitude
misinterpretation
mismanagement
misunderstanding

5.3 Problems

abnormality
breakage
breakdown
defect
fault
flaw
weakness

5.4 Solutions

compensation
guarantee
refund
reimbursement
replacement

5.5 Stating your case

	anger
	concern
express	dissatisfaction
	irritation
	regret
lodge	
make	a complaint
record	

threaten (legal action)

6 Description

6.1 Adjectives to describe character

aggressive
alert
approachable / unapproachable
arrogant
attentive / inattentive
audacious
boastful
boisterous
civil
conceited
considerate / inconsiderate
courteous / discourteous
deceitful
dedicated
deferential
determined
dominant
eccentric
enigmatic
expansive
flexible / inflexible
honest / dishonest
ingenious
inventive
knowledgeable
likeable
level-headed
mean
obsessed
offensive / inoffensive
organized / disorganized
outgoing
patient / impatient
polite / impolite
pompous
reclusive
reliable / unreliable
respectful / disrespectful
restrained / unrestrained
self-assured
self-centred
self-confident

self-possessed
sensitive / insensitive
single-minded
sloppy
sympathetic / unsympathetic
trustworthy / untrustworthy
unflappable
vacant
vain
zealous

6.2 Adjectives to describe a book / film / play

Note: many of these adjectives collocate with the intensifying adverbs listed in 9.3.

appealing
brutal
callous
compelling
excruciating
exhilarating
exquisite
extensive
fast-moving
gloomy
horrific
impressive
innovative
intense
intimate
intricate
intrusive
lively
moving
phoney
powerful
preposterous
pretentious
prying
stunning
subtle
threatening
tranquil
trivial
unconvincing
under-rated
vivid
wooden
zany

6.3 Adjectives to describe a place

air-conditioned
claustrophobic
classical
cluttered
confined
cramped
derelict
full-sized

fully-equipped
high-tech
historical
idyllic
isolated
large-scale
lively
luxurious
magical
neglected
open-plan
oppressive
overcrowded
overgrown
peaceful
refurbished
restored
run-down
spacious
spectacular
splendid
suburban
tranquil
undiscovered
well-preserved

6.4 Identifying and specifying position

along the edge
alongside this
at the top / bottom / side
close to
immediately behind
in between
in front of
in the foreground / background
in the top left hand corner
near
next to
on the left / right
on top of
to the left / right / side

7 Evaluation

7.1 Benefits and drawbacks

chief	advantage
great	asset
major	benefit
primary	concern
	difficulty
	disadvantage
	drawback

7.2 Stating what is typical

as a rule,
broadly,
by and large,

for the most part,
generally,
normally,
typically,
usually,

8 Information (giving and requesting)

8.1 Introducing topic-specific information

Culturally, you cannot fault New York – it offers everything.

culturally
financially
historically
intellectually
legally
morally
physically
politically
psychologically
scientifically
technically
technologically
visually

8.2 Referring to content

comprise
consist of
concentrate on
elaborate
focus
highlight
outline
underline
deal with
refer to

8.3 Requesting information

find out about
inquire about
investigate
give (someone) advice about
give (someone) details about
seek information

8.4 Text elements

conclusion
example
introduction
paragraph
quotation
section
statement
summary

9 Opinion

9.1 Expressing your opinion

in my   opinion
            view
my impression is
from my perspective

9.2 Highlighting your opinion

*In spite of my reservations, the play was **actually** very good.*

actually
additionally
admittedly
especially
mainly
notably
particularly
predominantly
primarily
really
specially
surely
understandably

9.3 Intensifying your opinion

*He is **amazingly** generous with his money.*

*It is a **considerably** longer production than previous ones.*

amazingly
considerably
exceedingly
extraordinarily
extremely
highly
immensely
noticeably
radically
remarkably
significantly
totally
truly
utterly

10 Persuasion

10.1 Persuading someone

assure
convince
encourage
entice
persuade
reassure

10.2 Suggestions

invite
offer
plan
proposal
proposition
strategy

11 Reporting

aggressively	argue
angrily	assert
furiously	declare
	demand
	deny
confidently	agree
eagerly	announce
	boast
	claim
	urge
hesitantly	admit
reluctantly	recognize
	reveal
patiently	explain
politely	agree
tactfully	remark
	suggest

12 Recommendation

12.1 Making recommendations

*I strongly **advise** you to accept his offer.*

*Paul is highly experienced and I thoroughly **endorse** his application for the job.*

advise
endorse
recommend
support
urge
have no   hesitation
           reservations

12.2 Reacting to recommendations and suggestions

*I will have to **consider** your offer carefully before making a decision.*

consider
contemplate
reflect on
think about / over

Appendix

Student's Book Answers

Unit 9
Speaking 3 page 116

1C This is normal, acceptable behaviour in the US amongst social equals. B is also acceptable although it would be more common if you were older or richer.

2C South Africans take their rugby very seriously and as you have been invited into someone's home, it is rude to make a show of supporting the opposition. It is much better to appear as if you are only interested in the skills being displayed.

3C Children are regarded with reverence by Thais but age is also greatly respected in the Far East so B is also possible.

4C Loss of face is a serious issue in the Far East and you should avoid doing anything which might cause it.

5B It is very important to realize that your host is really asking for a compliment and has actually spent a great deal of time and effort in seasoning the dish correctly.

6C Britons will often say 'sorry' even if the action is clearly not their fault. It is a way of minimizing the embarrassment that might be caused. Shyer individuals may act as in A!

7A Amongst the older generation it would be considered rude to take a bottle of wine as the hosts would have spent time and effort selecting the appropriate wine to compliment the meal. However, things are more relaxed these days, although it would usually be considered impolite not to take anything.

Unit 13
Listening 4 page 162

1e   2f   3b   4a   5d

Unit 14
Introduction 2 page 170

1 False. The average is two-man years and this is getting shorter.

2 True. The fastest robot holds the 38.4 kph land-speed record for a legged robot vehicle, and has the size and appearance of an ostrich.

3 False. It actually weighs ten times this – 20 tons – and is used on oil platforms.

4 False. In fact, the smallest robot weighs less than 30 grams and is smaller than a human thumbnail.

5 True.

3A

4A

You saw up to six UFOs – you can't be sure about the exact number because they were moving too fast.

They were spherical in shape and metallic-looking.

It was 11.30 at night – you know that is correct because a radio programme you were listening to on your personal stereo had just finished.

You had been inside your tent but came out when you heard your friend – you were worried by the hysterical screaming.

5A

6A

6B

6C

6D

6E

6F

3B

4B

You definitely saw eight UFOs – you counted them.

They were like large oval discs of light, very colourful.

It was well after midnight.

You were outside as you couldn't sleep – you had walked down to the lake and were on your way back to the tents.

You felt very calm when it happened.

5B

7A

12A

Invite him to play tennis and he will probably decline, because he fears that he will look foolish – he prefers to play games in the office where he is a proven winner. If he has a holiday home, or stays in a plush hotel, he will be on the phone six times a day, doing what he does best. Relaxing is for wimps.

So what can a 'leisure adviser' do for him, or increasingly, her? The basic task is to change attitudes, and gradually introduce him to various leisure activities. Some experts believe in playing what is known as the 'fear card'. The executive is warned of the risk of 'burnout' and told that if he doesn't take care of his health, the business will suffer.

13A

14A

6A

6D

6B

6E

6C

6F

7B

12B

But I believe in a more positive approach. A good start is to persuade him that holidays are a good 'psychological investment', and that it is perfectly feasible to combine business with pleasure. This has to be done step by step.

They can take work with them. They can call the office, though the aim must be to reduce the number of calls as the holiday progresses. They can have faxes sent to them. They can be persuaded to take up golf. Once the initial leisure training period has been completed he may well end up making a happy discovery: leisure *can* be fun.

13B

14C

13C

14B

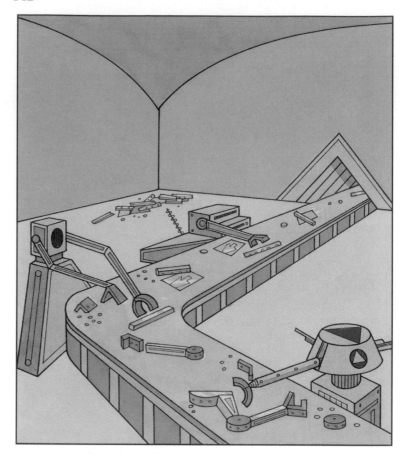

14D

14E

14F

14G

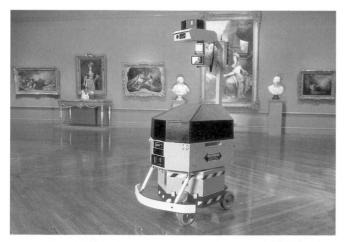

14H

Tapescript

Unit 6

Introduction 2 page 78

Interviewer   For me, any film by writer-director David Mamet is something to savour. His vastly under-rated second film, *Things Change*, starring Don Ameche and that archetypal Mamet-man Joe Mantegna, is currently experiencing a revival. It's the story of a lowly New York Italian shoe-repairer, Don Ameche, who, bearing a striking similarity to a member of the New York mob, is approached and asked to become his double and take the rap for murder. His promised reward is the fishing boat of his dreams, once he's served the due time in gaol. Michael Pond, your views on *Things Change*?

Michael Pond Well, I must start by saying I share your admiration of Mamet's work. To me, he is a maker of poetic myths and this film is no exception. It's a poignant and moving story, lovingly crafted, with quite magnificent acting by both Ameche and Mantegna.

Interviewer   Yes, and clearly Mamet also epitomizes that very American duality between hardness and sensitivity – which is a core theme in this film?

Michael Pond Yes, very much so. In fact, you could say that he constantly divides his male leads into two types: the pivotal figure who has to take a tough moral decision – in this film the Don Ameche character – and the flash guy who talks big, who always attracts the star actor (Al Pacino in *Glengarry Glen Ross* and Joe Mantegna as the vulnerable mobster here in *Things Change*). And I think the reason why the film is so good, so powerful, lies in the dynamics of the relationship between these two protagonists.

Interviewer   Anna Railton, can I bring you in at this point. A powerful film?

Anna Railton   I suppose it is – I can't deny that it has a rather unusual intensity. And the two leads certainly have presence. My reservation is that the film is marred by the absence of any significant female characters, which is unfortunate, to say the least.

Michael Pond Presumably this is part of the realism? Organized crime is a man's world, where women are viewed as adornments, or as practical providers, as in the exquisite portrayal of the housekeeper-cook in Chicago.

Interviewer   So you'd say that all in all the film is completely authentic in terms of its characterization?

Michael Pond Yes, and…

Anna Railton   Well, I'm afraid I can't accept that. Quite frankly, some of the minor roles were definitely phoney, and in the case of the junior mobsters, the depiction bordered on caricature with a capital C. Absolutely unconvincing at times.

Interviewer   Mmm, you might have to agree to differ there. But, er going back to Michael's point, although Mamet writes mainly about men, he's not what you would call a macho dramatist, Anna.

Anna Railton   No, that's true. And I certainly liked the way he brought out the frail ego behind the bravado in the Joe Mantegna part – that was clever, he pulled it off well. But the fact remains that this is a film about men and as such, I couldn't respond to it in a wholly positive way.

Interviewer   And what of the theme encapsulated in the title itself, *Things Change*?

Michael Pond Well actually, that for me is the finishing touch. The film has so many subtle shifts and balances, all of which are very convincing – and indeed compelling. One of the scenes I remember most vividly is the return from that fishing trip, where you have two men from very different walks of life standing on the jetty, trousers rolled up and everything else stripped away. But, of course, as the title says things change – the big man returns to his house and his role within organized crime, while the little man has to meet his own fate.

Interviewer   Not entirely as you might expect, perhaps ... but we mustn't reveal that final delightful twist in the plot. Anna Railton, Michael Pond, thank you. *Things Change* is back on general release for a limited period – don't miss it.

Oxford University Press, Great Clarendon Street, Oxford OX2 6DP

Oxford New York

Athens Auckland Bangkok Bogotá Buenos Aires Calcutta
Cape Town Chennai Dar es Salaam Delhi Florence Hong Kong
Istanbul Karachi Kuala Lumpur Madrid Melbourne Mexico City
Mumbai Nairobi Paris São Paulo Singapore Taipei Tokyo
Toronto Warsaw

and associated companies in Berlin and Ibadan

OXFORD and OXFORD ENGLISH
are trade marks of Oxford University Press

ISBN 0 19 453427 8
© Oxford University Press 1996

First published 1999
Third impression 2000

Printed in China

Acknowledgements

The authors and publisher would like to thank the following for permission to use
extracts and adaptations of copyright material in this book:

Asia Week Ltd: for extract from 'It's Only Rock'n'Roll' in *Asia Week* (28.4.93); **The Big
Issue**: for extract from 'Classless Education' in *The Big Issue* (16–29.10.92); **A & C Black
(Publishers) Ltd**: for extract from *Writing for Children by Margaret Clark (A & C Black,
1993); British Telecommunications PLC: for extracts from* 'An Overview of Teleworking'
(1992); **Cambridge Green Belt Project**: for information leaflet; **Careers and
Occupational Information Centre (COIC)**: for extract from 'Working in Music', © Crown
1992; **The Centre for Alternative Technology**: for extract from 'Alternatives for the
Future'; **Paul Devereux**: for extracts from *Earth Lights Revelation* by Paul Devereux,
(Blandford Press); **Focus**, Gruner & Jahr: for extracts from 'Hype or Hyper-reality' by
John Browning & Phil Barrett in *Focus* (Dec. 1993) and from 'Keyhole Surgery' by Ann
Kent in *Focus* (May 1993); **The Guardian**: for extracts from *The Guardian* – 'Scanner
"ends checkout woes"' by Nicholas Bannister (6.1.94), 'These children are taught to
survive' by Esmerelda Greenslade (14.4.94), 'French rail computer gives skiers booked
for ghost train a slalom ride' by Andrew Gumbel (3.1.94), 'Islands look to future of tele-
cottage industries' by Martyn Halsall (15.3.93), 'Big boys do cry... and they're heroes' by
Liz Hodgkinson (10.7.92), six interviews about career advice by Robert Leedham, 'The
Beauty Myth' by Patricia MacNair (7.1.92), 'Police pelted with stones by travellers
blocking the M5' by Paul Myers (31.5.93), 'Great balls of fire' by Paul Simons (22.10.92),
'All that's left is a band of gold' by Robyn Skinner, (18.6.94), 'Voice of Carnival Culture' by
Robin Thornber (14.7.92), 'A career as a careers officer' by Graham Wade (21.7.94), from
The Guardian Weekend - 'Room for Revolution' by Marion Cotter (10.5.92), 'The small
thief' by Nick Davies (2.1.93), 'The dirty dog', Urban Myths no. 6, by Healey & Glanville
(1992), 'Freight Expectations' by Trader Horn (15.10.94), and from *The Educational
Guardian* - 'The Eye' by Cathal Morrow (15.12.91) and 'An ecological disaster' (3.12.91),
all copyright © The Guardian; **HarperCollins Publishers Ltd**: for extract from *The
Shogun Inheritance* by Michael MacIntyre (Collins/BBC, 1981); **Harp Publications Ltd**:
for advertisement; **Health and Safety Executive**: for extracts from leaflet 'Passive
smoking at work'; **The Independent**, Newspaper Publishing plc: for plot summary for
'Save the Earth', *IOS* (11.7.93) and adapted extracts from 'The professionals who prefer
Mcjobs' by Sue Webster, *IOS* (7.8.94); **IPC Magazines Ltd**: for adapted extracts from
Living magazine, 'Why you should never diet again' by Isabel Walker, (June 1992), and
from *Practical Health* magazine, 'Me and my health' by Maureen Lipman, (March/April
1992), and 'Body language' by Sheena Meredith, (July 1991); **Labyrinth Publishing**: for
extracts from *Nostradamus – the End of the Millennium* by V J Hewitt and Peter Lorie
(Bloomsbury, 1991); **Lemon Unna & Durbridge Ltd**, 24 Pottery Lane, Holland Park,
London W11 4IZ, Fax 0171 727 9037: for 'Lost Consonants' cartoon by Graham Rawle in
The Guardian © Graham Rawle 1993; **Multimedia Books Ltd**: for extract from
Explaining the Unexplained by Hans J Eysenck and Carl Sargent (Prion); **National
Magazine Company**: for adapted extracts from *Cosmopolitan* magazine, 'The politics of
gift giving' by Kate Saunders (Dec. 1992), and from *She* magazine, 'Sick blokes' by
Geraldine Lynn (Feb. 1992), all © National Magazine Company; **National Youth Agency**:
for extract from *Young People Now* (April 1994); **New Woman**, EMAP Women's Group Ltd:
for extract from 'The Love Map' by Jane Alexander in *New Woman* (June 1994); **New
Scientist**: for extract from 'The future of work': it's all in the mind' by Charles Arthur in
New Scientist (16.4.94); **The Observer**: for adapted extract 'The Infinite variety of
lateness' by Patrick Marber in *The Observer Life Magazine* (5.6.94), copyright © The
Observer; **The Pountney Clinic**: for advertisement; **Premier Magazines**: for extracts
from British Airways magazines, 'Up Front' (Oct. 1992), 'News from BA and beyond'
(Nov. 1994) from *Business Life*, and Easy does it' by William Davies (Nov. 1991) from *High
Life*; **Runner's World Magazine**: for adapted extracts from 'Melting Pot' by John Hanc,

Runner's World (Nov. 1993), copyrighted 1993, Rodale Press Inc., all rights reserved;
Sainsbury's *The Magazine*: for photographic competition article; **The Skyros Institute**:
for extracts from brochure; **Teen Magazine**, Petersen Publishing Company: for 'Star
Gazing' by Pamela Dell in *Teen* (July 1993); **Times Newspapers Ltd**: for adapted extracts
from *The Sunday Times*, 'Schlock of the new' by Frank Whitford (23.2.92), © Times
Newspapers Ltd 1992, and 'The Care Label' by Margarette Driscoll (2.5.93), © Times
Newspapers Ltd 1993; **University of California Press** and the author, William Lutz: for
extract from chapter by William Lutz 'The World of Doublespeak' in Christopher Ricks &
Leonard Michaels *The State of the Language* (Faber/University of California Press, 1990
ed), copyright © 1989 The Regents of the University of California; **World Society for the
Protection of Animals** (WSPA): for cover of 'The Zoo Inquiry' leaflet.
Despite every effort to trace and contact copyright holders before publication, we have
been unsuccessful in these few cases. We apologize for any apparent infringement and
if notified will be pleased to rectify any errors or omissions at the earliest opportunity.

'Au Pair America' advertisement, and 'New Future' advertisement (page 95); 'Your
Business' article by Tom Edge (page 148); Meiling Jin: 'World Geography and the
Rainbow Alliance' from *Black Women Talk Poetry* (1987) (page 111).

Illustrations by:

Alex Ayliffe/2d, Before the advent of television (p85) © Glen Baxter, Russell Becker/
Artist's Partners, Brett Breckon, Linda Combi, Bob Dewar, Nicki Elson, David Eaton
Mikey Georgeson, Spike Gerrel, Neil Gower, Andy Hammond/The Garden Studio, Sue
Hillwood-Harris, Sarah Jowsey, Kevin O'Keefe/Cartoon City, Ian Kellas/Cartoon City,
Belle Mellor, Oxford University Press Technical Graphics Department, Pantelis Palios,
Sharon Pallent/Maggie Mundy Agency, David Pike, Georgina Platt, Lost Consonants
(p90) © Graham Rawle, Simon Stern/The Inkshed, Alex Tiani, Harry Venning.

The publishers would like to thank the following for the permission to reproduce
photographs:

Action Images; **Allsport**: Sean Botterill, Phil Cole, Gary Mortimer, Mike Powell, Anton
Want; **BBC**; Bob Battersby; **Henrietta Butler**; **Bruce Coleman Ltd**: Geoff Dore;
Colorific!: Sylvain Grandadam; **The Hulton Deutsch Collection**; **Mary Evans Picture
Library**; **Eye Ubiquitous**: Frank Leather; **FLPA**: C Fields, R Jennings, NASA, T Whittaker;
The Fortean Picture Library; **Robert Harding**; **Hutchinson Library**: Sven
Arnstein, Crispin Hughes, Eric Lawrie, Trevor Page, Nick Vaccaro; **Image Bank**: Deborah
Gilbert; **Impact**: Piers Cavendish, Anita Corrin, Brian Harris, Caroline Penn, Dominic
Sansoni; **Kobal Collection**: Heather O'Rourke; **The Billy Love Historical Collection**;
Moviestore Collection; **Network Photographers Ltd**: Kay Brimacombe, Roger
Hutchings, Justin Leighton, M Horacek Bilderberg; **Oxford Picture Library**: Chris
Andrews; **Pictor**; **Popperfoto**; **Quadrant**: Auto Express; **Redferns**: Leon Norris; **Rex
Features**: Peter Brooker, Alan Davidson; **Science Photo Library**: Tim Beddow, Labat/
Lanceau, David Lean, Damien Lovegrove, R Maisonneuve, Peter Menzel, Hank Morgan,
David Parker, A C Twomey; **Tony Stone**: Chris Baker, Beryl Bidwell, Ken Biggs, Peter
Cade, Paul Chesley, Ary Diesendruck, Chris Haigh, David Hiser, Paul Kenward, Mitch
Kezar, John Lamb, Peter Lamberti, Renee Lynn, Michael O'Leary, Barry Lewis, Pascal
Rondeau, Dave Saunders, Kevin and Rat Sweeney, Charlie Waite, Baron Wolman, Jeremy
Walker; **Sygma**: Benito, D Boursellier, Brooks Kraft, JP Lafont, M Polack; **Telegraph
Colour Library**: Alexander Arakian; **UPPA**.

And for permission to reproduce book covers:
A Bittersweet Promise, Grace Green reproduced with the permission of **Harlequin
Enterprises Limited**, copyright © Harlequin Enterprises Limited; *Hollywood Kids*, Jackie
Collins (Pan Books); *The Lady in The Lake*, Raymond Chandler, cover design by Accident
(Penguin Books); *The Secret History*, Donna Tartt (Penguin Books); *Sweeney Astray*,
Seamus Heaney, illustration by Chris Wormell (Faber and Faber).

Location photography by: Susie Barker

Studio photography by: Mark Mason, The Pack Shot Co (dinosaurs)

We would like to thank:

The Big Issue; The Cambridge Green Belt Project; Hoar Cross Hall; Bob Linney (jazz
leaflet p90); MTV Asia; The National Youth Agency; British Nuclear Electric; Psion;
British Sky Broadcasting Ltd; Skyros Holidays; Slim Images Ltd; The World Society for
the Protection of Animals, 2 Langley Lane, London SW8 1TJ (p127 ape).

Every effort has been made to trace the owners of copyright material in this book, but
we should be pleased to hear from any copyright owner whom we have been unable to
contact in order to rectify any errors or omissions.

The authors and publisher would like to thank all the teachers and students who
contributed to the research and development of the course. The following people
deserve special thanks:

Clare Anderson and Diana Fried-Booth for helpful advice and comments on the
manuscript; Simone Aronsohn; Paul Carne; Caroline Coate; Hugh Cory for useful
suggestions; Victoria Davis, International House, San Sebastian; Diana Fleming; Sue
Inkster, British Institute, Paris; Rosalie Kerr; Steve Lynden, Eurocentre, Barcelona; Clare
McGinn, King Street College, London; Renee O'Brate, London Language Centre,
Barcelona; Louise Perry for Unit 7 'gap year' recording; Kathy Pitt, The British Institute;
James Roy; Sarah Rumbolt, International House, Rome; staff and students at Eurocentre,
Cambridge, where the material was first trialled; Fred Tinnemann, British Council,
Barcelona; Clare West; Jan Whetstone; Ann Whitfield.